SAVANNAH

PRESTON RUSSELL

AND

BARBARA HINES

SAVANNAH

A HISTORY OF HER PEOPLE
SINCE 1733

FREDERIC C. BEIL

First published in the United States by
Frederic C. Beil, Publisher,
414 Tattnall Street,
Savannah, Georgia 31401.

Library of Congress Cataloging-in-Publication Data
Russell, Preston, 1941–
Savannah: a history of her people since 1733/by Preston Russell and Barbara Hines
p. c.m.
Includes bibliographical references, map, and index.
ISBN 0-913720-80-1 (hardcover)
ISBN 0-913720-81-X (softcover)
1. Savannah (Ga.)—History.
I. Hines, Barbara, 1947– . II. Title.
F294.S2R87   1992
975.8′724—dc20   91-45219   CIP

The illustration on the cover depicts Lafayette's 1825 visit to Savannah as he reviews the local militia from the balcony of the Richardson-Owens-Thomas House. Preston Russell painted the illustration.

The frontispiece is a print of Chief Tomochichi and his nephew, Toonahowi, from the 1736 portrait by Willem Verelst. Courtesy of Paul Blatner and the Savannah History Museum.

Beil books are available at special discounts for bulk purchases for sales promotions, premiums, fund-raising, or educational use. For details, contact the publisher.

Composition by the Design Press, Savannah College of Art and Design
Typesetting output by Savannah Color Separations, Inc.
Color separations by Kennickell Printing Co.

Printed in the United States of America

TO OUR FAMILIES

CONTENTS

PREFACE

"How to write a virgin history! Should the scholar's appetite for minutiae be indulged? Or rather should the need for a *popular* text be a major consideration? Balance in all things is a good motto to follow. . . ." This opening lament from the book by Rabbi Saul Jacob Rubin, one of our many sources, poses an incisive question as to what a "history book" should be. In our case we chose a popular text over appetite for minutiae.

Such a decision, however, is no excuse to write a narrative history based on inaccurate details. As listed in the bibliography, dozens of sources were read, compared, and collated in order to arrive at this condensation of their information. Occasionally the minutiae of several sources contradict one another in the well-known "fog of history." It is fortunate that such clashes are over rather trivial details in a sweeping story.

Beyond the primary gratitude to the many fine works in the bibliography, there are also individuals who gave of their expertise and personal time. Malcolm Bell, Jr., in particular used his eagle eye line by line through the first six chapters, seizing on errors and awkward syntax. His advice, based on his own experience, plus his encouragement, meant very much at an important time. We also would like to thank Arthur Gordon, who gave initial constructive criticism on style; our publishers, Deric and Mary Ann Beil, who provided their professional guidance that overcame periodic despair, known to occur among writers; Colonel Walter Wright, who read the manuscript and contributed colorful material related to family letters during the Reconstruction era; Carl Espy, who also contributed a family letter; and William L. Fogarty, who shared his time and expertise on Savannah's Irish tradition.

We are also grateful to Hank Ramsey, Marion Levy, Walter Hartridge, Emory Jarrott, Rita Trotz, Katherine Keena, Paul Blatner, Talley Kirkland, David Guernsey, Jr., William W. Waring, Harry James, Jim Pitts, Carroll Greene, Willis Hakim Jones, Jr., Peter and Helen Steward, and Virginia and John Duncan—all of whom endured our endless search for illustrations. With exceptional skill and diligence, Brenda Richards developed the many prints for the illustrations. Emma Adler, Beth Rieter, Fran Powell Harold, Eleanor Guerry, Stephen Bohler, Stephanie Churchill, Professor Gaye Hewitt, and W. W. Law took the time to answer our questions or to critique our writing. Anne Smith and Jan Flores of the Georgia Historical Society never faltered in their helpfulness. And we are grateful to the many people like Esther Shaver, who recognized the need for a short history of Savannah and encouraged its writing. And last, but not least, we thank Nancy Graham, who cheerfully typed chapters—deciphering a doctor's penmanship—without which we could never have progressed.

INTRODUCTION

Ask almost any citizen in "The Separate State of Chatham"—you just can't figure Savannah out. In following her history since 1733, the crazy quilt of Savannah's peoples reveals the threads of her eccentricity; she was a boisterous American microcosm over four decades before America was born. As tourists note, Savannah and Charleston remain nearly alone in modern America as still having a palpable historic persona. In haughty rivalry for over 250 years, Charleston's heritage seems loftier; her massive mansions still stand to buttress her *little London* description during the American Revolution. At that comparable time, Savannah was a sandhill of tiny clapboard houses on the edge of a pine wilderness.

If Savannah's origins are by comparison humbler, they are as noble and identical to the verse we all remember on the Statue of Liberty, put into action beside a vast river 150 years before the verse was written: *Give me your tired, your poor,/Your huddled masses yearning to breathe free,/The wretched refuse of your teeming shore,/Send these, the homeless, tempest-tossed, to me.*

As one such legacy of the city's ethnic diversity, a joke among Savannahians is that the Jews own it, the Irish run it, and the Crackers enjoy it.

From humble beginnings, Savannah has had over a quarter-millennium of intermingling to embellish her own heritage. If Charlestonians are like the Chinese because they eat a lot of rice and worship their ancestors, it is jested that one is not from an *established* Savannah family until your first and last names are the same: Just ask Sheftall Sheftall, Jewish revolutionary veteran.

Today as tourist and native walk through Savannah's delightful colonial squares, many plaques and markers explain that on a given date so-and-so first did this or that. It is the attempt of this book to try and catch a glimpse of *why* those so-and-so's did this or that.

Their actions are recorded here, with motives not always clear, but told in their own words where historical opportunity permits. Listen to just some of the voices that echo through Savannah's rich past. It is a moving story of love and hate, filled with fools and heroes, the sacred and the profane, saints and sinners, delight and despair. We believe you will recognize yourself in the past, as in biblical words of Paul—if *through a glass, darkly; but then face to face.*

This day I see the Majestry of your face . . . I am come over in my old Days, and I cannot live to see any Advantage to myself (Tomochichi, 1734); *I shook off the dust of my feet, and left Georgia, after having preached the gospel there not as I ought, but as I was able* (John Wesley, 1737); *You may be advocates of liberty; so am I; but in a constitutional and legal way* (Royal Governor James Wright, 1775); *Let our conduct show that we are not lawless . . . we do not complain of law, but of oppression* (the Reverend John Zubly, 1775); *I was a very great rebel* (Mordecai Sheftall, 1778); *I have a deep wound, which is not in your power to cure* (Count d'Estaing, 1779); *I would freely suffer death for the cause of Jesus Christ* (black minister, Andrew Bryan, 1790); *Called upon Mrs. Green . . . and asked how she did* (George Washington, 1791); *What! Allow such a trifle as that to worry you? Trust a woman's wit for the cure, and turn the cylinder* (Mrs. Greene, helping Eli Whitney perfect the cotton gin, 1793); *The greatest compliment we could bestow was to give her three cheers* (sea captain in 1819 being passed in mid-Atlantic by the steamship *Savannah*); *Well-fitted to inspire a melancholy sentiment of the shortness, uncertainty and insignificance of life* (Dr. William R. Waring during the 1820 yellow fever epidemic); *Ah, I remember!* (Lafayette, 1825); *That spot of Spots! That place of places!! That city of cities!!!* (Robert E. Lee, 1830's); *Niggers and cotton—cotton and niggers: these are the law and prophets to the men of the South* (Savannah visitor, 1844); *If any man is to peril life, fortune and honor in defense of our rights, I claim to be one of those men. Let it come now, I am ready for it* (Francis Bartow, 1860); *As soon as I saw Mrs. Davis' face . . . I knew it all . . . I knew it before I wrapped the shawl about my head* (Mrs. Francis Bartow, 1861, on learning of her husband's death at Bull Run); *I beg to present you as a Christmas Gift, the City of Savannah* (General Sherman to President Lincoln, 1864); *I shouldn't wonder if my papa did it. He has shot lots of Yankees!* (Juliette Gordon Low, founder of the Girl Scouts, at age five to General Sherman); *Nervous? Not a Bit* (last words of Savannah's last duelling victim, 1870); *Savannah is a beautiful lady with a dirty face* (Lady Astor, 1946); *that most magical of cities . . . that earthly paradise* (Conrad Aiken, poet and author).

SAVANNAH

Eighteenth-century print of Oglethorpe—a conventional portrait with anachronistic armor. His prominent nose is the most consistent feature of diverse likenesses.

THE COLONIAL PERIOD

Non Sibi Sed Allis
The English Pipedream Called Georgia
1728–1733

GEORGIA FOUNDERS' DAY: FEBRUARY 12, 1733. The weak winter sun illuminated a river bluff sheltered by five arching oaks, a bluff so high it *put a man out of breath before he can reach the Top.* The area was called Yamacraw by the Indians. It soon would be renamed Savannah, perhaps also derived from a long-ago Indian tribe, the Sawanwaki.* On that plateau two foreign cultures tentatively met. Below them, the slow green river flowed past vast tan marshes toward the Atlantic. On oozing brown mud banks, alligators watched with the expressionless hypnotic eye of eternity.

From one of four large tents on the bluff, an Englishman, James Edward Oglethorpe, thirty-seven years of age, stepped forth. With hawkish nose and angular face framed by mouse-colored long tresses, his searching eye looked across the sandy expanse commanded by Indians. The other English colonists clustered behind him. Having previously seen these aborigines, Oglethorpe again sized up their *mico,* or chief—a tall, erect, ageless Creek named Tomochichi. His bare chest

---

*According to Dr. Julian Kelly of Savannah, the Sa-wan-wa-ki were part of the Shawnee tribe prior to 1674. No one contests the city was named after the river, called the *Sabina* as of 1696. *Savano* and *Savanna* were English derivatives. The competing theory is the name comes from *Savanna,* derived from Spanish *sabanna,* still meaning a vast grassy plain.

marked by sweeping black tattoos of bear claws, he stood majestic in his bearskin robe. Beside him stood his queen, Senauki, generally impressive in a calico jacket and petticoat, but *barring the Want of an Eye . . . lost . . . with the Spaniards*. Around them was Tomochichi's feathered court, their black painted faces crowned by black shining hair cropped about the ears. Some had nose bobs, others *sliced ears*.

From this foreboding group one stepped forth. As hypnotic as the alligators, *a man dancing in antic postures with a spread fan of which feathers in each hand as a token of friendship, which were fixed to small rods about four foot long, set from top to bottom with small bells . . . which made a jingling, whilst the king and others followed making a very uncouth hollowing*. The medicine man, with his fans of holy eagle feathers, pranced and sang his way toward Oglethorpe. For a timeless fifteen minutes he *came close and waved his fans over him and stroked him on every side with them*. After this strange, sanctifying ceremony, *the king and all the men came in a regular manner and shook him by the hand*. Oglethorpe invited the principal Creeks into his tent. He seated Tomochichi on his honored right. John Musgrove, a local Indian trader, interpreted the first friendly talks.

Oglethorpe described Tomochichi and his tribe as *A little Indian Nation, the only one within fifty miles . . . not only at amity but desire to be subject of the Trustees, to have land given them and to breed their children at our schools. Their chief and his beloved man, who is the second man in the Nation, desire to be instructed in the Christian religion.* A few years later Oglethorpe would learn to his horror that Tomochichi's father had been "converted" to Christianity—burned at the stake by the Spaniards.

This meeting was the start of a beautiful friendship, sustained—amid the fractures of colonization — by the mutual respect these two men had for each other. One hundred fourteen English colonists were here; soon Portuguese Jews, German Salzburgers, French Huguenots, pacifist Moravians, and Gaelic-speaking Scots would follow. And many more. Briefly Welsh and Arabic would compete amid sixteen languages in the thirteenth and last colony of the British Americas. The first years of this outpost, named Georgia for His Majesty George II, would prove a tower of Babel in more ways than one.

THE CONCEPT
ENGLAND WILL GROW RICH BY SENDING HER POOR ABROAD

Twenty-one Englishmen back home conceived of this venture. How did they—haltingly—pull it off? That shall be explored, step by pitiable step with the first who dared. Why was Oglethorpe here, seeming personally to fulfill Georgia's motto, NON SIBI SED ALLIS (*not for ourselves, but for others*)? That's a personal story, one worth knowing, since it emotionally struck the collective spark.

Except for the unnecessary loss of a young friend, Oglethorpe might have remained an obscure member of Parliament in London, or blithely tended his impressive family estate in Godalming, Surrey. Or worse. At twenty-six years of age an intemperate Oglethorpe wounded two partisans in a fight over his first election campaign. A month later, in a drunken tavern brawl, Oglethorpe *drew his Sword and gave the Fellow a mortal Wound in the Breast.* He went to prison. Mysteriously he emerged five months later to take his first seat in the House of Commons in 1722.

Oglethorpe had served six years in Parliament when his friend Robert Castell met his doom—a doom that was to have a profound effect on Oglethorpe's life. The young architect had tried to publish his work, *The Villas of the Ancients Illustrated.* Being unsuccessful, Castell went into debt. As the law permitted at the time, a creditor had him thrown into London's Fleet Street debtor's prison. Such institutions were corruptly run on a fee system, by which the warden—in this case, Thomas Bambridge—could charge exorbitant *lodging fees.* Such places were popularly called sponge houses for the way the remaining funds of the already destitute disappeared in a hopeless cycle of bribes.

Being banished to pest holes rife with *gaol fever* was the last rung for many debtors, and so it was for Castell. He was exposed to dreaded smallpox and promptly died. Sir Kenneth Dover, dean of Corpus Christi College, which Oglethorpe briefly attended, best tells what happened in remarks delivered 250 years later: *A friend of Oglethorpe's, laden with debt which he could not pay, was thrown into the Fleet Prison and died there of smallpox under horrifying conditions. Few among us comprehend suffering and injustice until they are thrust under our eyes by the experience of someone we know, and we like to be judged by what we do then, without too close a scrutiny of what we failed to do before. . . . Oglethorpe's reaction to the death of his friend Robert Castell was to ask Parliament to appoint a committee which would visit the London prison and make recommendations for reform. Some (not enough) of the guilty were punished and some (not enough) regulations were made to correct abuses in the future; at any rate, the curtain which hid the fate of the desperate from the eyes of the secure and prosperous was torn and would never again be patched up.*

Certainly the curtain was torn forever for James Oglethorpe; it was this emotional epiphany that gave the rest of his life an iron-willed commitment. Not incidentally, half of the twenty-one Trustees later appointed for the new colony of Georgia were members of Parliament's prison reform group under Oglethorpe.

William Hogarth's print of Oglethorpe's prison reform committee, formed in 1728 to inspect the squalid circumstances in debtors' prisons. To the left of the table stands Warden Thomas Bainbridge, under the accusatory glare of Oglethorpe and his group.

THE EXECUTION

Given this committed reformist nucleus for the new colony, it would seem an easy leap of deduction that the first colonists would be a shipload of recycled dregs from prison dungeons. This is not the historical fact. Not one of the original 114 pioneers had a record of being in debtor's prison. Indeed, seeking unknown creditors who might wish to block a colonist's passage, news journals printed lists of proposed colonists.

If not sentenced debtors, certainly the first colonists came as a result of *charity to distressed persons,* as Oglethorpe wrote to Irish clergyman George Berkeley. Beyond Christian appeal, this letter illustrates only one of many attempts by the Trustees to divert religious funds to help underwrite the new colony. In this case Berkeley controlled £20,000 promised him by the government for the founding of a missionary college in Bermuda. Might he consider a reallocation? No—the usual response to similar attempts to secure designated charitable funds.

As five of the Trustees were clergymen of the Church of England, English pulpits were utilized in propaganda sermons. After months of such charitable appeals, around £2,000 was collected, often in one-pound donations. The Archbishop of Canterbury gave £10 for the conversion of Indians. But this all fell far short of the £10,000 estimated minimum that was needed. More popular than coin of the realm were donations of used odds and ends, particularly religious tracts. Reams of works were contributed, with austere titles like *Duty of Man, The Great Importance of a Religious Life, Showing How to Walk With*

God, *The Young Christian Instructed,* and *Help and Guide to Christian Families.* If all else failed, there were fifty volumes of the *Christian Monitor—and Answer to Excuses.*

All of the Trustees had had exposure to the works of Dr. Thomas Bray, founder of the Society for the Promotion of Christian Knowledge (S.P.C.K.). An inveterate organizer from the time the Trustees were in swaddling clothes, Bray and his expanding realm controlled funds for such diverse causes as aiding English prisoners to the Christian instruction of slaves in America. Included were significant sums for relocation of oppressed Protestant Europeans, such as Germans from Salzburg. The parallel paths of the Trustees and Bray would soon dovetail in the colonization of Savannah, but it was hardly an immediate leap of faith. Capital from S.P.C.K. did not plop—in spite of attempts—into the lap of the English Trustees.

This partnership was fortuitously woven into a larger, infinitely more subtle scheme, netting the Trustees the English crown and ultimately hundreds of thousands of parliamentary pounds. The strategy was a combined appeal to ethnic heritage, religious politics, geopolitical imperialism, and—astutely—to majestic vanity. It was packaged in an irresistible silk purse made of sow's ear pragmatism, with the added sheen of Christian purity. This silken purse promised to yield just that—tons of raw silk to allow England to profitably turn up its nose at imported silk from its eternal enemy, France.

England will grow Rich by sending her Poor Abroad, chirped Oglethorpe's promotional journal—specifically, £100,000 richer per year in silk alone, according to the ecstatic Trustees. Their careful calculations showed that a poor London family earned approximately £10 per year—but regrettably ate or otherwise consumed twice that amount. In the new Eden this same family would produce £600, consume only £200 of it, leaving a net balance for trade of £400—all multiplied by hundreds of families loyal to the crown.

The collective components magically fell into place from diverse efforts. Hanoverian George II was, after all, more German than English. His father, George I, could barely speak English. George II ruled over a fiercely anti-Catholic Parliament. What petition could be more reverently tailored than one establishing a colony to sustain displaced Protestant countrymen, fellow Germans exiled for their beliefs with no possessions other than the clothes on their backs? Additionally the project would provide for the Christian resurrection of England's distressed *in decayed circumstances.* Furthermore, Mother England would make a handsome profit and seal off Spanish expansion to boot. Just one signature—and perhaps a little seed money from Parliament—and how appropriately smashing to name the whole enterprise after His Majesty.

King George II, namesake of the Trustee colony of Georgia. Being of German blood, he was influenced to sign the 1732 Georgia charter as a haven for his displaced German countrymen, the Salzburgers.

On April 21, 1732, George signed the charter for Georgia. Most influential in obtaining this courtly signature was the well-connected head of the Georgia Trustees, John Percival, who became earl of Egmont in 1733. Another Trustee, James Vernon, had connections with both S.P.C.K. and Sir Robert Walpole, head of Parliament, where the money was. Both Percival and Vernon must have played their roles consummately. They procured a windfall of £10,000 (earmarked for Salzburgers) from Parliament, the allocation arranged by Walpole's brother Horace Walpole, in the House of Commons. The motion was introduced by Sir Joseph Jekyll, namesake of Georgia's Jekyll Island. More money would come. By the end of the private charter (twenty-one years), the government would pump in over £400,000, far exceeding the *combined* total for all her other North American colonies.

The charter was promulgated on June 20, 1732, solidifying all prior elements *to increase the trade, navigation and wealth of these our realms* to benefit *many of our poor subjects*—these subjects now to include foreigners willing to become British citizens. Additionally a defensive southern barrier protecting thriving South Carolina's borders would be in place—and what a buffer. "Georgia" would consist of an endless rectangle serenely starting east between the Savannah and Altamaha rivers, sweeping westward *in direct lines to the South Seas*—that is, from Atlantic to Pacific. Within, *the military strength of the Province is particularly to be taken care of*—particularly since most of this unsettled wilderness was claimed by Spain.

One provision of the charter was without precedent. Not one Trustee could receive any *salary, fee, perquisite, benefit or profit whatsoever. NON SIBI SED ALLIS*—indeed! Georgia was to be a religious haven for all of God's oppressed—as long as they were not Catholic.

Colonial seal with *not for ourselves, but for others* motto in Latin. It shows the importance first placed on the silk-worm industry as the main export income. This enterprise never materialized, and was replaced in the 1750's by the rice industry and its requisite, slavery.

PROMOTION
"THE MOST DELIGHTFUL COUNTRY OF THE UNIVERSE"

Publicity would be needed to rally recruits and private funding. Typical of such shameless Eldorado boosterism are excerpts from Oglethorpe's *New and Accurate Account of the Provinces of South Carolina and Georgia* (1733), descriptions of a swampy, sandy, steamy wilderness that he had never laid eyes on: *The Air is healthy* [false] *being always serene, pleasant and temperate* [ditto], *never subject to excessive heat* [rank lie] *or cold, nor to sudden changes* [except annual hurricanes]. . . . *The soil . . . is impregnated with such a fertile mixture that they use no manure. . . . They have oranges, lemons, apples and pears, besides the peach and apricot; . . . these are so delicious, that whoever tastes them will despise the insipid watery taste of those we have in England; and yet such is the plenty of them, that they are given to the hogs in great quantities.*

One not in the mood to raise livestock or hunt may simply purchase meat from the Indians; forty-pound turkeys at two pence and whole deer at six pence. Word had it that an Indian chief in nearby Florida was three hundred years old—survived by his father fifty years his senior!*

Projections in *The Gentleman's Magazine* speculated that colonists could *raise white mulberry trees and send us good raw silk*. Since clergymen were part of pulpit salesmanship, parish after parish reported that *Gentlemen were so fully convinc'd of the Charity and Excellence of this Undertaking, that they resolv'd, with great Unanimity, to collect from House to House for the Promotion of it.*

Only a few years after on-site experience in Savannah, Oglethorpe was giving a more accurate warning to prospective colonists. In spite of free land and sustenance, there would be *great Hardships in the Beginning . . . hot in Summer . . . Flies in Abundance . . . Gnats and Flies which are troublesome to the face . . . little red Vermin called Potatoe Lice which in Summer time crawl up the legs of those that lie in the Woods, and if scratched raise Blisters*—not to mention a few other little problems beyond chiggers and gnats. Fifty on the first boat of 114 passengers in 1733 were dead by their second year.

After recruitment Oglethorpe and a few colleagues began screening those *in decayed Circumstances, and thereby disabled from following any Business in England; and who, if in Debt, had leave from their Creditors to go, and such as were recommended by the Minister, Church-wardens, and Overseers of their respective parishes.*

John Percival, earl of Egmont. As head of the Trustees, Egmont had the most influence in Parliament. After he resigned, trust colony status went from troubled to terminal. (Courtesy of V. and J. Duncan Antique Maps and Prints, Savannah.)

THE FIRST FRUITS

Around six hundred men were interviewed, whittled down to one hundred finalists three weeks later. A final choice of thirty-five families resulted. The men generally ranged from thirty-five to fifty years of age, old enough to be proficient in their trades but young enough to bear arms. Since none but Oglethorpe had any significant military experience, males were drilled in the use of *Musquets, Bayonets, and Swords* while crossing the Atlantic. Some vocations among the group

*Such "our future Eden" language is a rehash of a similar tract, *The Design'd Establishment of a New Colony to the South of Carolina in the most Delightful Country of the Universe (1717)*. Oglethorpe and the Trustees were actually fourth in line with their vision. In 1717 Sir Robert Montgomery of Skelmorly had the identical concept, silk and all. The area was to be named "Azilia," but the plan had gone down with the South Sea Company crash in 1720. Next came Sir Alexander Cuming of Coulter, who in 1730 proposed a colony of 300,000 Jews in Indian territory. It didn't hurt promotion to point out that the area *lies in the same Latitudes with Palestine Herself, that promis'd Canaan*. A Swiss adventurer, Jean Pierre Purry, was already established just north of the Savannah River by 1731. Just brought to light, in the same year Oglethorpe signed a secret document with Purry (in French) exchanging personal land grants to Oglethorpe for his support of Purrysburg. Oglethorpe appears to have been covering his *NON SIBI SED ALLIS* bets.

were carpenters (five), sawyers (two), tailors (two), apothecary, engineer, wheelwright, farmers (five), cloth worker, stocking-maker, merchants (two), baker, gardener, vintner, flax and hemp dresser, and nine *servants*. The presence of two wig-makers and one unsuccessful writer testifies to occasional impractical choices. However, Paul Amatis, an Italian self-described as skilled in the silk industry, was a vital addition, as was Timothy Bowling, an artisan in potash production, an envisioned new export. The Reverend Henry Herbert *charitably offer'd to go without any allowance* (around £70 a year), as did surgeon William Cox.

Unexpectedly Oglethorpe decided to accompany the colonists. He was the only Trustee to do so, having no official authority, such as being appointed colonial governor. In fact no legal code for the colony yet existed, except the general agreement to follow English common law. A remarkable aspect of Georgia's settlement was the decision to allow no lawyers; life would be contentious enough without them.

Egmont was pleased with Oglethorpe's decision, but felt the first expedition premature, *that they should send any away so soon*. The whole venture was, and remained, underfinanced. For his part Oglethorpe donated two dozen chairs, a mahogany table, and eight maps—plus himself.

Aboard the two hundred ton galley ship *Anne*, Oglethorpe loaded personal equipment and one dog, a black bitch, that got "lost" at sea—believed to have been thrown overboard by the crew. The captain was John Thomas, and passage was £4 per head. Provisions for a six-week passage listed *10 Ton of Alderman Parsons' best Beer*, allowing two quarts per week for each adult. Presumably passengers would not sip it while reading the 1,122 religious tracts hauled on board, including those fifty copies of the dreaded *Christian Monitor—and Answer to Excuses*. On November 17, 1732, the *Anne* weighed anchor and departed, very slowly, from Gravesend, England. The voyage took fifty-eight days, and the ship arrived safely in Charles Towne, South Carolina, on January 13, 1733, with only the loss of two infants. A child was born at sea, named Georgius Marinus Warren by Oglethorpe, who was his proud godfather. The thirty-five families slept as units in large wooden cradles, the lower decks washed down with vinegar. On January 13 Oglethorpe joyfully recorded: *We are now within nine miles distant and can, from the deck with the naked eye, discover the trees just above the horizon, no disagreeable sight to those who for seven weeks have seen nothing but sea and sky. We have had a very favorable passage.*

Since the projected voyage of forty-two days was somewhat extended, provisions ran low. Oglethorpe dipped into his own resources to cover expenses—a first instance that would exceed £100,000 by the end of his Georgia experience. As pondered in Webb Garrison's book, appropriately named *Oglethorpe's Folly*, the larger mystery was from what deep pocket he kept pulling out those personal pounds.

"I HAVE LAID OUT THE TOWN"

South Carolinians were delighted to welcome others to settle between them and the Spaniards—especially since the new colony offered little competition, having banned slavery and rum. Many of Savannah's place names reflect her gratitude for Carolina's first aid: Johnson Square for Robert Johnson, governor of South Carolina; Broughton Street for Lieutenant Governor Thomas Broughton; Bull Street for Colonel William Bull; Drayton Street for Ann Drayton, who lent four sawyers for new building. Whitaker, St. Julian, and Bryan streets memorialize others who lent personal assistance, including the loan of slaves for labor and construction.

Even before February 12, 1733, Oglethorpe had personally selected the site. He ignored strong suggestions from Carolina to found Savannah on the Altamaha River, above present Saint Simon's Island at what is now Darien. Instead, as he wrote on February 10: *I went myself to view the Savannah River. I fixed upon a healthy situation about ten miles from the sea. The river there forms a half moon, along the South side of which the banks are almost 40 foot high and upon the top a flat which they call a bluff. . . . Ships that draw twelve foot water can ride within ten yards of the bank. Upon the riverside in the center of this plain, I have laid out the town.*

THE TOWN PLAN, 1733

Over 250 years later Savannah can justly claim to be America's first planned city. Her checkerboard symmetry, punctuated by now price-less squares, was an audacious design to ambitiously hack out of a pine wilderness. Oglethorpe had designed the plan before leaving England. But what was his inspiration? Most logically, the veteran of European military campaigns remembered the traditional designs of fortresses and military camps repeated since the Renaissance. Or was it inspired by the design of Peking? The functional symmetry of streets leading to unit blocks, blocks to wards, wards to precincts, and so on was certainly an efficient way to run a Brave New World colony. For the first decades life in Savannah much more resembled future Chinese collective communism than pell-mell American democracy. Some romantics, however, sentimentally suggest the inspiration from *Villas of the Ancients*, perpetuating the work of Oglethorpe's friend, Robert Castell, who died in debtor's prison.

If exact inspiration for form remains up for grabs, function did not. A square was a self-contained unit, individually defensible from attack by,

Map of Savannah after Peter Gordon in 1734, with Bull Street going down the center. Four squares are shown with the river bluff, *almost forty foot high and on top flat.*

say, ambitious Spaniards or French-incited Indians. Progressive squares were also wonderful units for arranging neat, equitable divisions of labor.

Oglethorpe envisioned a sequence of wards centered around squares, laying out six (present Johnson, Wright, Telfair, Ellis, Reynolds, and Oglethorpe squares) before he returned to England in 1743. Four *trust* lots, reserved for public buildings and churches, formed the east-west sides around the squares. The north-south sides around the square contained four *tything* lots for colonists' private homes. Each tything had ten lots, individually measuring sixty-by-ninety feet, onto which a twenty-by-thirty-foot house was built. Forty home sites thus resulted around each square; the first—Johnson—not so coincidentally equalled the nearly forty families on the *Anne.*

FUNCTION FOLLOWS FORM

Each tything of ten families had a tythingman, responsible for conduct and welfare. Ten males in each tything were trained to bear arms, taking watch every fourth night. The four tythingmen reported to a constable, responsible for the ward of forty families created by each square and its appendages. Forty soldiers were thus available from each ward. Colonist Isaac King Clarke soon wrote in exasperation, *I am obliged to attend the guard upon all occasions, to mount guard, to do day duty, to relieve guard &c.*

Today the central squares often have a church or temple as part of the ambience. Although he himself did not attend church regularly, Oglethorpe shared the collective mentality of the founders that religion was essential in establishing the type of colony that they had planned.

The first and remaining legacy of this is Christ Episcopal (then Anglican) Church on its original 1733 trust lot in Johnson Square. The others that followed—Jewish, Lutheran, and Presbyterian—are integral to Savannah's origins.

With the help of Colonel Bull and other Carolinians, four houses were underway in the first month. A year later there would be forty, for a general population of 260, the buildings made of *Timber & Clap board, with Shingled roofs,* according to Peter Gordon, an active first settler. Colonist Thomas Christie wrote: *The town [Savannah] is greatly increased, so that, whereas at first I could hardly see any thing but trees, I can now scarce see any trees for houses.* Although Oglethorpe might be expected to have had his pick, he chose to live a life of spartan inspiration, remaining in one of the tents originally set up by the river (the site now marked by a marble bench on Bay Street in front of the Hyatt Regency Hotel).

It did not displease him that most colonists soon addressed him as Father Oglethorpe, acknowledging the usually benevolent dictatorship he exercised—sustained without one whit of official authority. For the good of the cause, thou shalt move over *here* or do *that*—despite thine own experience there with barren soil or diseased climate. Few challenged him in the first years.

Satellite hamlets lost to history briefly ringed Savannah. The tempo-

Christ Episcopal Church, on its original 1733 site in Johnson Square. The first structure was destroyed by Savannah's first great fire in 1796. The present structure dates from 1838, rebuilt within its original walls after a fire in 1898.

rary existence of Joseph's Town, Acton, Abercorn, Highgate, and Hampstead is a reflection of how settlements should work—according to projections on a map—despite the inhospitable conditions found by the reluctant settlers assigned there. The fishing community of Thunderbolt is an exception. Set up as a defensive bastion for Savannah's eastern flank, it is still viable today. The other exception is the lighthouse on Tybee Island, a legacy of a ninety-foot-high beacon to put the area on the mariner's map. The first wooden tower, however, had collapsed by 1741, along with much of the first decade's efforts.

TRUSTEES' GARDEN
"MOST THE TREE STUMPS I HAVE ROOT UP"

A public garden was a necessity. Trustees' Garden, a ten-acre tract, was laid out along the river at the east end of Bay Street. The Trustees sent two botanists, William Houston and Robert Miller, to Madeira and the West Indies to gather plants and seeds, which never reached Savannah. Other cuttings came from France and Italy. A temporary nursery was set up in Charles Towne under Paul Amatis. Joseph Fitzwalter, the public gardener, toiled away mightily in the new Savannah garden. By 1735 he proudly wrote Oglethorpe: *Most the Trees Stumps I have Root up, planted the front walk with Trees of Oranges Six foot Hight which will Bear fruit some This Year. . . . Of Mulberry plants I have Eight Thousand. Some of them this last Season Shott to fairly fifteen foot. . . . I have meet with Some Cotton Seeds from Guinea which from it I have Raised a Thousand plants. . . . Rice I have had, very good Indian Corn, and pease in great plenty.*

The olive trees had also grown. In his pet project area, the kitchen garden, wheat grew, plus barley, rye, oats, and beans. Nearby flourished hemp, flax, indigo, cochineal, alfalfa, clover, and rye grass. And fruit trees—oranges, apples, pears, figs, pomegranates, and coconuts—abounded, even peach trees, traditionally claimed to be the first fruits of Georgia's most famous symbol.

Fitzwalter happily gave away the garden's bounty, believing that to be its purpose. Oglethorpe appointed young John Goddard to help Fitzwalter with his growing green cornucopia.

Mainly through the labor of Fitzwalter, Savannah thus established America's earliest agricultural experimental garden. But in Fitzwalter's same letter describing his trees leaping up all around him, he struck a first note of discord: *Mr Amatis hath been hear . . . Since the beging of September and is not for planting of any thing of Kitching Stuff att all in the Garden, which I always Apprehended was to be Carried on.* When Amatis returned to Savannah from Charles Towne, he and Fitzwalter—like two cooks in a kitchen—couldn't work together. Colonist Thomas Christie wrote in 1734: *Mr Amatis & Mr Fitzwalter have had Some*

Differences together concerning their Authority wch we have had Some Difficulty to Reconcile. Things got to the point that Amatis threatened to shoot Fitzwalter if he even entered the garden. According to Amatis in his letter to Oglethorpe, *I have found on my arrival here the garden in disorder and that since your departure almost nothing has been done.* Amatis complained that the servants weren't working, but instead were enjoying *in a few words, the pleasure of hunting, fishing and other pleasures.* Amatis would not further relocate his plants from Charles Towne until Oglethorpe *decided if Mr Fitzwalter ought to be the master of the garden, as he says he is, since he has insulted me two different times.* Whatever the facts of the matter, Fitzwalter was relieved of his post and Amatis returned to Charles Towne, where he died suddenly in 1736.

By 1738 heavy frosts and draughts began to take their toll. The excessive sun had long since caused the wine grapes to shrivel up and perish. When William De Brahm saw the gardens in 1751, all that were left were a few olive and fruit trees. In 1755, under Royal Governor John Reynolds, the tract was converted to residential use. It would be restored again as just that in 1945—still called Trustees' Garden.

OGLETHORPE'S "AGRARIAN EQUALITY"

The slavish, parceled uniformity that quaintly looks neat—even planned—centuries later is a pen-and-plumb-line legacy of a utopian classless society. Like Camelot, it didn't last long. In Oglethorpe's model of *Agrarian Equality* each small house and lot reflected a classless group of up-by-the-boot-straps artisans and yeoman farmers. Tending their little fifty-acre plots outside town, the group was coerced into all-for-one communal service by the Trustees' subsidy—at least for the first years of New World existence. Soon a subclass of entrepreneurial merchants would evolve—so envisioned the Trustees—profiting the whole with products like silk, wine, and potash sold back to Mother England. All would be trained in the use of *Musquets, Bayonets, and Swords*—just in case the Spaniards came up from Florida.

ADVENTURERS AND SERVANTS

An early problem, one that swelled the population to five hundred in mere months, were *Adventurers.* These were people, indeed like Oglethorpe, who had fundamental talents and bravery, but no economic necessity to submit to the communal dole and yoke. In addition to refusing to live on bureaucratically parceled land, they also brought along troublesome things like servants; a handful had arrived on the *Anne,* but only because they were near-members of the thirty-five families chosen. Indeed, even the Trustees subverted their own vision, amending the charter to give five hundred acres of land to anyone bringing over ten white servants at their own expense. The hapless colonists with their assigned fifty acres ground their teeth.

This opened the door for a flood of Adventurers—with their indentured servants. The ethnic stock of the servants was mixed—Dutch, German, Irish, Scottish, Welsh, and English. When their work term was over, they were granted land. Acton and Vernonburg were largely settled this way. Hampstead was mainly German; Joseph's Town, Scottish; and Highgate settled by French-speaking Huguenots. A French-speaking minister regularly visited down-river from Purrysburg to conduct services in Savannah.

Out of expedience, Oglethorpe himself contributed to the problem. In 1734 the population was increased by forty Irish convicts near starvation, the survivors of a shipload hurled into Savannah by a storm. With no place left to go, Oglethorpe purchased them at £5 each, putting them to work on the communal farms around Savannah. In February 1735 there was an attempt led by the Irish servants to take over the town by force. They were quickly overcome.

ANTISLAVERY, 1733–1750

What about the last rung below indentured servants—slaves? No! Absolutely not—unanimously from the Trustees through Oglethorpe. Never mind that the base of the economic pyramid in the other English colonies was slavery. But as Oglethorpe wrote: *If we allow slaves we act against the very principles by which we associated together, which was to relieve the distressed. Whereas now we should occasion the misery of thousands in Africa, . . . and bring into perpetual slavery the poor people who now live free there.*

But for Georgia in 1733, the reasons were more practical than humanitarian. First, a slave cost £30, enough to sustain a free colonist for a year. Worse, slaves and servants would promote sloth and the spotty beginnings of an idle upper class. As Oglethorpe wrote, *The idle ones are indeed for Negroes.* The Trustees concurred; *they would destroy all Industry among the White Inhabitants.* Slaves were also a potential for violent uprisings—for example, in 1739 the Stono Rebellion occurred in South Carolina. Finally, the Spaniards already had regular success in inducing many slaves in Carolina to run away to Florida; ergo, slaves, if allowed in Georgia, would surely be the first to defect if any enemy were to invade the colony and promise "freedom."

These points aside, the physical requirements of the land far exceeded the resources of the first colonists to meet it. Consequently a growing proslavery chorus bombarded the Trustees. With uncomprehending moral irony, Peter Gordon wrote: *It is morally impossible that the people of Georgia can ever get forward in their settlements or even be a degree above common slaves, without the help and assistance of Negroes.* In 1737 the Reverend George Whitefield argued that to settle Savannah

William Hogarth's print of *A Midnight Modern Conversation* in the eighteenth century. Such searing depictions by Hogarth began to shock England about the social destruction of alcoholic excesses.

without slaves was *little better than tying their [the colonists'] legs and bidding them to walk.* Thomas Stephens agreed: *It is as clear as light itself, that negroes are as essentially necessary to the cultivation of Georgia, as axes, hoes, or any other utensil of agriculture.*

In as artful an argument as possible, ninety-four colonists in 1740 crafted their second long petition to the Trustees, blaming the climate in quasi-scientific eloquence: *Unless we are in a proper temperature of air, we cannot go through the proper functions of life required. Unless our fluids have a due and natural circulation our constitution will quickly dwindle to nothing. . . . How terrible must such a sight be to any man who has the least grain of compassion with him! . . . Let him turn his eyes 'round to the Negroes in the same fields. There he will see the reverse. He will see the utmost vigours exerted in every act. They go through their work with pleasure. They welcome the rising sun with their songs and when in his meridian their spirits are at the highest. They are far more happy here than in their own country. There they are abject slaves. . . . Here it is true they are property of particular men but their lives are in no danger.*

Regardless, the Trustees maintained an official ban against slavery until 1750, almost their entire Trustee period before the crown took over in 1753.

ANTI-RUM, 1733–1742

"HE THERE DRANK RUM PUNCH . . . AND DYED"

Amid all the austerity real and invented, what about an occasional pint of rum, just like back home or up in Carolina—or illegally at John Musgrove's trading post? Oglethorpe tried to curb strong spirits as consistently as slavery, even though he permitted ale, beer, and wine. Ample beer, after all, came over on the *Anne*. Wine was intended, like silk, to be a chief export commodity. In 1738 Oglethorpe wrote the Trustees: *We want beer here extremely. I brought over twenty tons of beer, which I believe will be gone before I can receive a supply. . . . It will be a better remittance than even bills, since beer's being cheap is the only means to keep rum out of the colony.*

The reasons for the rum ban were multiple, some stemming from Oglethorpe's own prejudices. Britain was just beginning to look at the effect of alcohol excess on its social fabric, as witnessed by William Hogarth prints of the day. Among the many stern tracts sent over were also two hundred copies of *A Friendly Admonition to the Drinkers of Gin, Brandy and Other Spirituous Liquors.* Oglethorpe himself had once been imprisoned because of his own excess. Local Indian chiefs now saw the same excesses on their own people and requested curbs.

The Musgrove trading post ignored Oglethorpe's war against demon rum, a profitable item, especially for their Indian customers. Colonist Elisha Dobree wrote in 1735 that *the workmen at Tybee are almost continually drunk and that the lighthouse is not like to be quickly built.* Even on the first night in 1733, a colonist had slipped over to the Indian camp, got drunk, and *laid naked*, according to Peter Gordon, who, fearing a bad example, yanked him away.

Beyond the amorality of it all, Oglethorpe became convinced of another fatal link besides terminal liver failure. Strange fevers—*Augues*—in the first hot summer had killed over ten percent of the colonists. The very first victim was Savannah's only physician, William Cox. To Oglethorpe, rum was the cause, as he wrote of the death of Thomas Millidge: *Our best carpenter is dead of a burning fever which on his deathbed he confessed he contracted at the Indian trading house. He drank there rum punch on the Wednesday, on Thursday was taken ill . . . and on the seventh day . . . died. Poor Overend . . . is also dead with rum, to which most of the rest owe their deaths.*

Thus in 1734 the only three formal laws ever enacted in the twenty-one-year Trust period were bans against *Importation and Use of Rum and Brandies, Importation and Use of Black Slaves or Negroes,* and a statute requiring compliance with *the Law for maintaining the Peace with the Indians.* The latter two were well regulated. By 1742 the sieve-like regulation against rum importation was dropped by the Trustees. Since Oglethorpe spent almost all his time in Frederica by then, he presumably tried to glare down rum in that settlement. Desperate Elisha Dobree, who also moved there, wrote from Frederica in 1737: *When people are driven to poverty, distress or expectations of &c. they will drink when they can get it to keep up their courage. . . . Our people are almost mad and I am obliged to drink with them.*

Lawyers Banned, 1733–1755
"That Pest and Scourge of Mankind"

In Savannah, lawyers were forbidden *to plead for Hire*. Georgia, it was decreed, should be *free from that pest and scourge of mankind called lawyers*. Oglethorpe and the Trustees detested them, trusting each colonist could plead *his own Cause, as in old times in England*. When questioned about the details of the legal system, Oglethorpe is said to have responded: *Such laws as the Trustees think proper, what business have poor people to do with laws?* If this sounded quaint even for 1733, soon legal thickets sprang up. In 1734 Richard White and Alice Riley, two Irish servants, were sentenced—by English common law in the absence of a Georgia law—to be hanged for the murder of William Wise. White preceded her to the gallows, as Riley was found to be pregnant and her execution thus delayed until one month after she gave birth to a son. In 1735 Edward Jenkins wrote Oglethorpe that White *was led immediately to the gallows and declared to the last he was not guilty of the murder and by all appearance died a Roman*. As for Riley—*the woman was hanged yesterday, and denied the murder of Wise*.

But was it legal? Common law justice was getting ad lib; indentured servants were being whipped in public, and one woman was afterward dragged up and down Bull Street behind a cart.

For that matter, was the awkwardly named *tail-male* system of land inheritance legal? Highly unpopular, tail-male barred women from inheriting improved land. The Trustees' rationale was utopian, if not straight out of Plato's *Republic*. If a landowner died or quit the colony without a male heir, his land went back to the Trust for a new colonist. Primarily this insured each landholder was a male available for military service. Perhaps the grant might revert to the Trust anyway if the owner had not made required improvements. In a long petition to the king in 1740, ninety-four colonists argued the contrary logic of the military intent: *No free men or even tenants can be supposed to fight and put their lives in jeopardy for houses and lands that they have no title to. . . . Can it be imagined any free man will stay in a frontier colony, where he is every hour liable to be knocked o' the head.*

Four of the first colonists chosen in 1732 had stayed home in England after mulling over the possibilities. Now prospering colonists were leaving Georgia for areas with less restrictive land laws—lands also free of bans on slavery. In 1739 the English Trust greatly curtailed the tail-male system, in spite of Oglethorpe's militant objections, and abolished the system completely by 1750. Maximum individual holdings had jumped from an "official" five hundred acres to two thousand acres. By 1750 one could buy about as many acres as desired on a *fee-simple* basis.

THE JEWS, 1733
"WE OPENED THE SYNAGOGUE"

The religious tolerance of the embryonic Anglican colony was quickly tested. Only six months after settlement, on July 11, 1733, a storm-tossed boatload of forty-two Jews arrived in Savannah's port, having fled Portugal because of lingering ripples of the Spanish Inquisition. In Savannah they were received with courtesy, even delight, when one turned out to be a physician, Dr. Samuel Nunes Ribeiro. Deadly fevers in Savannah had already killed over twenty colonists, including the only physician, William Cox. Oglethorpe gave Samuel Nunez (as his name is more popularly spelled) credit for saving the colony by *cold baths, and cooling drinks since some of the sickest experienced wonderful recoveries.* He was Savannah's first civic hero.

Providence challenged Oglethorpe. Since there was no legal representation yet in Savannah, he checked with Charles Towne lawyers to be sure that the charter indeed only banned *papists* and *slaves.* He then welcomed the Jews to Savannah with no recorded blink of an eye. He knew his decision would not please the Trustees. Three Jewish agents working with the Trustees had left a bad taste in their mouths. The agents refused to apply funds they raised for general use in the colony, but, instead, used the money to help only Jewish refugees. Additionally such an exotic grafting might upset the fragile Anglican economic crop just planted over in the Trustees' Savannah hothouse. Oglethorpe received the following Trustee instruction: *Use your best endeavor that the said Jews may be allowed no kind of settlement with any of the grantees, the Trustees being apprehensive, they will be of prejudice to the trade and welfare of the Colony.*

Oglethorpe ignored the Trustees' instruction and helped the Jews to locate in Savannah, predominantly in the area around Ellis Square. Included in the ship manifest were two family names still thriving today in Savannah, Sheftall and Minis. Philip Minis was the first male child conceived and born in the colony. He would guide the French in their attack on the British forces holding Savannah in 1779; his descendant and namesake would fight a famous duel a century later. The Sheftalls would also grow to play important roles in Savannah's Revolutionary War period.

Almost two years to the day after they arrived, Benjamin Sheftall recorded on July 12, 1735: *The Jews meet together and agreed to open a synagogue, which was done immediately, named K.K. "Mickva" Israel. We opened the synagogue and made the proper officers.*

Relocated several times, Mickve Israel synagogue now proudly sits on Monterey Square. It houses the South's oldest Jewish congregation, the third founded in America. Inside is the group's priceless Torah brought with them from Portugal. A marble monument at the corner

The original 1733 Torah of Congregation Mickve Israel, part of the priceless artifacts at the present temple on Monterey Square. (Courtesy of Congregation Mickve Israel and Alex Gilmore, Savannah.)

A marker of the first Jewish grave sites at Bull Street and Oglethorpe Avenue—the plot granted by Oglethorpe in 1733. In the background is Independent Presbyterian Church, on its locale since 1819.

of Bull and Oglethorpe streets marks the site of the original Jewish burial ground established in 1733. Sheftall Cemetery, still existing a quarter mile west of there, would see its share of revolutionary blood shed around it in 1779. It was later popular as an area where gentlemen settled affairs of honor.

By 1738 John Martin Bolzius, the Salzburger minister, wrote: *The German Jews have in Savannah the same liberties as any Englishman. They drill with a rifle, as all the soldiers do. They have no other profession besides farming or dealing in small trade. . . . They even have a doctor who has the permission of the Trustees to cure them when they are sick.* When Bolzius mentioned *dealing in small trade*, perhaps he was referring to the firm of Salomons & Minis, opened in the same year.

The Salzburgers
"Cheerful and Pious, Laborious, Sober People"

Following the Jews, the first group of Salzburgers arrived in Savannah on March 12, 1734. The Germans, under the leadership of Baron Georg Philipp Friedrich von Reck, received gifts of fresh meat, vegetables, and fruit. Oglethorpe wrote: *I have bought a sow, a cow, two fowls, ducks and geese for each of them. . . . The ministers are very devout and the eldest is a very wise man. The whole are a religious, industrious and cheerful people.* Pastor Bolzius was among them, initially hitting it off with Oglethorpe before their mutual strong wills clashed. They both, however, held identical views on the use of slaves as a corrupter of local initiative, as Bolzius wrote in 1739: *I take this freedom to beseech the Honourable Trustees not to allow any Negro men or women to be carried to and employed at our place or neighborhood, seeing that the consequences of it would be very bad and the ruin of poor labourers.*

Print of the Reverend John Martin Bolzius, minister of the Salzburgers, who settled Ebenezer. (From George White's *Historical Collections of Georgia*, courtesy of the Chatham-Effingham-Liberty Regional Library.)

The 1769 Salzburger Church at Ebenezer, near present Rincon. In spite of molestations by the British in 1778 and by Sherman's troops in 1864, it is the oldest standing church in Georgia.

The charter presumption of the Georgia haven for all oppressed creeds was that they lose their ethnic identity by becoming British subjects. The king's English would certainly be a minimum requirement, and assimilation by intermarriage was assumed. Neither suited the Salzburgers, and their stay in Savannah proper was short.

Again dealing with reality over intent of the charter, Oglethorpe helped the displaced Germans relocate. According to von Reck, the site was *21 miles from the town of Savannah, and 30 miles from the Sea, where there are Rivers, little Hills, clear Brooks, cool Springs, a fertile Soil and plenty of Grass.* They named it Ebenezer, *the Stone of Help.* Less than two years later the Salzburgers abandoned the site because of infertile soil and constant flooding. In spite of setbacks, a colonist described the Salzburgers as *still cheerful and pious, laborious, sober people.* Bolzius wrote *to report well of them, that they dwell in the fear of*

God, practice soberness and other Christian virtues and labour so earnestly that some of them have, by the much troubles and heavy works, sickness and death among themselves. Childbearing mortality was appalling in the first years, as colonist John Vat wrote in 1735: *It is very observable that hitherto all our childbearing women are delivered of their children before their full growth, and that most of the women died.* Vat and the women believed *the present soil is pernicious both to the growth of children and seeds.* As pitiful testament, he listed the last eight names of deaths in only two months related to childbirth.

New Ebenezer was established on a red clay bluff on the Savannah River, outside of present Rincon. The colony thrived, adding much to Savannah by its eternal diligence. In a 1739 letter to Oglethorpe the Salzburgers described their routine for beating the heat: *We find it tolerable and for working people very convenient, setting themselves to work early in the morning 'till ten o'clock and in the afternoon from 3 to sunset.* The Salzburger beehive rejoiced at the mild winters: *People in Germany are hindered by frost and snow in the winter from doing any work in the fields and vineyards.*

There was estimated to be over a thousand Germans in Georgia by 1741. In the coming years nearly half of the colony's silk production as well as early cotton came from the Salzburgers. They founded a small orphanage in 1738—America's first—which closed around two decades later. Their prerevolutionary church and museum now stand as a gathering point for annual fall reunions of some of Savannah's oldest families. From 1769, the structure, with hand prints in the homemade brick, is the oldest standing church in Georgia.

The Moravians

Another German-speaking people who settled nearby were the Moravians. Around forty-five of the stoic pacifists arrived in 1736. A year earlier the earl of Egmont had described them as *a lot of enthusiasts, miserably persecuted by Papists, [who] desired only land and that we would defray the charges of their passage, intending to convert the Indians and relying on Providence.*

All true. The Morivians' serene reliance on Providence during a violent storm at sea so impressed young Anglican John Wesley that he later credited this incident as his first important conversion. Within eighteen months the Moravians started a school, named Irene, for Indian children on the Savannah River five miles above town. Indian children soon enrolled; Tomochichi visited frequently and was greatly impressed. In 1736 colonist Benjamin Ingham wrote to Sir John Phillips: *I believe in a little time we shall have a good number of scholars. The Indians . . . now are very willing to have them [the children] taught and even some of the men seem to have a desire to learn.*

Like the Salzburgers, the Moravians were eternally diligent, certainly in the opinion of Ingham: *I heartily wish they [S.P.C.K.] would contribute towards bringing over some more of the Moravian brethren . . . for they are not only the most useful people in the colony, but also they are certainly the holiest society of men in the whole world.*

When the Moravians, however, became interested in evangelism among the slaves in South Carolina, the plantation owners there did not view the endeavor with favor. And the Moravians' refusal to bear arms made them unpopular locally in Savannah. They thus drifted away to Pennsylvania to less militant climes, not leaving a trace of their Georgia beginnings. By 1740 the Reverend George Whitefield wrote: *The Moravians, by far the most pious and industrious people in the province, are now all gone.*

The Wesleys, 1736–1737
"Think of It No More"

The Wesley brothers' sojourn in Savannah can be simply summarized. They came; they saw; they hated it! The former founders of *the Holy Club* at Oxford University in 1729 (derided as *methodist* because of stern, methodical piety) disapproved of Savannah. The feeling was mutual, compounded by John's peevish, bizarre behavior and Charles's loose tongue.

Their father was the Reverend Samuel Wesley, an old friend of Oglethorpe's in England. The sons heard directly from Oglethorpe that many in Savannah were *ignorant and licentious.* What could be better for Georgia than two Anglican brothers interested in saving the heathen, also tending the English Anglican flock? The Reverend Henry Herbert, Savannah's first pastor, had not had popular success, being ill most of his brief stay. Samuel Quincy, his successor, was recalled by the Trustees after he officiated at the marriage of Joseph Fitzwalter, the hard-luck gardener, to an Indian maiden—Georgia's first interracial union. Without success, Oglethorpe wrote the Trustees explaining: *The generality of the people thought they had done a very pretty thing in getting an intermarriage.*

The brothers arrived in 1736 on Oglethorpe's second visit, on one of two ships loaded with 490 more Salzburgers and those first Moravians, who particularly impressed John Wesley. He began to study German for closer ties, his interest enhanced by their common concern for Indians and that legendary episode of Moravian faith in the face of shipwreck.

The Wesleys came ashore at Cockspur Island, site of present Fort Pulaski, where a large monument now marks the site where John first gave thanks for deliverance on New World soil. In less than two years the brothers were praying for deliverance back to England. In the case

Charles Wesley, who lasted less than a year in Georgia. His many later hymns include *Hark the Herald Angels Sing.* (Courtesy of V. and J. Duncan Antique Maps and Prints, Savannah.)

of Charles, deliverance would be only five months hence. As he wrote on landing in Georgia: *In vain have I fled from myself to America. . . . Go where I will, I carry my Hell about me.*

Since Oglethorpe rarely wrote back to the Trustees explaining anything—especially galloping expenditures—Charles was assigned as his secretary. Diverting him for the religious needs of the colony, the chore embroiled Charles in Georgia-Carolina conflicts over Indian trade. He accompanied Oglethorpe to the new community of Frederica on Saint Simon's Island. Cold and sick with dysentery most of the time, Charles stayed there in a shabby house on bare ground.

Ill and emotionally drained, Charles became vulnerable to local gossip about Oglethorpe. The upshot was that Charles accused his leader of adultery—*simultaneously* with two married women. Wesley later recanted his charges. Things, however, weren't quite the same as before, when they were already abysmal. His Frederica "Anglican" congregation shrank to two Presbyterians and a Baptist (or Catholic no less, as another source states). John visited his brother in Frederica and offered to switch congregations. So Charles limped back to Savannah, and shortly thereafter—upon the "friendly advice" from Oglethorpe, a bachelor himself—left for England to take a wife to become a better minister.

True to form, Charles's ship almost sank on the way. It was diverted to Boston by bad weather, where Charles was received by the clergy. *I cannot help exclaiming,* he exclaimed, *O happy country that cherishes neither flies, nor crocodiles, nor informers!* When Charles finally reached England, his first visit was to a friend who had read of Charles's death in the papers. Appropriately, Charles entered in his journal: *Happy for me, had the news been true!* After his evangelical conversion in 1738, he is estimated to have written over six thousand hymns. One of the first was justly named *And Can It Be.* Today his best-known standards are *Hark the Herald Angels Sing* and *Christ the Lord Is Risen Today.*

John's experience was not much happier, although he was pleased when twenty people were at his first Savannah service on March 13, 1736, near Johnson Square. Since he soon began to seek separate instruction of the children, tradition credits John Wesley with founding the world's first Sunday school. He worked hard—too hard for the locals. He led the congregation through 5 A.M. and 7 P.M. services each day before and after sweaty communal toil.

One devoted attender was attractive young Sophey Hopkey, who flirted with Wesley. Between giving her private French lessons and winding up on a boat with her for five days and nights, Wesley developed a growing moral crisis. (In case one wink, on the boat he is said to have entertained Sophey by reading her Patrick's *Prayers and History of the Church*). Wesley sought advice from his austere Moravian friends.

John Wesley, a troubled young enigma while in Savannah, spent the remainder of his life in England as the central founder of Methodism. (Courtesy of V. and J. Duncan Antique Maps and Prints, Savannah.)

John Wesley monument in Reynolds Square, erected in 1968 in proximity to his 1734 parish house. In the background is the portico of the Pink House Restaurant, the prior 1789 home of Liberty Boy James Habersham, Jr.

Frowning on the prospect of marriage, the Moravians cast lots. Wesley drew the slip that said: *Think of it no more.* In his spiritual self-flagellation, Wesley's demands on his flock grew even sterner, if such was possible.

But it was not Wesley's self-flagellation that was remembered more than forty years later by a generally spiteful colonist from 1736. Phillip Thicknesse (called *Dr. Viper* by his later biographer) recorded that *J.W. and C.W. both are dangerous snares to many young women.* Writing about John Wesley, Thicknesse said that Sophey and *some other females,* went constantly home with Mr. Wesley to his lodgings, in order to be further instructed; . . . *Surely, said I, my soul is of as much importance as theirs; and if I am to be excluded a "part" of the benefit, I will withdraw myself altogether; and did so.* Thicknesse accused Wesley of writing Sophey letters that *contained an "olio" of Religion and Love.* He also charged that Wesley wrote the beautiful, but deaf, daughter of John Hutton letters *to mingle Love and Religion into one Mess, so as to leave an artless innocent Girl at a Loss to separate the Ingredients.*

But *Dr. Viper* most rejoiced in telling of John's joust with Beata Hawkins—in at least four different versions over the years. Traditionally attributed to the pen of Thicknesse, one Sunday Wesley's hair was *so long on one side, and so short on the other, that those who saw him on the "worst side" might have observed, "What a cropt head of hair the young parson has on!"* This was the most visible result of a physical confrontation with Beata, who was said to have held a pistol in one hand and scissors in the other. As Wesley tried to stop her, he reported that she swore *she would either have my hair or my heart's blood.* She also had— or had not—chewed off Wesley's shirt and *bitten large pieces of flesh in her rage.* Wesley later wrote to Oglethorpe that Beata *fixed upon my arm.* Her father and eight spectators finally pulled her off.

As a matter of public record in the matter of Wesley's involvement with Sophey, she switched her attention from Wesley to another suitor, named William Williamson, whom she soon married. When Sophey became less attentive to church duties, Wesley felt it his duty (or something) to deny her Holy Communion. This resulted in a court battle for defamation of character, abetted by Sophey's uncle being Thomas Causton, second in command of the colony. Wesley claimed that as a priest he wasn't bound by civil authority; chief magistrate Causton settled that nicety by setting a court date. Against Causton's legal order, Wesley circuitously left Savannah by night in the company of a wife beater, a bankrupt constable, and a defaulting barber. His final diary entry on December 2, 1737 speaks for itself. *Being now only a prisoner at large, in a place where . . . every day would give fresh opportunity to procure evidence of words I never said, and actions I never did, . . . I shook off the dust of my feet, and left Georgia, after having preached the gospel there, . . . not as I ought, but as I was able, one year and nearly nine months.*

Two years later John had his most famous conversion on Aldersgate Street in London, still under the general influence of Moravian friends. He is estimated to have given 40,000 sermons and traveled over 250,000 miles during the remainder of his life. Today 250 million Methodists worldwide are the fruits of his labor. A nine-foot-tall monument of Wesley is in Reynolds Square, located near the site of his parish house.

George Whitefield, the charismatic populist preacher who ceaselessly raised money for two decades in order to sustain his orphanage and school. Today he would be a smashing television evangelist. (Courtesy of V. and J. Duncan Antique Maps and Prints, Savannah.)

GEORGE WHITEFIELD, 1737
"GOD HELP ME—GOD HELP US ALL"

In response to a request from the Wesleys, George Whitefield, a colleague of the brothers in the derided Oxford Holy Club, ironically was crossing to Georgia as John Wesley was returning to England. In spite of the advice of friends to remain in England, the charismatic young preacher had decided to immigrate to the New World. James Habersham, a wealthy Englishman converted by Whitefield's forceful sermons, accompanied Whitefield. Savannah would greatly profit from the friendship.

In 1740 Whitefield and Habersham together started America's first orphanage, which is still in continuous operation. They named it Bethesda, meaning House of Mercy. Whitefield wrote: *On Friday last God brought me hither. Mr. Habersham before I came had looked out a proper tract of land near Skidaway on which I propose building the Orphan House as soon as possible and to take all the orphans in general into it.* Habersham, along with Charles Delamotte, became Savannah's first teachers, since Bethesda was soon as much a school as orphanage.

The daily routine as described in 1740 appears spiritually daunting as well as exhausting. The children were awakened at 5 A.M. for fifteen minutes of silent prayer. Sixteen hours later they were put to bed with the same ritual—*each boy, as in the morning, is seen to kneel by his bedside, and is ordered to pray from his own heart for a quarter of an hour.* In between were two church services, two work periods that involved *spinning, picking cotton or wool, sewing, knitting. Others serve in the store or kitchen; others clean the house, fetch water, or cut wood.* And then there were four hours of school lessons. The day ended with an examination by Mr. Whitefield to *instruct the children by way of question and answer. . . . His main business is to ground the children in their belief of original sin, and to make them sensible of their damnable state by nature.* Lunch period mercifully had no holy rigors, *but no time is allowed for idleness or play, which are Satan's darling hours to tempt children to all manner of wickedness, as lying, cursing, swearing, uncleanness &c.*

Whitefield spent nineteen years working on Bethesda and with his persuasive sermons raised funds on both sides of the Atlantic. Even Benjamin Franklin was seduced, the wry old agnostic emptying his pocket for the cause; both pockets, so his story goes. He later became a trustee of Bethesda.

Whitefield was the most charismatic preacher of his day, but, unlike Wesley and other eighteenth-century revivalists, his intent was not to start some new purified sect. Quite the opposite. In his rhetorical way Whitefield would cry out: *Father Abraham, whom have you in heaven? Any Episcopalians? No! Any Presbyterians? No! Any Independents, or Seceders, New Sides or Old Sides, any Methodists? No! No! No! . . .*

We don't know those names here! . . .

A sketched layout of Bethesda Orphanage, founded in 1740 by James Habersham and George Whitefield. The systematic austerity was carried over to the crushing daily routine. The structure was destroyed by fire in 1770. (Courtesy of V. and J. Duncan Antique Maps and Prints, Savannah.)

Oh, is that the case? Then God help me, God help us all, to forget having names and to become Christians in deed and in truth!

George Whitefield died in 1770, the same year Bethesda was hit by lightning and destroyed by fire. In Savannah, upon news of his death, *All the black cloth in the stores was bought up,* as the town went into mourning.

THE SCOTS, 1735

As individuals, Scots were in Savannah from the first. The earliest colonists of Scottish extraction, mostly Lowlanders, settled primarily in the hamlet of Joseph's Town. Names like Tailfer, Sterling, Grant, Douglas, Baillee, and Anderson were the nucleus of the St. Andrew's Society, loosely founded in 1734. According to their many Anglican enemies, this crowd—wearing their distinctive laced bonnets—could chiefly be found down at Edward Jenkins' *Publick House* or tavern, tippling and spreading sedition against the Trustees. They were also accused of dancing *with each other,* racing horses and *betting* on them, putting on silly *plays,* and even walking down the streets *arm in arm*—instead of working. Causton called them *Grumbletonians.* The Scots's loudest howls were over the bans on slavery and rum, the latter freely consumed in denouncing the former. New Trust Secretary William Stephens minced no words about them—*that insolent Club . . . Riff Raff . . . Sheep Excrements, which are numerous & much of a size.* When this grumbling group, known as *the Club* or *Malcontents,* eventually forsook Savannah for South Carolina in 1740, Stephens gloated—*Thus we at last see an End of that cursed Club, which has so long been the very Bane of this place.* Stephens would later cringe when his own son, Thomas Stephens, became a leader of the Malcontents and later carried the club's list of grievances all the way to England. When the Trustees were completely cleared of the charges on the list, Stephens was repri-

St. Andrew's Society monument on Oglethorpe Avenue, placed in honor of its 250th anniversary. In the background is the Juliette Gordon Low Girl Scout National Center.

manded by the speaker of Parliament, kneeling at the speaker's feet for a half hour. At first Stephens had only dropped to one knee. The speaker thundered—*Both knees!*

Unlike the Lowlanders, the nearly two hundred Sutherland Highlanders, led by John Mackintosh and Hugh Mackay, were welcomed when they arrived in Savannah in 1735. With their tartans and Gaelic-tinged speech, they proved as clannish as the Salzburgers (after all, being literally clannish). They soon founded the town of New Inverness, later called Darien. This town was adjacent to Fort King George, the crumbling southern British bastion against the Spaniards. The Highlanders' backgrounds made them the only veteran fighters in the colony, as well as the group most consistently faithful to Oglethorpe's political and militant designs. They vocally abhorred slavery, describing it as a *Scene of Horror* in their rebuttal to a petition supporting slavery submitted by their Grumbletonian kith and kin in Savannah.

The Darien Highlanders were described vividly with their *Plads, broad Swords, Targets* [shields] *and FireArms*—plus those screeching bagpipes. (An old British definition of a gentleman is someone who can play the bagpipes, but, of course, does not.) There were bagpipes for weddings, bagpipes for funerals, bagpipes for parties, bagpipes for dancing, and bagpipes for war. The Highlanders' efforts in the last department would prove indispensable against the Spaniards in 1742. When Oglethorpe visited he would disappear among them in his *Highland Habit*, as the residents *cried out, "Mr. Oglethorpe, Where's Mr. Oglethorpe?" not knowing him from the rest of their brethren.* For whatever image-conscious reason, Oglethorpe refused the offer of an indoor bed, even in the bitter cold. Instead he wrapped himself in his tartan and slept under a large tree.

Such behavior might lead one to conclude that Oglethorpe was too loyal to all things Scottish. The English Trustees did. The Trustees and those in much higher places strongly suspected Oglethorpe was a Jacobite. If so, he was an English traitor, a supporter of the Scottish rebellion of the Old Pretender, James III Stuart, and his son, Bonny Prince Charlie. Oglethorpe's family back in England oozed Jacobean allegiance. Several sisters were married into the Catholic French court, where the Stuarts took refuge. Bonny Prince Charlie himself would take refuge at Oglethorpe's estate, Westbrook, south of London, in the bad old days to follow when the prince almost toppled England in armed conquest. Not one whit of historical evidence, however, indicates that Oglethorpe was anything but a loyal Englishman, promoting the interests of the crown in Georgia. Sometimes, however, he was forced into confusing alliances to keep his English colony in one piece.

The Jacobean climax would come at *the Forty Five*—in 1745—at Culloden, when the king's brother, the duke of Cumberland, trounced Stuart and his frenzied clans with *Plads, broad Swords, Targets and FireArms.* The Jacobean Rebellion was over. After *the Forty Five,* even wearing a tartan was outlawed. Later this same duke, who was never convinced that Oglethorpe was not a Jacobite, would help bring Oglethorpe down through court-martial. In an irony of place names and history, Oglethorpe named Cumberland Island at the southern extreme of the Georgia coast for the duke, who, after *the Forty Five,* was known to all Scots as Butcher Cumberland. That Darien is so close to Cumberland Island adds to the irony.

King Tomochichi Visits King George, 1734
"What Stranger This? and From What Region Far?"

If affairs were confusing in Savannah, the English Trustees back home were pulling their hair out, or at least tugging on the huge wigs of the day. Quasi-secretaries or no, Oglethorpe rarely wrote, and when he did the letters had no financial particulars. *Cannot send particulars . . . so much hurryed . . . have been obliged to make many new expences here.* Et cetera. He freely admitted that he did *not understand Accounts.* In a brief year he had written unexplained drafts exceeding £5,000, which would exceed £100,000 by the end of his tenure. Oglethorpe was always on the wing, as described by colonist Hector Beaufain—*I had much ado to follow Mr. Oglethorpe, for he walks the wood like an Indian.*

From this black hole of financial mystery, the Trustees occasionally received such New World money-makers as *the stem of a large Vine, 64 Hogsheads and 112 Barrels of Tar, a hundred weight of the Bark of a Tree, rattle snake Root, Et Cetera.* Georgia did send 268 barrels of rice for resale—only because Oglethorpe had overbought supplies from Carolina. Only the many deer skins obtained from Indian trade were actually profitable. A few pounds of raw silk and one magnificent old

Detail from the Willem Verelst painting related to the 1734 visit of Tomochichi and his entourage to England. The child Toonahowi in civilian clothes impresses the big-wigged Trustees, flanked by Oglethorpe and a proud Tomochichi. John Musgrove stands behind him as interpreter. (Courtesy of the Henry Francis du Pont Winterthur Museum Library.)

Indian, however, would set the stage, winning the favor of the king and setting all England on its ear in renewed romance.

Oglethorpe knew that he was in trouble back home vis-à-vis the Trustees' accountant mentality. He needed a publicity stunt. If he couldn't bring back that three-hundred-year-old Indian down in Florida whom he had mentioned in his first promotion, he at least could present Tomochichi and his court to England as living proof of Savannah's fountain-of-youth ambience. By legend Tomochichi was one hundred years old, but he looked half that age. As a bonus, his young nephew, Toonahowi, could recite the Lord's Prayer, the Ten Commandments, and reams of Anglican rote in eager English.

On May 7, 1734, Oglethorpe left for England on the man-of-war *Aldborough,* carefully coaching his nine-member regal Indian court during the trip. There were the king and queen, Tomochichi and his wife, Senauki; Toonahowi, Tomochichi's nephew and heir prince; and Hillispylli, the war chief of the Lower Creeks. Also along were five other chieftains: Apakowtski, Stimaleechi, Sintouchi, Stingwykkie, and Umpychi, Senauki's brother.* Tomochichi would remember to pause periodically to allow time for interpretation by John Musgrove. (Musgrove would get drunk at one treaty conference in England. It recessed promptly; nobody could comprehend what anybody said until Musgrove sobered up.)

The Indians were received royally—mainly by being themselves. The earl of Egmont noted, *They will not put on breeches . . . their breasts and thighs and arms open, but they wear shoes of their own making of hides*

---

*This was the second Indian group to be presented to George II, the first being in 1730. Sir Alexander Cuming of Coulter, he of the new Zion in Georgia, brought six Cherokee Indians to London. They too caused a sensation.

that seem neat. He described Senauki, however, as an *old ugly creature.* The London papers went crazy, including poetry inspired by Tomochichi:

> *What stranger this? And from what region far?*
> *This wondrous form, majestic to behold.*
> *Unclothed . . . yet Awed by no slavish fear,*
> *By no vile passion blind.*

The Georgia entourage did it all, riding around in the king's own carriage pulled by six white horses. They visited the Tower of London, Windsor, Hampton Court, the Royal Gardens, Greenwich. The king personally directed the changing of the guard for his feathered guests. At Eton, Tomochichi caused pandemonium when he suggested a holiday visit to Savannah for the cheering students. What most arrested the wide-eyed guests was a lion in the Tower of London. In exchange for gifts of many furs and a dugout canoe, could the Indians possibly have a painting of the lion to hang in their lodge back home? Instead, they got two swans—present status unknown.

For the reception by King George II and Queen Caroline at Kensington Palace, the principal Indians dressed in scarlet with fur trim. Others had their faces painted black, or with little triangles on their chin simulating impromptu goatees. Tomochichi, by now an established demimonarch, addressed his royal counterparts via his interpreter John Musgrove, *speaking in an elevated tone and in the strange accents of the Indian orator.*

This day I see the Majesty of your Face, the Greatness of Your House and the Number of Your People. I am come for the good of the whole Nation call'd the Creeks, to renew the Peace which was long ago had with the English. I am come over in my old Days, and I cannot live to see any Advantage to myself. I am come for the Good of the Children of all the Nations of the Upper and of the Lower Creeks, that they may be instructed in the Knowledge of the English. These are the feathers of the eagle, which is the swiftest of birds and who flieth all around our nations. These feathers are a sign of peace in our land. They have been carried from town to town there; and we have brought them over, to leave with you, O great king, as a sign of everlasting Peace.

Tomochichi then addressed the queen: *I am glad to see this Day, and to have the Opportunity of seeing the Mother of this Great People. As our People are joined with your Majesty's we do humbly hope to find you the common Mother and Protectress of us and all our Children.*

King George responded in kind, ending with: *I shall always be glad of any Occasion to shew you a mark of my particular Friendship and Esteem.* Toonahowi then recited the Lord's Prayer for the queen, who embraced him with evident emotion. Later Toonahowi received a gold watch from the king's brother, the duke of Cumberland, *to call upon Jesus Christ every morning when you look at it.* Remembering this, it was Toonahowi who later suggested to Oglethorpe the name for Cumberland Island.

As Webb Garrison put it in his book, *Oglethorpe's Folly,* "Tomochichi and his tribesmen had brought victory. It was time to crush the opposition with silk."

Eight pounds of silk, all home grown, were made into a dress for Her Majesty, Caroline. Delighted, she wore it to celebrate the king's birthday, forgoing official royal finery. As icing on the cake, Sir Thomas Lombe declared to eager journalists that the Georgia product was far superior to the imported stuff from France. The crown gladly footed the bill for the entire visit, with change to spare.

To mar the delight of the memory, one of the chieftains, Umpychi, sickened and died of smallpox. He was buried at Westminister in St. John's cemetery (the site now long gone because of construction in central London). Tomochichi was ready to return home anyway. He marveled at, but was puzzled by, the stupendous buildings. Why should anyone build a house that would live longer than the occupant? He was also shocked by the corruption of London, supposedly saying to Oglethorpe: *What swarms of fools there are in this country! . . . Here you see some in fine clothes, bridling like turkey-cocks; there, others drawn about in cages; I see a parcel of insolent savages, that lord it over others, of whom they make slaves. I think this is a damned country, and that if you will take my advice we will be gone out of it as soon as we can.*

In 1739 Tomochichi finally succumbed to his years, whatever their number. Oglethorpe wept at the news. At Tomochichi's own request and as a sign of eternal friendship, Tomochichi was buried in Savannah. Oglethorpe arranged a funeral with full military honors and was himself a pallbearer. The grave site is in present Wright Square (old Percival Square), where Oglethorpe erected Savannah's first monument, a stone pyramid. This first monument, long since gone, is now commemorated by a large boulder in the square. The legacy of this friendship would endure through Oglethorpe's tenure, with Indian allies serving him well in his jousts with the Spaniards.

BLOODY MARSH, 1742

Receiving word that Lord Walpole almost had his Parliament ready to concede Georgia to Spain as an expedient to pressing global politics, Oglethorpe rushed home to England in 1736. He barely convinced Walpole to reverse his stand and send a professional regiment to Georgia. The Forty-second Regiment was stationed at Frederica in 1738. As the new *General and Commander in Chief* of both Georgia and Carolina, Oglethorpe used his clout in the nearly successful attempt to take Spanish St. Augustine in 1740. The next clash, however, was the totally successful repulse of the Spaniards near the marshes of Saint Simon's Island in 1742. Called the Battle of Bloody Marsh, it produced only around fifty casualties—mostly Spanish. If a microscopic battle by any standard, it still has been designated one of the fifteen most strategic engagements in military history. To wit, the Spaniards never again harassed Savannah or any other English colony. It indeed fulfilled Georgia's mission of being a southern military buffer.

Whitefield correctly wrote that *the deliverance of Georgia from the Spaniards is such that it may be paralleled but by some instance out of the Old Testament.*

Living It Up—So to Speak

Amid the rigors of man against nature and his fellowman, there was surprising—if limited—frivolity. There were no theaters or libraries— still decades away—but taverns were abundant. On special days, such as the king's birthday, the taverns were filled with folks dancing or eating free cold buffets. Meanwhile, cannons boomed while many toasts to George II's health were given. As an indication of Father Oglethorpe's status, his birthday was also a holiday (December 22, 1696). Even Founders' Day was commemorated from 1733 (current Georgia Day, then celebrated on February the first by the old calendar). St. George's Day in April and St. Andrew's Day in November were also excuses to quit work and party. Cricket games filled the squares, but William Stephens frowned when raucous Scots raced horses from the Trustees' Garden to Johnson Square and loudly exchanged bets. Stevens blamed *Dr. Tailfer and his Associates [the Malcontents]* for *the odd Humour being lately sprung up among some of our People for Horse-Racing.*

In spite of the so-called rum ban, several citizens hinted at a morning "eye opener," which occasionally helped them muddle through the day. In 1735 Samuel Eveleigh blithely wrote Oglethorpe of his visit to Sir Francis Bathurst: *I carried with me two bottles of punch and two bottles of red wine. The former we drank after breakfast, the latter I left with him and in the last glass we drank his cousin's health.* In the same year Francis Piercy wrote a Reverend Forester recommending a form of Indian tea: *Now all the gentry of the town drink it frequently, and I find that it does me more good than when I drank rum. For now I am married. Instead of drinking rum in a morning, I drink tea with my wife.*

In the same year Paul Amatis tattled to the Trustees about the many violations of the rum ban, mainly because *Mr. Causton fined me £7 Currency for selling a few gallons of rum.* Amatis then listed others who sold rum: *Mr. Edward Jenkins, Mr. John Fallowfield, Mr. Patrick Houston, Mr. James Gould, chief clerk of your Public Store, Mr. Christie, Mr.*

John Ambrose, all the public houses . . . and several others; and Amatis added: *The reason some of the above gentlemen do not pay a fine is because they are intimate to Mr. Causton. I don't say because they are Freemasons.* Thomas Christie added a new twist to push his bottles—*he called the same bottled beef, so that "Christie's Bottled Beef" is a common proverb.*

THE GREAT DECLINE, 1740–1753
"IT IS A MELANCHOLY THING"

Savannah was drastically changing, now only a pipe dream of the Trustees' utopian vision. Her population dropped ghost-like, perhaps fulfilling John Wesley's parting curse that Sodom-like Savannah would revert to *a settlement of oppossums, raccoons and the like inhabitants.* In 1741 Joseph Fallowfield, a Savannah bailiff, wrote: *The Town is full of Buildings but thin of Inhabitants, three houses are empty through the Town for one that has a family in it.* A new colonist named Henry Garret wrote: *I got into a very bad corner of the world, where poverty and oppression abound to such a degree that it's become proverbial this way to say as "poor as a Georgian."*

In 1740 those Malcontents under Patrick Tailfer sat up in Charles Towne, *mean pitiful Wretches* amid their slaves and rum, watching Savannah's decline. They gloated: *The inhabitants are scattered over the Face of the Earth; her Plantations a Wild, her Towns a Desart, her Villages in Rubbish, her Improvements a By-Word, and her Liberties a Jest; an Object of Pity to Friends, and of Insult, Contempt and Ridicule to Enemies.*

In Savannah even optimist James Habersham feared for the colonists' survival. *They droop under these difficulties, grow weary of the colony, get into idle and refactory company. . . . The colony, without some proper remedies, must dwindle away into nothing. . . . Many are already gone to other provinces to seek their bread, and those who remain have laid out their all.*

The cooperative and benevolent attitude of Carolina toward Georgia had begun to die after the death of Governor Johnson in 1735. His successor, the contentious Thomas Broughton, lacked Johnson's and Oglethorpe's belief that Georgia and Carolina could be mutually beneficial for each other.

Savannah's standards were declining. Colonists were stealing vegetables from each other's gardens. There was *profanation of the Lord's Day. When at church in the time of divine service, can hear continual firing of guns by people that are shooting at some game.* In 1740 Oglethorpe personally led a voluntary clean-up crew to rid the squares of an *offensive Weed* that grew shoulder high, full of *troublesome Insects and Vermin. Very nearly two hundred* able-bodied men participated; Oglethorpe

Opposite, Oglethorpe monument in Chippewa Square, by sculptor Daniel Chester French. Dedicated in 1910, it was placed facing south—to keep a watchful eye on the Spanish.

rewarded them with a beer party. He was already spending money on cash prizes to perk up individual incentive. By the next year, however, colonist John Terry wanted *to get out of Savannah, for there are here human snakes, much more dangerous than the rattle ones.*

By 1741 the colony had split—Savannah, the northern half, was led by William Stephens; and Frederica, the southern half, was led by Oglethorpe. Oglethorpe's visits to Savannah were infrequent; he would part forever on July 22, 1743. He didn't even stop by Savannah for a last farewell. Perhaps he did—or didn't—give Mary Musgrove as a parting gift a ring, which in her words was worth £1,000. She had certainly done her part as interpreter and all-around free spirit. Much married by then, wags would speculate she may have "parlayed" with Oglethorpe in his big tent back in the spartan old days down on Bay Street. (That would total at least three accusations of normal—if illicit—attraction to the opposite sex; history records no convictions. Oglethorpe married the year after he left Georgia.) By 1749 *Cousaponakeesa*, a.k.a. Mary Musgrove/Matthews/Bosomworth, would try to add another name, *Empress.* For services rendered the colony under Oglethorpe, she presented William Stephens with a bill for £1,024. She and her latest husband, Thomas Bosomworth, also demanded three Golden Isles—St. Catherine, Ossabaw, and Sapelo. They backed up their demand with a siege of Savannah by threatening Indians. (After a decade in court, they wound up with £2,100 and St. Catherine Island. In 1765 most of the island was purchased for £5,250 by Button Gwinnett, future signer of the Declaration of Independence.)

As Phinizy Spalding describes in his biography, *Oglethorpe in America*, lightning shattered two of the remaining five oaks where Oglethorpe first tented on Bay Street, only a week before he left forever. The new Trustee representative, William Stephens—long suffering under Oglethorpe's thumb—felt the trees had remained as a *Standing Monument* to where the Moses-like leader had first *pitched his Tent.* Now Oglethorpe, the oaks, and his act of settlement were gone. But, as Spalding concludes, Stephens "failed to add, however, that the surviving pines still stood, symbolic of the boldness and strength of James Oglethorpe and symbolic, too, of the permanency of the colony he founded, settled, protected, and led."

In the famous words of the Irish poet W. B. Yeats, *Things fall apart; the centre cannot hold; . . . and everywhere the ceremony of innocence is drowned.* By 1750 the Trustees' antislavery law was overturned; three years later the colonial population was one-third slaves. Without Oglethorpe's on-site touch with the Indians, lucrative trade with them shifted back to Carolina.

After Oglethorpe's departure, only 172 new colonists arrived, compared to 2,499 *Adventurers;* but the considerable number of indentured servants that they brought with them tended to drift elsewhere after servitude, in search of less repressive landowner policies. Worse, two-thirds of those who left the colony were not servants, but subsidized colonists. Charitable contributions dropped from thousands in the idealistic 1730's to £10 by 1742. The Parliament and crown finally cut off all funds in 1751.

If any other index of the decline was needed, the fatigued Trustees—their membership turning over and meeting less often—surrendered their charter to the crown a full year before it was due on June 23, 1753. Egmont, once chairman and anchor of the dream since his association with Oglethorpe in the prison-reform days, had long retired by 1742. He wrote: *It is a melancholy thing to see how zeal for a good thing abates when the novelty is over and when there is no pecuniary reward.*

In their final two years the Trustees made land grants right and left, some to friends in England. Over seventy-five thousand acres were handed out in 1752 alone. *NON SIBI SED ALIIS* had fallen on its nose. The dream was long since dead, but Savannah was here to stay.

THE ROYAL CROWN CITY
1751–1775

EMBRYONIC SELF-GOVERNMENT, 1751

A vital action on the eve of transfer from Trustee to crown status was the beginning of self-government. Previously the Trustees in England managed the colony, with Oglethorpe on-site periodically being his autocratic self. Incapable of delegating authority, Oglethorpe had colonists viewing his few officials as mere ciphers from the beginning. Thomas Causton supervised in Oglethorpe's absence, amassing charges of corruption. After 1741 William Stephens became the more steady local conduit of the Trustees' orders. As early as 1738 Stephens had Causton's account books examined by Thomas Jones, who succeeded Causton. Dismissing Causton as public storekeeper, Oglethorpe fretted about the potential scandal looming over the colony: *I cannot as yet find that Causton has been guilty of getting for himself, though he has unaccountably trifled away the public money. . . . (I know not what name to give it).* The only other local administration was a general court of three judges called bailiffs, set up to enforce the handful of statutes on the books. Gripes and grievances against them were also endless.

A prime motivation for strong—or any—government was the prospect that South Carolina would annex the colony in the vacuum left by the departing Trustees. The threat was real. This would not be the last time friendly Carolinians would try to embrace Georgia out of existence.

A council first met in Savannah on January 15, 1751. Composed of sixteen deputies sent from any settlement with over ten families, the group assembled a list of eleven grievances. Most of these issues were corrected by the Trustees back in England. The most tangible result was the construction of a decent wharf along the river, completed by 1760. The Trustees even encouraged another meeting—provided each elected delegate have at least one hundred mulberry trees on his fifty acres of property.

A local militia was approved, headed by Captain Noble Jones, who had been one of the original colonists on the *Anne* and served with Oglethorpe at Bloody Marsh. Any man with three hundred acres and a horse could be in the cavalry, provided he showed up at the musters on horseback. Those without horses would be de facto infantry. Commander Jones counted around 220 men in the Savannah militia's first parade on June 13, 1751. The manpower was drawn from the seven hundred to eight hundred white males estimated to be in the whole colony. Jones proudly wrote, *they behaved well and make a pretty appearance.*

The Savannah Assembly, 1755

The transition from Trustee colony to royal province was consummated by the meeting of the first Royal Assembly in Savannah on January 7, 1755. Discussions had begun in 1751, with official transfer of the charter in 1752. What evolved from this fermentation period was a power structure similar to the other British colonies, beginning with Virginia in 1607.

The king would appoint a royal governor to rule over an assembly. The assembly in turn would have an upper and lower house, simulating Parliament's House of Lords and House of Commons. The lower house was elected, with their actions passing to the upper house, or council, community leaders appointed by the crown. There were limited checks and balances between "the people's" elected common house and the council, the latter skewed by their appointment process to check any excess of democracy. Only the lower house could initiate money bills and approve bills before they became law. They alone could elect their own speaker. The twelve-member upper council was all prestige and persuasion with no teeth. They stood at shoulder level with the governor to—momentarily—delay a bill by a frown, and generally smile along with the governor over his land grants and appointments. There was an implied advise and consent process, but only at the whim of the governor, who could convene, recess, or dissolve the whole body at his pleasure. He was also the final chief justice and sole head of the military—appointed and paid by Mother England to act in her interest.

Georgia was upgraded from colony to province, since provinces and their minions had more prestige. The province was divided into eight parishes by 1758, with Savannah being in the parish called Christ Church. Many new laws would be needed; lawyers were—at last—openly admitted to Georgia. A flourishing Savannah Bar Association soon appeared. One of the first acts of the assembly was to adopt a legal Slave Code in 1755.

JOHN REYNOLDS—FIRST ROYAL GOVERNOR
"HE DON'T COMMUNICATE TO THEM"
1754–1756

On October 29, 1754, Georgia's first royal governor, John Reynolds, sailed past Oglethorpe's crude lighthouse on Tybee Island to be welcomed with ringing bells and booming cannon. *The lower Class of People unwilling to lose their Share of Rejoicing made a Bonfire of the Guard House, and had nigh done the same with the old Council-House.* Perhaps the lower class was psychic. John Reynolds would make Captain Bligh look magnanimous.

Upon landing, Reynolds noted that there were *about 150 houses, all wooden ones, very small, and mostly old,* including the old council house on present Wright Square, *in great Danger of falling.* So it was. In the council's first meeting *one end fell down whilst . . . we were all there.* No one—physically—was hurt. Reynolds would continue to bring down the house.

Reynolds was a diplomatic disaster from the beginning. He immediately declared war on his leading councilmen—James Habersham, Noble Jones, and Patrick Graham. Snorted Reynolds at the whole advise and consent process: they—zounds—*would fain have all things Determined by Vote.* Soon Reynolds set up his own written dictates, which councilman Alexander Kellett described: *He don't communicate to them . . . otherwise than by Reading these himself in an unintelligible manner.* When first affronted by opposition, Reynolds' written bristling retort began: *I expect that no Member of this Board will presume again to tell me in Council.* As only a minor detail of his style, he ordered that a man be hanged two days before his appointed legal time.

Flaunting the laws that didn't suit, Reynolds simply altered the legislative minutes to cover his illegalities. He soon enlisted his deputy, William Little, to handle such things for him. A ship's surgeon under Captain Reynolds for twenty years, Little was installed over the assembly, the main perk being to rig who would be elected. Little twice failed to convey on bills passed by the assembly on account of his own sense of their *Insignificancy and Non-Importance.* In retaliation the assembly formed a grand jury and declared Little a public nuisance, *a man of bad head and worse heart.* Reynolds then dissolved the assembly. Councilman Jonathan Bryan demanded Reynolds be recalled.

Reynolds also decided to relocate the settlement of Savannah to the Ogeechee River. He reasoned: *There are many objections to this town of Savannah being [the capitol], besides it being situated at the extremity of the province, the slowness of the river, and the great height of the land, which is very inconvenient in the loading and unloading of ships.* Reynolds drew up plans and proposed the new name of Hardwicke, after a relative. He progressed as far as unloading twenty-seven lots to associates. But he also kept one eye on the English Board of Trade. When he finally got the pay raise he sought, he returned to England as a sea captain in 1756. There he became an admiral in the Royal Navy. (The French have a tongue-in-cheek expression, *pour encourager les autres,* "to encourage the others." It derives from Voltaire's wry observation in 1757 that the English shoot an admiral from time to time—*pour encourager les autres.* Perhaps they had Reynolds in mind. The French captured Reynolds on his return voyage from Savannah to England—but released him.)

HENRY ELLIS—SECOND ROYAL GOVERNOR
"A RECESS WOULD BE AGREEABLE AT THIS SEASON"
1757–1760

Opposite in temperament to Reynolds was the next governor, Henry Ellis, thirty-six years of age, who arrived on February 16, 1757. Born in Ireland, Ellis was described as *rational, benevolent, and pleasant,* vowing that *if unfortunately my wishes and endeavours prove fruitless, to be the first to solicit my recall.* He was endlessly curious, especially about natural and scientific phenomena. Earlier, as an explorer, he participated in the search for the Great Northwest Passage to the Orient via the Hudson River. He had sailed to both polar areas, Africa, and the West Indies. He was a member of the prestigious Royal Society and knew Oglethorpe, by then a fellow member. In Savannah people watched in amazement while Ellis trudged the sandy streets, a thermometer attached by a string from his parasol hanging at the exact *height of his nostrils.* Aha, concluded Ellis, Savannahians breathe *a hotter air than any other people on the face of the earth.* As historian William W. Abbott wrote: "His deductions and conclusions are always logical, plausible, stimulating, and delivered with clarity and pungency. Unfortunately they are nearly always mistaken."

Unlike Reynolds, Ellis was no political fool. If he had been, he might have missed the strong message manifested by the *lower class* burning of William Little in effigy on the day Ellis arrived. Astutely Ellis immediately took a peek at Little's handpicked assembly. Blaming the weather, Ellis then suspended the group, *finding a recess would be agreeable at this Season of the Year*. Even in mid-winter Ellis sensed things needed cooling down: *This suspense will give time for mens passions to subside & for truth to appear through the cloud of party prejudice that at present obscures it . . . every publick office that either existed or were likely to be established, were filled with [Reynolds'] Creatures*. In less than six months Ellis had worked political magic, restoring an upbeat harmony in the province with new appointments loyal to him; Ellis knew how to play the game.

Ellis next focused on the defenses of the province. Since the French and Indian War had broken out in 1756, his first undertaking was to build log forts along the southern frontier in case Spain decided to join France in the global conflict. His fears were well founded, but no local repercussions resulted. As Ellis wrote to William Pitt in general explanation, *It is not probable that it [Georgia] will ever be properly settled . . . unless some effectual measures are taken for putting the province in such a state of defense so as not to be at the mercy of its savage neighbors.*

After Ellis shored up Georgia's southern defenses, he turned his attention to the new Indian problems. Oglethorpe had had a steady, honest touch with the Indians, but after his departure they became progressively less friendly. An estimated eight thousand hostile braves ringed Savannah, according to the alarmed new regime. At least this was the reason that the assembly gave for sending no military support to Mother England in her fight against the French in Canada. Since Savannah was desperately poor, they sent no material aid either. In fact, Reynolds had previously requested £28,000 from Parliament to bolster Georgia's own defenses. As for the colony actually sending aid, Reynolds had bluntly responded in his usual whimsical way: *I beg leave to acquaint you that Georgia is so very thinly inhabited that there is not the least probability of my being able in any degree to effect it. This I had the honor to represent to you before, by my letter of February 7, in answer to yours of October 26.*

In the eight months since his arrival, Ellis had personally welcomed over 1,300 Indians with grievances into his chambers or home on Telfair Square. On October 25, 1757, Ellis gathered important Indian chiefs, along with Governor William Lyttleton of South Carolina, for a climactic powwow in Savannah. The Indian delegation had refused to meet in Charles Towne. At the meeting relations were sufficiently mended, sparing Savannah the ravages of the extensive Cherokee War that followed in 1761. William Abbott put his finger on Ellis' political genius when he called him "chameleon-like," able to adapt to any situation for the salvation of his province. Even Oglethorpe had wisely suppressed any little ego problems in order to ingratiate himself with South Carolina's Robert Johnson. So too, Ellis could work in subordinate harmony with Governor Lyttleton—little brother to big brother.

Sir James Wright, royal governor from 1760 to 1782. Although respected as an individual, he was progressively dragged down by the rebellious movement that ended in the American Revolution. Exiled, he is buried in Westminster Abbey, London. (Courtesy of the Georgia Department of Archives and History.)

As Ellis wrote in 1757: *By address, by bold, but honest arts, & by doing my duty in a way unusual here, I have at length been able to change the temper of my opponents to my wishes.*

James Wright—Last Royal Governor
God Save the King
1760–1776

Suffering ill health, Ellis requested a leave of absence to sail back to England after three years in the province. He complained that the *intense heats* allowed *very little enjoyment of life*. Ellis never returned, feeling—correctly—he left the province *in full as good a situation, as could reasonably be expected*. One month before Ellis left in the fall of 1760, the third, last, and longest serving royal governor would arrive. Characteristically Ellis spent the interval smoothing the new governor's way.

Coming full cycle from Reynolds, James Wright was personally likable and respected—even by those burning him in effigy a decade later. He was similar to Ellis, but with a decade more experience and the resultant clout of maturity. With his Reynolds-like recessive gene, however, Wright would progressively view growing opposition as lack of respect for his position. Wright was first described by the assembly as having *Integrity and Uprightness joyned with solid sense and sound Judgment*. Although Wright was educated in England, he was born in South Carolina, serving as her attorney general for twenty years before coming to Georgia. Prophetically he took office in the year that the colonial namesake, George II, died—to be followed by "Mad" King George III.

The First Prosperity—Rice

During Wright's term as governor, Savannah would continue to establish herself as the social, political, and cultural center of the province. Augusta, Darien, Frederica, Midway, Sunbury, and New Ebenezer were the other settlements that had taken root. The prominent factor in Savannah's first boom was the emergence of the rice trade. The industry required tide-irrigated low country, and—like the rice center next door, South Carolina—demanded massive amounts of manual labor—namely, slaves.

In 1751 William DeBrahm had observed *scarce three Dozen of African Servants* in Georgia. After the Trustees' antislavery law was overturned, the total population of the colony (around three thousand to four thousand) was nearly one-third slaves by 1753. By 1760 the population was six thousand whites and 3,500 slaves. In just six more years there would be sixteen thousand slaves in Georgia. (An estimated four thousand slaves would depart Savannah with their Loyalist masters after the Revolution. Slavery was a national institution by the Revolution: 15,000 in New York, 80,000 in Maryland, 75,000 in North Carolina, and 110,000 in South Carolina.)

With the emergence of the rice trade, a prosperous plantation society arose, living on elegant estates with romantic names like Silk Hope (James Habersham), Wormsloe (Noble Jones), Mulberry Grove (Patrick Graham), Fair Lawn (James Wright), Brampton (Jonathan Bryan), Isle of Hope, and Wild Heron. By 1773 Wright recorded 1,400 plantations, averaging around 850 acres each. The richest Savannahian of all was said to be Wright himself, whose property was estimated at £80,000 among his eleven plantations. He was closely followed by his lieutenant governor, John Graham (25,000 acres), and James Habersham (10,000 acres). Wright and Habersham respectively owned 523 and 198 slaves.

Cotton was not yet king, but a first shipment of eight bales would reach Liverpool from Savannah in 1764, exported by Habersham, courtesy of the Salzburgers. The next year the *Friendship* left Savannah with a heartening £18,000 load of goods. The cargo included deer skins, lumber from Darien, indigo, and silk. By 1770 Savannah's exports would exceed £100,000.

James Habersham wrote to former Governor Ellis that *We have now near 40 square rigged Vessels before town. . . . I am loaded with Business.* Fifty-two ships cleared Savannah in 1755, to triple in the next ten years. By then there were over a dozen merchant warehouses along the river on *commerce row* (now Factor's Row). Habersham and Francis Harris had opened the first commerce house in 1744, sending their first £2,000 cargo of foreign trade by 1749.

The transition from silk to rice is mirrored in the history of a structure called the Filature on Reynolds Square. In 1751 this large wooden building was the first silk factory built in America. From a zenith of 40,000 mulberry trees planted around Savannah in the 1730's, by 1764 over half the dwindling silk came not from Savannah, but Ebenezer. In 1758 the Filature burned down, containing over 7,000 pounds of silkworm cocoons. By 1764 it was rebuilt and contained another 15,000 pounds of cocoons. But in the face of the transition to the rice trade the silk industry so declined over the next two years that the Filature was converted into a large assembly hall in 1766.

High Society, 1760

Socially and materially Savannah began to emulate Charles Towne, itself described around that time as *a little London*. Savannah squares now saw carriages, satin bonnets, fine wigs, white silk gloves, painted hose, and gentry festooned with fine jewelry. By the 1760's Savannahians were buying locally such books as *Gulliver's Travels, Robinson Crusoe, Aesop's Fables,* and Shakespeare, along with Greek and Latin classics. Three subscription libraries were present, to be followed by the Savannah Library Society in 1774. A post office opened in 1764. The well-off were posing for their portraits by Thomas Bembridge and Jeremiah Theus. Most of this same strata attended Christ Church and listened to Georgia's first pipe organ by 1758. The building was eight years old.

Besides Trustee-era cricket, horse racing, and pub crawling, other semblances of lighthearted society appeared, as illustrated by the resurfaced St. Andrew's Society. A quarter century before, the malcontent little nucleus of Scottish *sheep excrement* had been shoveled out of Savannah into South Carolina. By 1762 the society was officially reborn, with thirty members meeting at MacHenry's Tavern. Comprising the social gentry, membership in the society was no longer limited by station or nationality. It has remained vibrantly active. In 1771 James Habersham described the annual banquet that easily could describe the one last year or next year: *Tomorrow I am to dine with a Merry Saint, St. Andrew. I am a Member of the Society, and as I am told our Friend John Graham will preside there, I am of Opinion, he will send many of the Saints Votaries away with Sare Heads. I do not mean our Friend John likes Sare Heads, because I know him to be one of the most temperate and at the same time one of the best Hearted Men in this Province, but for the Honor of his Saint and Country, I think he will on this occasion particularly exert himself.*

In 1758 the Savannah assembly adopted the Church of England as the official provincial religion under the long, strong leadership of the Reverend Bartholomew Zouberbuhler, a man fluent in English, French, and German. Membership was not compulsory; Jews, Lutherans, Presbyterians, Baptists, and others could still practice their own faiths—as long as they all paid the new tax to finance the salaries of the Anglican clergy. Catholics, of course, remained scarce—still not allowed to vote as late as the revised laws of 1776.

In 1763 James Johnson started the first colony newspaper, the *Georgia Gazette,* on Broughton Street. He published it from his printing and book shop with his jingling profits from sales of *Gulliver's Travels,* ink, stationery, and legal forms. By the late 1760's, thirty-two merchants had advertisements in his paper.

Prelude To Revolution, 1763

For Savannah in 1763, the principal consequence of the Seven Years (French and Indian) War was that Florida was now English, an outcome that certainly must have pleased that old Spainophobe, Oglethorpe.* The other consequence was that England, in winning

---

*Spain had joined France just before she lost the war, losing Florida as a minor chip in reshuffled geography. England would surrender Florida back to Spain in 1783, when the Spanish backed the winning Franco-American side in the Revolution.

the war, doubled her national debt. Ah, there's the rub—one to progressively cause friction for the next fifteen years.

New monies must be raised to recoup. Certainly the colonies could understand—especially Georgia, who hadn't sent any men nor contributed any money or material to the common cause. Besides, new taxes would help sustain England's military strength in the colonies, the best insurance to have on hand against Indians gone wrong—remember the sweeping Cherokee War of 1761. In spite of his success with the Indians, Ellis had warned that the province was *still on a very ticklish footing* with the Creeks.

Of course Georgia was not the only colony to chafe at this taxing posture of arrogant self-interest and paternalistic noblesse oblige. One easily recognizes the decade-long preamble to the revolution: TAXATION WITHOUT REPRESENTATION.

THE REVOLUTIONARY PERIOD

THE DREADED STAMP ACT, 1765
"MY WRETCHED SITUATION"

Parliament passed the notorious Stamp Act in 1765, bureaucratically charging a tax on all marriage certificates, deeds, contracts, notes, bonds, university degrees, cargo manifests, pamphlets, books, almanacs, and newspapers. The tax hit everybody—most immediately James Johnson, who quickly closed down the *Georgia Gazette* (later to be reborn as the *Royal Georgia Gazette*). This same year, when Savannah celebrated its traditional Guy Fawkes Day, things got a bit out of hand. Sailors paraded one of their shipmates dressed as the mock *Stamp-master* on a scaffold through the streets. He was progressively *abused* as the celebration wound up in front of MacHenry's Tavern. There fantasy and reality became blurred in a rum haze—and the poor fellow was actually strung up. The *Gazette* recorded that the crowd was *highly diverted by the humor of the tars.*

General outrage promptly resulted in a protest meeting of the Stamp Act Congress in New York. Wright, described as *universally respected by all the inhabitants* [who] *can hardly say enough in his praise,* was able to cajole Savannah into not sending any representatives, although an observer went—against Wright's objections. Since Georgia was among the few provinces that did not officially participate, from the first she was labeled a Loyalist Milquetoast. Carolina propaganda howled at *the weak and unpatriotic Georgians who refused to join in support of the fight for American freedom.* This lambasting only intensified as Savannahians, *like Esau of old, sold their birthright for a mess of pottage.* The Liberty or Death Boys up in Charles Towne vowed to stop trade with

Doctor Lyman Hall, the most firebrand signer of the Declaration of Independence for Georgia. He tried to lead his Midway parish to secede to South Carolina because Georgia was too slow in getting revolutionary fever. (Courtesy of the Hargrett Rare Book and Manuscript Library, University of Georgia.)

the pantywaists in Savannah, calling them *unworthy of the rights of freemen.* By 1775 St. John's Parish (Midway, south of Savannah) was fed up with Georgia's unpatriotic foot-dragging; by then Georgia was the only province not to attend meetings in Philadelphia. Midway tried to secede from Georgia and join South Carolina. Physician Lyman Hall, Midway's most ardent delegate, failing to swing the deal, went off to Philadelphia alone. Settled in 1752 by Puritans originally from Massachusetts, Midway was the firebrand of Georgia. Wright sneered at the uproar of *these Poor Insignificant Fanatics.*

While Charles Towne, and everybody else, defiantly maintained a free port, Governor Wright strictly upheld the shipping stamp law. Sixty vessels jammed the Savannah harbor, waiting for the arrival of the H.M.S. *Speedwell* with its load of little coarse blue stamps of tobacco paper for pasting on exports. Amid the growing tension, Wright wrote of his increasing *wretched situation,* as Georgians *have been seized with their strange enthusiastic ideas of Liberty and power.*

THE LIBERTY BOYS, 1765
"FATHER AGAINST SON AND SON AGAINST FATHER"

Not all Savannahians were pantywaists. The same year the Stamp Act emerged, so did Savannah's Liberty Boys, or Sons of Liberty—called *the Sons of Licentiousness* by Wright. Over the next decade the club's membership would be in the hundreds, the roster including such famous Savannah and regional names as Noble Wymberley Jones, Joseph Habersham, James Habersham, Jr., Archibald Bulloch, Peter Tondee, John Houstoun, Edward Telfair, John Milledge, James Jackson, Samuel Elbert, Joseph Clay, Lachlan McIntosh, Button Gwinnett, George Walton, Lyman Hall, and Jonathan Bryan.

Jonathan Bryan was the son of Joseph Bryan, colonial namesake of Bryan Street. Such were the times that began to try men's souls. Future Americans, who were Englishmen in transition, turned from their Loyalist fathers in the colonial past to embrace the new fight for freedom. The anguished schism between fathers Noble Jones and James Habersham and their respective sons epitomizes what has been accurately called America's first civil war—rebel brother against Loyalist brother, father, son, uncle, and neighbor. In 1775 James Habersham, cofounder of Bethesda Orphanage, wrote: *Father against Son, and Son against Father, and nearest relations and Friends combatting with each other . . . cutting each others throats, dreadfull to think of much less to experience.*

Other excerpts of letters by Habersham touch on the growing heartache. In 1766 he wrote to his old friend George Whitefield, cofounder of Bethesda: *My very Flesh trembles while I am writing to you, at, I must say, the Madness of the People here. . . . I have had an incendi-*

ary letter written to me, have been threatened to be mobbed at Night . . . surely we are no longer Freemen, than the Laws of our Country can freely operate to protect them . . . My Heart bleeds . . . P.S. The People at Bethesda are all well. Four years later James Habersham wrote to his own son, Joseph, on the brink of Liberty Boy leadership: *Thus my dear Joe, it is easy to inflame the populace, which when once done . . . is frequently productive of the most terrible Effects. . . . God grant that it may not be repeated by the present Generation. . . . I am dear Joe Your Truly Affecate [sic] Father.* James Habersham would watch his sons Joseph, James, and John, along with nephew Joseph Clay, help lead the Liberty Boys to the ultimate split.

As for the *Speedwell* full of stamps in 1765, the Liberty Boys, up to two hundred strong, threatened to seize the stamps, but were backed down by Wright with his own musket and fifty soldiers. If not thwarted, the Savannah Stamp Party would have preceded the Boston Tea Party by seven years. However, by way of the stamps, and the newly arrived English stamp agent, George Angus, most ships were officially cleared out of port. Of course this only made the local Liberty Boys appear even more ineffectual, particularly when Charleston Liberty Boys managed to seize and destroy two of the ships cleared by those very stamps. In Savannah, James Habersham had to seek refuge in the governor's house, while the governor himself, along with the stamp agent, were hanged in effigy. This was only the beginning.

James Habersham had sound business instincts and was one of the wealthiest colonists behind Governor Wright. Most loyal to Wright's wishes, Habersham watched in anguish as his three sons drifted over to the cause of the Liberty Boys. (Courtesy of Rita Trotz, The Printed Page, Savannah.)

Benjamin Franklin—Georgia Representative

Affairs were paralyzed in the elected Savannah assembly. The lower house, loaded with Liberty Boy Whigs, split with the upper council, all of whom were either Loyalists or undecided. The issue was whether to send a representative to England to speak for the province. What was the point? Obviously nobody listened over in the mother country.

In lieu of having taxation with no representation at all, in 1768 Benjamin Franklin volunteered to do double duty in London for Georgia and his native Pennsylvania. He would also end up representing New Jersey and Massachusetts, making him in essence America's colonial ambassador. Savannah's gratitude endures in the name of Franklin Square, among other personal ties. Georgia would commemorate his service by originally naming their state university Franklin College. Now located in the rolling hills of Athens, the University of Georgia was founded in 1785 and is the oldest state university in the United States. John Milledge of Savannah donated the land.

Yielding to American outrage, Parliament repealed the Stamp Act in February 1766. William Pitt, earl of Chatham (namesake of Chatham County), led the debate. If Pitt himself could exclaim to the king, *This kingdom has no right to lay a tax on the colonies. I rejoice that America*

Benjamin Franklin, namesake of Franklin Square, assumed Georgia's representation to England in 1768 because the royal colony refused in a huff to send more agents to face the British Parliament's arrogance. (Courtesy of V. and J. Duncan Antique Maps and Prints, Savannah.)

has resisted, then such only fanned the local flames of independence. The now happy colonists responded to Pitt: *To you grateful America attributes that she is reinstated in her former liberties.* The assembly happily wrote to Wright vowing their *most dutiful acknowledgements to the best of Kings for his paternal and princely attention and regard manifested to his faithful subjects in these remote parts of his dominions.*

New Taxes and Turmoil, 1767
"They Bellow'd on Their Rights and Privileges"

The victory did not last. The Stamp Act was followed by one similar in design, the Townshend Act. It taxed all imports of glass, lead, paper, painter's colors—and tea. For a kicker, search and seizure—without warrant—could be imposed by British soldiers on any place at all that might harbor such untaxed goods. The Quartering Act of 1765 also was irritating, demanding local tax money to garrison those same soldiers right next to where you lived—occasionally in the very house you lived.

The Savannah assembly refused to implement the Quartering Act. In 1769 the group balked again, under the fearless leadership of Jonathan Bryan. The members drew up a statute boycotting all British imports, including *any negroes that shall be brought into this Province from Africa* by English slave runners. Any dissenters *were not only to be treated with contempt, but deemed enemies to their country . . . that it may be detested and abhorred.*

Doctor Noble Wimberley Jones, ardent Liberty Boy, who repeatedly was rejected by head Loyalist James Habersham as the elected speaker of the rebellious Savannah Assembly. (Courtesy of V. and J. Duncan Antique Maps and Prints, Savannah.)

As elected speaker of the assembly, Dr. Noble Wymberley Jones led the resistance until Governor Wright dissolved the body on February 22, 1770, complaining that they *Bellow'd on their Rights and Privileges, and the Plenitude of their Powers.* Wright had first dissolved it in December 1768 after a squabble over the Townshend Act, which he dismissed as a *Distinction without a Difference.*

In 1771 Wright departed for England on a huffy leave of absence, putting James Habersham in charge. During Wright's absence, Habersham twice vetoed Jones's reelection in 1772. Substitute Liberty Boy Archibald Bulloch was eventually elected speaker on the third attempt. But when Habersham saw the minutes of the assembly showing Jones had been the first choice for the third defiant time, he dissolved the body over crownly principle and personal affront. The assembly retorted—*This act of dissolution is regarded as unjustifiable interference. . . . It's effect is perplexing and deleterious.*

Ultimately Parliament would limit the Townshend tax to tea alone. But the fuse was lit, to burn along in Tondee's Tavern.

Tondee's Tavern, 1766
"The Wars of Bacchus"

Born in Switzerland, Peter Tondee was raised as one of the first children in James Habersham's Bethesda Orphanage. Indeed, he was an early member of the Union Society. This fund-raising board for the benevolent refuge couldn't have been more ecumenical: Tondee, a Catholic; Richard Milledge, an Anglican; and Mordecai Sheftall, Jewish patriot. (Tondee was possibly a Huguenot, according to recent scholarship.)

As an adult, Tondee and his Acadian wife, named Lucy Mouse, built a tavern on what is now the northwest corner of Broughton and Whitaker streets. The tavern was a family gathering place where parents drank ale while their children played a game called quoits. Still a recognizable game today, quoits was a contest to toss a ring around a peg—with money riding on the outcome in the adult version.

This early Savannah bistro soon became popular, even with Governor Wright—before a politically active group calling themselves the *All Saints Quoits Club* began to meet there. Increasingly so did the Liberty Boys, wearing their Liberty stocking caps. A Loyalist sneered that the group met there to fight *the wars of Bacchus* (god of wine).

Dissatisfaction in the colony was merely a dull roar at the time of "Sir" James Wright's return to Savannah in February 1773. He was even received on his landing by a temporarily cheerful group from the assembly. Wright noted *rather a pleasing Prospect of Harmony amongst the different Branches of the Legislature.* Basking in the prestige of his new title of baronet, he was applauded on all sides for his plan to purchase two million acres of Indian land, which would be the main magnet to draw "Crackers" from Virginia to Georgia.

Then, in 1774, England passed the Intolerable Acts. Boston Harbor was closed, partly as punishment for the Boston Tea Party three months before. The *Georgia Gazette* recorded the incident: *Two thousand chests of the East India Company's Tea, that were on board three vessels from London, have been stove and the Tea thrown overboard in the Harbour of Boston, by a number of people unknown.* (There were other tea parties along the coast, including one at Charleston. Savannah didn't happen to have any tea on hand with which to throw a party.) The Liberty Boys in Savannah hit the ceiling over the Intolerable Acts and summoned their first organized meeting on July 27 at the Exchange on Bay Street. A larger meeting would follow on August 10 at Tondee's Tavern. The *Georgia Gazette* of July 20 advocated a protest meeting over *the arbitrary and alarming imposition of the late acts of the British Parliament respecting the town of Boston.*

Peter Tondee, owner of Tondee's tavern at Whitaker and Broughton streets, where the Liberty Boys met to fight *the wars of Bacchus*, according to irate Loyalists. He was raised at Loyalist James Habersham's Bethesda Orphanage. (Courtesy of Walter Wright, Savannah.)

Wright called his council together and demanded the resignation of Jonathan Bryan, believed a prime instigator of the outcry. Bryan—stating he would *save them the trouble*—shoved his resignation into Wright's hand *in a style peculiar to himself for its candour and energy.* Wright next countered by issuing a proclamation, warning *all assembling and meetings of the people which may tend to raise fears and jealousies in the minds of his Majesty's subjects . . . are unconstitutional, illegal, and punishable by law . . . pay due regard to this my proclamation, as they will answer the contrary at their peril. . . . God save the King.*

Of course the Liberty Boys met. They sent over five hundred barrels of rice to Boston, but did not go as far as Lyman Hall had wished—a complete break with England.

Later a Loyalist dissent widely proclaimed the proceedings of August 10 at Tondee's Tavern rigged. It complained that the doors had been *shut for a considerable time, . . . and when several gentlemen attempted to join, the tavern-keeper, who stood at the door with a list in his hand, refused them admittance. . . . Such was the conduct of these pretended advocates for the liberties of America.*

The governor quickly drafted a petition protesting the meeting, collecting the signatures of Noble Jones and James Habersham against their sons. Other Loyalist dissent came from outlying settlements, worried over Indian attacks in the absence of British troops. One Loyalist wrote that his parish *would most certainly be laid waste and depopulated, unless we receive such powerful aid and assistance as none but Great Britain can give.*

Meanwhile the Liberty Boys were garnering support, and they now had a church committed to their cause. The Reverend John Joachim Zubly, the minister of Independent Presbyterian Church, was, like Peter Tondee, a native of Switzerland. Zubly was considered one of the most persuasive preachers in the province. His views were anti-England; and, like Thomas Paine in Boston, he turned out pamphlets of impassioned oratory against Britain. So powerful were Zubly's rebel-rousing sermons, the Anglican congregation often deserted Christ Church on Johnson Square to attend Independent Presbyterian on Bryan Street.

Words Lead to Action, 1775
"Give Me Liberty or Give Me Death"

It is in vain, Sir, to extenuate the matter. Gentlemen may cry "Peace, Peace!"—but there is no peace. The war is actually begun! The next gale that sweeps from the North will bring to our ears the clash of resounding arms! Our brethren are already in the field! Why stand we here idle? What is it that Gentlemen wish? What would they have? Is life so dear, or peace so sweet, as to be purchased at the price of chains and slavery? Forbid it, Almighty God! I know not what course others may take, but as for me, give me liberty or give me death!"

Those words came from another pulpit, one in Richmond, Virginia. Patrick Henry made his famous speech following reports of the *Shot Heard 'Round the World* at Lexington and Concord on April 19, 1775. News did not reach Savannah until May 10, where it immediately prompted a celebration. The revelry resulted in a raid on His Majesty's powder magazine on Reynolds Square. Six hundred pounds of powder were sent to Boston to be used against the British at Bunker Hill. Wright offered a £150 reward for the arrest of the leaders (Jones, Joseph Habersham, Joseph Clay, Edward Telfair, and John Milledge). No one stepped forward to claim it.

Agitation continued. On June 4 all of the cannon that Governor Wright had assembled to celebrate the king's birthday was spiked and rolled down the river bank. The next day a liberty pole appeared in front of Tondee's Tavern. On June 21 a Revolutionary Council of Safety was established, as in other colonies. Tondee provided a free dinner and sufficient drink to toast all thirteen of them. On July 29 a sailor named John Hopkins, who happened by and made some impertinent remarks, was tarred and feathered, made to kiss the liberty pole, and forced to apologize by exclaiming, *Damnation to all Tories & Success to American Liberty.* Wright wrote: *Soon after they brought him in a cart down by my house, and such a horrid spectacle I really never saw.*

In a letter from Wright to his patron in England, Lord Dartmouth, he described the deteriorating situation: *The Liberty Folks here assembled in the Town of Sav. and put up a Liberty Tree and a Flag and in the Evening paraded about the Town I am informed to the number of 300, some say 400. . . . The Liberty Tree and Flagg were kept up from Tuesday Morning till now and is still flying in contempt and defiance of the Court and of all Law . . . which . . . seems now nearly at an end . . . this is very "galling.". . . My lord I presume again to repeat my humble request to have leave to return to England.*

Another group, similar to the Council of Safety, was the Savannah Parochial Committee, headed by Mordecai Sheftall. Peter Tondee and Mr. Lyons, blacksmith, were among the other members. Too populist and pedestrian for Wright's titled tastes, he described them as *a Parcel of the Lowest People, chiefly Carpenters, Shoemakers, Blacksmiths etc. with a Jew at their Head . . . it is really terrible my Lord that such people should be suffered to overturn the Civil Government . . . and sport with Other Mens Lives, Libertys, and Propertys.*

The Reverend Zubly and the Law of Liberty—1775
"We Do Not Complain of Law, But of Oppression"

On July 4, prophetically the year before the Declaration of Independence in 1776, 102 delegates attended the second provincial congress at Tondee's Tavern. The group first went to Independent Presbyterian Church to hear the Reverend Zubly give Georgia's most important revolutionary sermon, *The Law of Liberty*. Zubly based the sermon on the Epistle of James, the letter that the Salzburgers' patron saint, Martin Luther, three hundred years before had called *An Epistle of Straw (So speak ye, and so do, as they that shall be judged by the law of liberty—* James 2:12): *We are to be judged by the law of liberty. . . . Every man is a rational, and therefore accountable, creature. . . . Every work and every man will be brought into judgment, and the judgment of GOD will never be otherwise than according to truth. . . . Never let us lose out of sight that our interest lies in a perpetual connection with our mother country . . . there are thousands in Great-Britain that think with us, and wish well to the American cause, and make it their own . . . but the breach is growing wider and wider, it is be come great like a sea. . . . I have but a few hints to give to my hearers in general. . . . Let our conduct shew that we are not lawless. . . . Let us convince them that we do not complain of law, but of oppression. . . . Let us act "as free, and yet not make liberty a cloak of maliciousness, but as the servants of GOD."*

The mixed emotions of these thoughts would cause a crisis of conscience for Zubly in Philadelphia.

Off to Philadelphia—1776
"When in the Course of Human Events"

After thirteen days of deliberations, the provincial congress sent another petition to His Majesty, asking him to control his *corrupt Parliament, despotic ministry, and army of mercenaries . . . we must take the liberty to speak before we die.* The congress announced to one and all— *A civil war in America is begun.* Wright was the true instigator—he had dissolved the assembly. (Wright did try to reconvene it, but members of the assembly refused to show up.) Georgians also learned that they had just voluntarily given up their *genial herb*—tea—for the good of the cause. Delegates were chosen to represent Georgia at the Continental Congress to be held in Philadelphia. Zubly was a natural choice, along with firebrand Lyman Hall from Midway, who had led his little parish's campaign for secesssion from Georgia to Carolina. Noble W. Jones, Archibald Bulloch, and John Houstoun were also picked. Button Gwinnett and George Walton would be selected at a later meeting.

For a variety of personal, business, or unknown reasons, the three Georgia names destined to immortality at the bottom of the Declaration of Independence were Hall, Walton, and Gwinnett. Today Button Gwinnett's exceedingly rare signature is easily the most valuable in American history. (Currently selling at well over $100,000—if it isn't one of many fakes. This market was abetted by Gwinnett's death in a

Button Gwinnett

duel a year later, leaving only around thirty-six known authentic Gwinnett signatures today.)

One name on our most viewed document in the National Archives is not Zubly's. When he got to Philadelphia and saw the action caused by words like his, he got Loyalist pangs. One day during mounting argument, Zubly blurted out: _A Republican government is little better than government of devils._ He was caught trying to warn Wright of impending separation. Confronted on the floor of Congress, he was forced to resign in disgrace. George Walton replaced him. Zubly came back to Savannah and converted his pulpit—and pamphlets—to support of the Loyalists under Wright and James Habersham. Later Zubly was banished to South Carolina and half of his considerable property confiscated. He returned to Savannah during the Revolution and died in 1781 on the eve of the final British eviction from the colonies.

"Sir James, You Are My Prisoner," 1776

Wright was increasingly isolated and powerless. By January 1775 he put his own fiber on the line, as expressed in these excerpts to the Savannah Commons House Assembly: _GENTLEMEN . . . Be not led away by the voices and opinions of men of overheated ideas; consider coolly and sensibly of the terrible consequences. . . . You may be advocates of liberty, so am I; but in a constitutional and legal way. . . . It is an indispensable truth, that where there is no law there can be no liberty. . . . Do not consider me as speaking to you as the King's governor. . . . I have lived amongst and presided over you upwards of fourteen years, and have other feelings. I have a real and affectionate regard for the people, and it grieves me._

By August of 1775, however, the Savannah port was closed to British vessels. By December the Council of Safety seized all the courts. Wright's personal gamble had failed. In the first month of 1776 he wrote: _There is hardly a shadow of government remaining. . . . It is really a wretched state to be left in. . . . The Powers of Government are wrested out of my hands._

On January 18, 1776, Joseph Habersham and a group burst into the governor's mansion (present site of the Telfair Academy) and arrested

Joseph Habersham, the Liberty Boy who boldly put Royal Governor James Wright under house arrest. (Courtesy of V. and J. Duncan Antique Maps and Prints, Savannah.)

Wright in mid-meeting with his councilmen. The twenty-four-year-old Habersham confronted Wright and exclaimed, *Sir James, you are my prisoner!* The patriots' Council of Safety had ordered the detention in order to prevent Wright's communication with three British troop ships off Tybee. The councilmen fled and Wright was put under house arrest. A month later he took a nightly stroll and, carrying the province seal, slipped off to Bonaventure Plantation, where his friend John Mullryne helped him aboard the H.M.S. *Scarborough.* From the ship he issued a few appeals back to Savannah—*in the King's name, the olive branch . . . to plead with them to consider well the course they had taken*—which were totally ignored. In retrospect the escape seemed absurdly easy, but appropriately so, as both friend and foe were happy Wright got away.

Loyalists James Habersham and Noble Jones also would never hear *we hold these truths to be self-evident* loudly read in the streets of the English Trustee city of their founding. Both died on the eve of 1776. Jones is buried in Bonaventure Cemetery, near the site of Wright's escape.

THE REVOLUTIONARY CITY

When in the Course of human events, it becomes necefsary for one people to difsolve the political bands which have connected them with another, and to afsume among the Powers of the earth, the separate and equal station to which the Laws of Nature and of Nature's God entitle them, a decent respect to the opinions of mankind requires that they should declare the causes which impel them to the separation.

We hold these truths to be self evident, that all men are created equal, that they are endowed by their Creator with certain inalienable Rights, that among these are Life, Liberty, and the pursuit of Happinefs. That to secure these rights, Governments are instituted among Men, deriving their just powers from the consent of the governed, That whenever any Form of Government becomes destructive of these ends, it is the Right of the People to alter or to abolish it, and to institute new Government.

On August 10, 1776, Tondee's Tavern celebrated the culmination of its patrons' efforts. Archibald Bulloch, the Council of Safety's president, read the Declaration of Independence four times—first to the provincial council inside the meetinghouse on Reynolds Square; next to the excited throng outside. The group then moved several blocks to Tondee's Tavern for a reading in front of the liberty pole. Gathering steam, the growing crowd then paraded to the old Trustees' Garden area for a fourth reading—just because it sounded so good—enhanced by the spirit-full celebration in the streets. (It was Savannah's soul mate, Benjamin Franklin, who helped Jefferson occasionally with a better sound. Franklin advised: *Here—on this line—"We hold these truths to be sacred and undeniable." It appears to me to be still stronger if we say that we hold them to be "self-evident."*) A holiday was declared as cannons along the Savannah River bluff boomed off a thirteen-gun salute to the new union. By that evening some citizens formed a mock funeral cortege with the effigy of King George inside the coffin. In front of the courthouse the crowd chanted: *Commit his political existence to the ground—corruption to corruption—tyranny to the grave—and oppression to eternal infamy, in sure and certain hope that he will never obtain a resurrection to rule again over these United States of America!* Tondee was already in his grave the year before, but his wife, Lucy, continued to do a brisk business in the tavern.

Wheels were quickly in motion, fashioning the new revolutionary state of Georgia. Archibald Bulloch was elected the first governor, and a constitution was completed on February 5, 1777. When Bulloch died mysteriously in the same month, Gwinnett replaced him as acting governor. The new constitution contained sixty-three articles and provided for a legislative and judicial branch. In order to vote one had to be twenty-one years of age, white, Protestant, own 250 acres, and be a resident for at least one year.

Archibald Bulloch, first governor of the new independent state of Georgia, died mysteriously in his first year of office. (Courtesy of V. and J. Duncan Antique Maps and Prints, Savannah.)

Since Savannah would surely be attacked by the British—a year later, in fact—troops became a prime concern. On hand were approximately 280 men, placed under the command of Colonel Lachlan McIntosh from Darien. A born military leader, McIntosh and most of his family had fought beside Oglethorpe at Bloody Marsh. He soon would be put in charge of all continental troops in Georgia and made a general.

Earlier the eccentric General Charles Lee had inspected Savannah and observed that no horses or boats existed to support grand defensive schemes of cavalry hordes and vast navies. He facetiously concluded: *I shou'd not be surpris'd if they were to propose mounting a body of Mermaids on Alligators.* The Council of Safety threatened to burn Savannah if forced to evacuate, *that rather the same be occupied by our enemies . . . that the same shall be burnt and destroyed.*

Gwinnett-McIntosh Duel, 1777
"A Scoundrell and Lying Rascal!"

Although he had had no military experience, Gwinnett fancied himself a military commander. His friend and cosigner, George Walton, declared that Gwinnett *like Alexander the Great, imagines himself to be lord of the earth.* As acting governor, Gwinnett was commander in chief in Georgia. The hodgepodge of troops in the region, already confused, often received rival or countermanding orders from Gwinnett and McIntosh.

Bad blood between the two came to a boil when Gwinnett arrested McIntosh's brother, George, for treason, at the request of John Hancock, president of the Continental Congress. George McIntosh was

Apocryphal 1876 print of the Gwinnett-McIntosh duel of 1777. Gwinnett grimaces in the foreground from the leg wound that would take his life. McIntosh looks appalled by his action, apparently unaware of the leg wound he also received. (Courtesy of V. and J. Duncan Antique Maps and Prints, Savannah.)

accused of helping buy rice to support British forces in Florida. Furthermore, Gwinnett refused to release McIntosh on bail.

Things were getting messy, including the already disorganized military situation in south Georgia. History was repeating itself. In the 1740's Oglethorpe had fallen on his face trying to take Florida from the Spanish. In 1777 this pratfall was repeated when Georgia troops tried to take Florida from the English. Masterminded by Gwinnett, McIntosh and Samuel Elbert were left wandering around in the southern swamps.

When the time came to replace the governor's vacancy left by Bulloch's death, John Adam Treutlen, an unblemished Salzburger patriot, was chosen over Gwinnett. Compounding the comedown, Gwinnett was called on the carpet along with McIntosh to explain the Florida follies. Being more facile of tongue, Gwinnett sidestepped most of the scolding. He even managed an approving resolution from the tribunal, *so far as these matters were laid before them.* McIntosh was not so lucky.

The general was enraged. The outcome of the argument is indirectly captured in the words of Lyman Hall; the secondhand nature of what really did—or didn't—happen still lingers today in local lore. *Here it was (in Assembly) that the Genl. called him (as 'tis said) a Scoundrell and lying Rascal—I confess I did not hear the words, not being so nigh the parties. A Duel was the consequence, in which they were placed at 10 or 12 foot Distance. Discharged their Pistols nearly at the same Time. Each wounded in the Thigh. Mr. Gwinnett's thigh broke so that he fell—on wh'h ('tis said) the Genl. Asked him if he chose to take another shot—was Answered Yes, if they would help him up (or words nearly the same). The seconds interposed* [Colonel James Habersham for McIntosh and George Wells for Gwinnett].

Mr. Gwinnett was brought in, the Weather Extremely hot. A Mortification came on—he languish'd from that Morning (Friday) till Monday Morning following & expired.

O Liberty. Why do you suffer so many of your faithful sons, your warmest Votaries, to fall at your Shrine. Alas, my Friend, my Friend.

The duel occurred at sunrise on May 16. Its locale was either to the south of present Colonial Park Cemetery or in James Wright's meadow near Thunderbolt. Legend has it that McIntosh limped over and that the two shook hands—never mind, *'tis said,* that Gwinnett wanted another shot at McIntosh, *or words nearly the same.* In great remorse McIntosh is also said to have broken off the handle of the pistol that mortally wounded Gwinnett.

Whatever remorse felt by McIntosh was insufficient for Lyman Hall, friend of Gwinnett. A murder trial resulted. McIntosh was found not guilty; even Gwinnett's wife cast no stones. However, after a petition that contained the names of five hundred of Gwinnett's friends was raised against McIntosh, he decided to go north and fight under General George Washington. A letter from Joseph Clay best sums up the atmosphere: *General McIntosh is called to the Northward, which I am very glad of, both for his own & the State's Sake. 'Twas impossible for him to have or to give any satisfaction here, prejudice was so strong against him.*

For his part McIntosh grumbled that Gwinnett's death *was evidently owing to the unskillfulness of his doctor.* Both men's graves are now about a pistol shot away in Colonial Park Cemetery. Probably—there is even minor controversy that Gwinnett's grave site, now replete with beautiful marble memorial by the D.A.R., is not exactly where he is buried.

British Capture Savannah, 1778

Savannah would be captured by the British in 1778 in an embarrassingly easy manner. It took about one day, as the British under Colonel Archibald Campbell landed below Savannah at Brewton's Hill on December 27 with three thousand troops. Opposing him, General Robert Howe of North Carolina had around seven hundred troops. Nevertheless, Howe was overheard by one of his subordinates, George Walton, to exclaim that the British were *composed of raw boys from the Highlands and of Delancey's [Loyalist] green-coats, who would not fight, and that he did not care if there were twice the number.* Although overly blamed for the disaster at Savannah in light of information clearing him

Lachlan McIntosh was a brave and dedicated soldier who finally outlived the recrimination of killing Button Gwinnett in a duel.

Archibald Campbell, British commander of the 1778 capture of Savannah, much later in his career. (Courtesy of V. and J. Duncan Antique Maps and Prints, Savannah.)

George Walton, one of the three Georgia signers of the Declaration of Independence, was wounded and captured in the 1778 conquest of Savannah. (Courtesy of V. and J. Duncan Antique Maps and Prints, Savannah.)

Mordecai Sheftall, the Jewish patriot who was captured and nearly *skivered* in the 1778 British conquest of Savannah, was head of the Savannah Parochial Committee, in charge of civilian authority. (Courtesy of Marion A. Levy, Savannah.)

at his later court-martial, Howe by some accounts was preoccupied by the fair sex—*a sort of woman-eater that devours every thing that comes his way, and that no woman can withstand*—in the opinion of Loyalist Janet Shaw.

Howe was concerned with how to block the British approach to the city. He chose a defensive position toward the sea with a creek in front, approximating the present intersection of Wheaton and Randolph streets. It was one of Governor Wright's plantations called Fair Lawn. Although outnumbered, Howe's position was strong, with both flanks naturally protected, and a low-lying, moat-like morass in front. Howe was vaguely aware of a way around his right flank guarded by a swamp and deep woods. Walton warned Howe of a path where he asserted, *Upon my honor, . . . that before the war I . . . have frequently crossed the pass . . . with young ladies, picking jessamines.* Howe set up a small patrol there, just in case, *to guard the desease of my position.*

An old black slave at Fair Lawn, Quamino "Quash" Dolly knew about the private gully. Induced *by a small reward,* he led the British right past the Americans to the rear of their defenses on December 29. The British had left their cannon back to distract the Continentals. With cannons now booming in front of them and muskets from behind, the Americans panicked and retreated back toward town.

Walton and around ninety Georgia militia took it upon themselves to hold off the British at the pass, arriving to find the redcoats approaching the swamp, *hopping over the little difficulties with great agility.* Walton was wounded and captured by Sir James Baird's troops. Howe's men, along with Governor John Houstoun, fell back to Musgrove Creek. The British fleet, under Admiral Hyde Parker's command, came up river to finish the job, taking another 126 prisoners and eleven American vessels, with the loss of only one English sailor.

The Americans, in full flight, found Musgrove Creek at high tide. Many made it over, except the last column under Samuel Elbert. Only strong swimmers escaped. Several dozen drowned, and around 186 more were taken prisoner. Among those captured were Mordecai Sheftall and his young son, Sheftall Sheftall, who did not know how to swim. According to Mordecai's account, the prisoners were marched into town to the courthouse and put under guard. As Sheftall recorded, he was called out by name, as *I was a very great rebel,* and put under separate guard. A Major Chrystie *ordered the sentry to guard me with a drawn bayonet.* Later, when Sheftall refused to divulge information on stores he knew of, he *was threatened to be run through the body, or, as they termed it, skivered.* This threat was almost carried out three times that night, before the Sheftalls were finally transferred to the prison ship *Nancy.* Over two-thirds of the American force had been captured or killed, often in a hasty manner. According to French witness Pierre Colamb, *Plunging their bayonets into the sides of the unhappy wretches, they [the British] continued stabbing until, on withdrawing their blades, they tore out their victims entrails.* According to a woman Loyalist, the Highland troops *ripped open feather beds, destroyed the public papers and records, and scattered everything about the streets.* A German officer observed, *It was a pity to see the finest furnishings . . . were smashed and lay around the streets.*

After two brief years of exile, the British Union Jack again flew over Savannah. A year later Governor Wright returned from England, along with his lieutenant governor, John Graham. Rebel governor John Houstoun fled Savannah in this thunderclap transition from Whig to Tory. The infant state of Georgia was again a British royal province.

Siege of Savannah, 1779

Savannah, before the storm. Standing on her high bluff and gazing over the cool slow river, one saw endless rice fields flooded by the tides. Looking the other way, there were unremarkable wooden structures around six squares. *No one building I can describe,* noted a visitor in 1778. Beyond, there was the beginning of pine forests that filled the vast wilderness that was Georgia, now stretching from the Atlantic to the Mississippi River. Toward the west was Ebenezer Road (present Louisville Road), leading ultimately to defiant Augusta, where the rebel government fled after 1778. To the east began Sea Island Road (present Wheaton Street) out to Bonaventure, Thunderbolt, Beaulieu (buuu-LEEE), and the Isle of Hope. Due south down central Bull Street one picked up Ogeechee Road on the way to Midway and Darien. The little jewel of Frederica at the end of the road had vanished.

The war had swollen the population to 750 whites, with thousands of slaves now on the surrounding plantations. And a new breed was about, soon to encroach on Savannah. *Crackers,* second-generation Americans usually of Scotch-Irish Presbyterian stock, had begun spreading far and wide from Pennsylvania, Virginia, and North Carolina. But they tended to live out of town, or *upcountry* on newly acquired Indian Lands. James Habersham sniffed, *idle People from the Northward, some of whom are great Villains, Horse Stealers etc . . . by no means the sort of People that should settle these lands . . . idle and disorderly Vagrants.* *

*Such villains, vagrants, and horse stealers were the wild and woolly militia that would crush the Loyalists like Habersham at Kettle Creek in 1779. Combining with their *Over the Mountain* cousins from Tennessee and North Carolina, they would further reverse the British fortunes at King's Mountain and Cowpens in 1780 and 1781. The name *cracker* is lost in lore. Usually it is explained that they cracked whips incessantly, or cracked a lot of corn, or ate a lot of crackers, or they spat a lot. The French verb *cracher* means "to spit."

General Augustin Prevost, the victorious British commander at Savannah in 1779, was called *Old Bullet Head* by his troops because of a dent in his left temple from a prior wound. (Courtesy of Margaret Prevost Wood.)

Luckless Charles Henri d'Estaing, momentary hero in the Caribbean and scapegoat on American shores, was twice wounded in trying to take Savannah. His bad fortune followed him to the guillotine in the French Revolution.

In Savannah, growing from forty houses in 1734, 450 buildings were now visible, although *poorly built mostly of wood—in Short the whole has a most wretched miserable appearance*, wrote a homesick British officer. The city limits were between present Lincoln and Jefferson streets to the east and west, and to the south, Oglethorpe Avenue (called South Broad). A Hessian soldier wrote that the wide unpaved streets *have white sand so deep that it is just like walking through fresh fallen snow a foot deep.... A man runs no small risk of being chocked [sic] by the clouds of sand and dust;* also by mosquitoes and sand gnats. Recorded the Hessian commander, Colonel von Porbeck, of the lethal fevers: *Savannah in the province of Georgia remains the death trap of human society. The third European generation reaches at most 34 years of age ... crocodiles, tigers, all kinds of game, snakes, mingle together.*

The largest structure in town was *ye great or English church* on Johnson Square, recorded naturalist John Bartram. Also notable were Wright's governor's mansion on St. James Square; the City Market; the old silk house, or Filature, on Reynolds Square; some taverns; and a new military barracks (where the De Soto Hilton Hotel presently is). On Bay Street since 1744 sat the prosperous commercial house of Harris and Habersham, with thriving profits in rice, indigo, pelts, and cotton. The headquarters of the British commander, General Augustin Prevost, was on Broughton Street. Swiss-born Prevost was called *Old Bullet Head* by his men because of a depression in his temple, the result of a glancing cannon ball at the Battle of Quebec in 1759. Evidence of recent political differences were the musket-ball holes in Wright's mansion, where patriots had taken potshots at him while he was under house arrest.

Wagonloads of slaves, helping to build new fortifications and defensive redoubts, moved through the dusty streets. The descendants of Tomochichi now took the king's shilling, plundering slaves from Carolina plantations for work in Savannah. With painted faces and in a torpor of grog and tobacco, they startled the ladies as they paraded their booty down the streets.

THE FRENCH ARRIVE

Before daybreak on September 8, 1779, Governor Wright was awakened by a message from General Prevost. Off Tybee bar *there were 42 Sail of French Ships of War in Sight, most of which appeared to be large Ships.* Four thousand troops were aboard, composed of French, Irish, and black volunteers from Haiti. The expedition was under the command of Count Charles-Henri d'Estaing, who the British had thought to be embroiled with their fleet in the Caribbean. Worse, Savannah's best contingent of British defenders, the Seventy-first Regiment of Highlanders under Colonel John Maitland, was presently fifty miles away in Beaufort, South Carolina. Additional American forces from Charleston were already on the march toward Savannah, cutting off the Highlanders' overland route.

The French troops debarked at Beaulieu onto a bluff on the Vernon River. Philip Minis of Savannah had recommended it *as the best place for landing.* Meeting no opposition, the only casualties were two troopers who accidentally wounded themselves in the dark. *Like blind men,* complained French officer Jean-Rémy de Tarragon, the troops scaled the steep bluff in the night. Some had been waiting in landing boats for three days. Morning light revealed a leisurely ascending trail within a hundred paces of the bluff. Exhausted, the troops gathered around a huge fire and enjoyed soup and the first fresh meat they had tasted in weeks. Later that night, however, they were soaked in a squall. The tents had not been unloaded. Out on the ships, sailors were dying by the dozens from scurvy.

A month later the French, Americans, and British would collide in one of the Revolution's three bloodiest battles—the one nobody remembers, if indeed they ever heard of it. Yet, as Alexander A. Lawrence points out in the period's definitive book, *Storm Over Savannah*, it "possessed qualities of drama and color unmatched elsewhere in American history . . . the best blood of Europe reddened the soil of Savannah."

Among the French expedition was Admiral DeGrasse, later hero of Yorktown. At his side was Admiral Bougainville, the Pacific explorer after whom islands and a flowering plant were named. Also present was Louis-Marie de Noailles, brother-in-law of Lafayette and another future Yorktown hero. Pierre-Charles L'Enfant, future designer of Washington, D.C., would almost be left for dead on the field before Savannah's defenses. Amid this titled glitter was a future king, a black teen named Henri Christophe. Wounded at Savannah, he would recover to become Haiti's first monarch a quarter century later. Other future Haitian revolutionaries would also serve at Savannah: Jean-Baptiste Belley, Andre Rigaud, Martial Besse, and Louis Jacques Beauvais.

THE AMERICANS CONVERGE

Coming overland from Charleston to meet the French were the Americans under General Benjamin Lincoln (namesake of Lincoln Street). Among the troops were fine old Charleston names like Thomas and Charles Cotesworth Pinckney; Daniel and Isaac Huger (*uuuu-GEE*, a Huguenot name); John Laurens, a favorite aide of Washington and son of Henry Laurens, head of the Continental Congress; Thomas Heyward, Jr., a signer of the Declaration of Independence; David Ramsey, future historian; Colonel Francis Marion, later famous as the *Swamp Fox*; Sergeant William Jasper, the hero of the 1776 battle of

Admiral Louise-Antoine de Bougainville, commanding the fleet while his sailors died offshore from scurvy. His name lives on from a Pacific island and a flowering plant encountered in his voyage around the world in the 1760's.

Rotund Benjamin Lincoln wrote a report of the defeat at Savannah so discrete that one would assume only a minor skirmish occurred. Captured with his whole army at Charleston a year later, he always landed on his feet.

Charles Cotesworth Pinckney in his South Carolina continental garb, an uncommonly correct depiction of a revolutionary uniform. He later was a prominent member of the Constitutional Convention in 1787. (Portrait by Henry Benbridge circa 1773. Courtesy of the National Portrait Gallery, Washington.)

Charleston. Also in this group was *the Jew's Company*, under Captain Richard Lushington. It was the only recorded Jewish military unit in the Revolution.

Coming from Augusta were the Georgia militia under Lachlan McIntosh. Among them were names who now anoint Georgia counties: John Houstoun, John Twiggs, James Jackson, John Baker, Joseph Habersham, David Meriwether, and John White. Another was a Cracker from the wild upcountry—Sam Davis, father of future Confederate President Jefferson Davis.

"Count" Casimir Pulaski, the Polish adventurer who was Washington's first calvalry commander, joined these forces with the lancers of his Pulaski Legion. The legion was largely raised in Maryland and financed out of Pulaski's own pocket. He was a colorful, impulsive leader. His glitz and *élan* are evident in this description of his recruiting capers in Baltimore: *The new soldiers were impressed with the handsome 30 year old general, who contributed to their morale by galloping at full speed on his horse, firing his pistol into the air, throwing his pistol ahead of the horse, swinging out of the saddle with one foot into the stirrup—and picking up the pistol before it touched the ground.*

Pulaski and Jasper would die here, along with hundreds of others. The two patriots are memorialized by their own beautiful monuments in Monterey and Madison squares.

SIEGE AND BOMBARDMENT

The large Franco-American force did not attack the British at once, which in hindsight they should have, since the Savannah defenses were poorly prepared and the defenders outnumbered four or five to one. Even a Hessian officer in Savannah wondered why his enemies did not immediately *storm and take this miserable sand pile with fixed bayonets.* Instead, a three-week siege commenced, replete with advancing French cannon batteries and relentless bombardment throughout the last week. Although a thousand shells were fired in anger at Savannah, the bombardment did not accomplish its purpose, especially if judged by this French diary entry: *At midnight . . . the bombardment begins. It ceases at two o'clock, by order of M. de Noailles, because the mis-directed bombs fell in great numbers in the trench which he commanded. This bad firing was occasioned by a mistake of a ship's steward who had sent to the cannoneers a keg of rum instead of a keg of beer. . . . At four o'clock in the morning, we begin to cannonade and bombard the city and the enemy's [British] works with more vivacity than precision, . . . the cannoneers being still under the influence of rum.*

On a night early in the siege, Colonel Thomas Browne, or "de Browne" as he styled himself, commanding the Dillon Regiment of Irish *Wild Geese* from France, set off an explosive assault against thin

The 1854 Pulaski monument in Monterey Square. Pulaski's remains were probably not relocated here years later, but most likely buried at sea. Rightfully a beacon of pride to Polish Americans, his name is perpetuated in place names across America.

air. In the doldrums of night watch during the siege, he had taken to the bottle and imagined a British counterattack. D'Estaing berated him because *without any motive and against no object had all this powder been wasted*. A week later Browne would be one of the first to die as he hurled himself over the British parapets into waiting bayonets.

Extensive property damage was done by the bombardment, but only one British soldier was killed, a young ensign named Pollard. Scarcely a house was without a hit. The other casualties—several score of women, children, and slaves—were slaughtered in collapsed cellars. American Major John Jones recorded: *A number of the poor women & children have already been put to death by our Bombs & cannon; . . . many of them were killed in their Beds and amongst others, a poor woman with her infant in her arms were destroyed by a Cannon Ball. . . . A more cruel war could not exist than this.* Like Browne and Pulaski, Jones (namesake of Jones Street) had a premonition of his own death; he too died in the dawn attack of October 9.

Without relief, the British would soon have to give in. General Prevost began boosting manpower by arming two hundred slaves, garrisoned with Indians across the river on Hutchinson Island. Children made six pence for each French cannonball retrieved in the streets and turned over to the British to be fired back.

Thomas Pinckney described much of the action he saw at the battle of Savannah, later becoming the governor of South Carolina and finally minister to Great Britain.

Maitland Saves the Day
"From Beaufort's Banks the Gallant Maitland Flew"

To the rescue—Colonel John Maitland from Beaufort. His land route cut off, Maitland somehow ferried his eight hundred troops by inland waterways to the Savannah River. But the French fleet was blocking the river's mouth, and there were still twenty miles of marsh and swamp

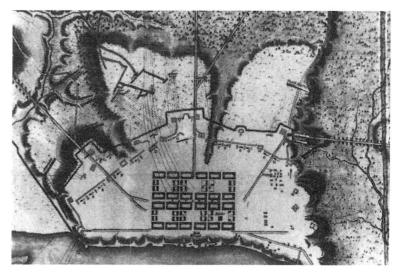

The English version of the 1779 battle map of Savannah. Their defenses ring the squares like a horseshoe. Near the eight o'clock position is the Spring Hill redoubt, with present Louisville Road heading due west from it. Here was the center of the carnage of one of the Revolution's two bloodiest battles. In the area hundreds of French and Americans lie together in mass graves lost to history.

John Maitland, commander of the Seventy-first Scottish Regiment, was the prime mover in the successful repulse of the French and Americans. Dying soon after of *the annual Fever of this Province*, he was buried in Colonial Park Cemetery. (Courtesy of the Lauderdale family, Great Britain.)

between him and Savannah. Black fishermen told Maitland in their local Gullah accent of a little-known shortcut between creeks, called Wall's Cut—a still-obscure passage that would also play a role in Savannah's downfall in the Civil War. Around noon on September 16, Maitland's battle-hardened troops began trudging up Savannah's bluff to the cheers of the besieged defenders. Their arrival brought *inexpressible joy*, said an English officer. *It made us about 2,000 strong and very saucy, as to refuse to let "Monsieur" [d'Estaing] and "Jonathan" [Reb] in.*

Poetry sprang up to remember this daring-do. *With rapid wings, but not before untried, From BEAUFORT'S banks the gallant MAITLAND flew.* Fly, indeed. Surely closer to reality was the reaction of an incredulous Charlestonian, who supposed Maitland *must have plunged through swamps, bogs and creeks which had never before been attempted but by bears, wolves, and run-away Negroes.* Galled, d'Estaing watched from a distance while his chances for an easy victory slipped through his fingers up the bluff. *I have had the mortification of seeing the troops of the Beaufort garrison pass under my eyes . . . a sight so vexatious that I began to bemoan bitterly.* Equally as mortifying, the corpulent Lincoln, also watching this *doleful sight*, promptly fell asleep in a chair. (He was said to even nap between sentences while dictating dispatches. The French and Americans sniped at each other ceaselessly.)

BLOODY DIRECT ASSAULT
"KILL THE RASCLES FRENCH DOCKS!"

Maitland's arrival did nip a British collapse, thus requiring a massive "surprise" attack by the allies on the dawn of October 9. At least that was the opinion of d'Estaing; most everyone else stood around grumbling about a direct attack. Only Noailles spoke up, saying that the

Harper's Weekly romanticized rendition of the death of Sergeant Jasper in 1860, on the brink of Civil War, called *Memories of the Union.*

attack was too risky. D'Estaing replied that Noailles' *views were those of an old man.* The charge was a disaster, the bloodiest single hour in the entire Revolution. With shouts of *Vive le Roi* ("Long live the French king, Louis XVI"), French troops staggering in the fog through bogs toward the western defenses at Spring Hill redoubt were met by the sound of bagpipes. This *lugubre harmonie,* in the words of d'Estaing, let all know that nothing was a surprise. Maitland and his Seventy-first Highlanders were loaded and waiting.

Through three valiant advances and the staggering retreat, French and Americans were slaughtered by land and naval artillery from Spring Hill redoubt and from the ships in the river, firing grapeshot *plus nails, bolts, scrap-iron, the blades of knives and scissors and even chains six feet long.* Of six brothers in the French LeBey family, five were killed in minutes and the sixth wounded. (Wounded Andrew LeBey ended up a prisoner at Ebenezer. He stayed on to marry a Salzburger and became a progenitor of the LeBey family in Savannah.) American troops, advancing after the French, *showed the greatest courage, remaining at the foot of the ditch exposed to the enemy's fire without wavering until they received the order of Monsieur le Comte d'Estaing to retire. . . . [The British] deliver their fire with their muskets almost touching our troops . . . after much Slaughter they were driven out of the Ditch.*

A French commander, Count von Stedingk, himself wounded in planting an American flag on a British redoubt, recorded that *the moment of retreat, with the cries of our dying comrades piercing my heart, was the bitterest of my life, [and I] wished for death. Of nine hundred choice troops I led into action, four hundred men and thirty-nine officers were dead and wounded.* In the midst of this hell, John Laurens, on

A miniature scene of the mortal wounding of Casimir Pulaski in a cavalry charge before Savannah's defenses. The unit flag has survived, presently quite faded in the Maryland Historical Society, the state where Pulaski raised most of his legion. (Miniature scene by the author, Preston Russell.)

viewing his fallen comrades all around him, is said to have hurled his sword to the ground in anguish, crying, *Poor fellows—I envy you!*

Groups still staggered back and forth in the deadly confusion. According to an account in *Rivington's Royal Gazette, When the second American column, under McIntosh, reached the Spring Hill Redoubt, the Scene of confusion was dreadful. They marched up over ground strewn with the Dead and Dying. The smoke of the muskets and cannon hung broodingly over the place . . . the Roar of Artillery, the Rattling of small arms, the sounded Retreat, the stirring Drum and the Cries of the Wounded blended startlingly together.*

Sergeant Jasper died in attempting to save his blue unit flag of the Second South Carolina Regiment. Although his unforgettable example would inspire hundreds of Irish Jasper Green militia in the next century, he failed to save the flag. The captured war prize has recently been purchased by the Smithsonian Institution from the English descendants of General Prevost.* Count Pulaski fell from his charging black horse, mortally wounded in a hail of grapeshot. The shot that killed him is now in the Georgia Historical Society on Whitaker Street. The memory of Pulaski's sacrifice lives on in the names of dozens of towns and counties nationwide, as does Jasper's. D'Estaing was twice wounded

---

*Recent evidence shows that Jasper may have upset several centuries of legitimate Irish pride by being German by birth. Jasper was not the only one to die in trying to save the priceless flag. So did Lieutenant John Bush of the Second South Carolina Regiment. Lieutenants James Gray and Alexander Hume were killed in successfully retrieving a second red South Carolina flag, its present whereabouts lost to history.

The beautiful Jasper monument in Madison Square is respectably accurate in its detail. Dedicated in 1888, predominately by proud Irish-Americans continuing a legacy of the Irish Jasper Greens.

leading the assault; his second in command, Count Arthur Dillon, took over. D'Estaing was carried behind the protective crypts of *the old Jewish graveyard* to escape further injury. The 1773 Sheftall Cemetery still stands on Boundary Street, near the looming shadow of the approach to the new Savannah River bridge.

From this same location the reserve of blacks, named the Chasseurs Voluntaires de St. Dominique (Haiti), maneuvered to save the remnants of the retreating army. A French officer described the reserve's

Likeness of Henri Christophe as the first ruler of free Haiti in the early nineteenth century. He was wounded as a teenager a quarter century before at the 1779 battle of Savannah. (Original portrait lost.)

Louis-Marie de Noailles, twenty-three-year-old aristocrat, led the reserves in a rear-guard action that *prevented the total destruction of our army*. He would help negotiate the British terms of surrender at Yorktown.

sangfroid under twenty-three-year-old Louis-Marie de Noailles: *When the Viscount de Noailles perceives the disorder reigning in the columns, he brings his reserve corps up to charge the enemy: and, when he hears the retreat sounded, advances in silence, at a slow step and in perfect order, to afford an opportunity to the repulsed troops to reform themselves in his rear. He makes a demonstration to penetrate within the entrenchments in case the enemy should leave them, and prepares to cut them off in that event [preventing] the total destruction of our army. . . . The fragments of the army hastily form . . . behind the reserve corps, and begin marching to our camp. M. de Noailles constitutes the rear guard and retires slowly and in perfect order.*

From the other side of the defenses, Colonel von Porbeck wrote home to relatives in Germany with a colorfully direct account of what he saw: *I was attacked first at four o'clock by a lieutenant colonel of the French-Irish Brigade* [probably Major de Browné] *with 400 men, then at four-thirty by Count D'Estaing with 600 men of the French Grenadiers. Fortunately, D'Estaing was wounded in the left arm and above his left breast by small musket balls, so that he had to crawl behind the nearby Jewish grave* [Sheftall Cemetery]. *Nevertheless, in French fashion, he called to his people, "Avances, mes braves grenadiers, tuez les pauvres* [kill the wretches].*" We answered "Kill the Rascles French docks* [dogs], *God save the King of Great Britaine!" . . . We also captured the rebel flag* [probably of the Second South Carolina Regiment]. *. . . By daylight the 60th Regiment came to our aid until the enemy retired. . . . Poulawski dies of his wounds . . . Lieutenant Colonel Maydland of the 71st Scots Regiment won from the affair of this day great honor and much thanks from his Britannic Majesty. . . . He died of the annual fever of this province* [two weeks later].

In less than an hour, one thousand casualties resulted, chiefly French and Irish; British losses were under a tenth of that. During a truce, hundreds of French and American soldiers were buried together in a mass grave on the battlefield where they fell. Although the exact site is not known, this hallowed ground is in the proximity of (perhaps under) the Savannah History Museum and Visitor's Center on Martin Luther King Boulevard. Appropriately, some of the programs and displays there remember *their last full measure of devotion*.

When word of the victory reached England, cannons in the Tower of London boomed in celebration. After recovering from his wounds in Thunderbolt, d'Estaing sailed back to France. Shutting himself up for three days, d'Estaing is said to have finally responded to a surgeon, *I have a deep wound which is not in your power to cure*, and pointed to his heart. He would later be beheaded in the French Revolution. Louis-Marie de Noailles would lose his wife, mother, father, and even grandmother to the Reign of Terror. Arthur Dillon and other French officers who fought at Savannah would also be beheaded. Dillon's last words on the scaffold of the guillotine were *Vive le Roi.* It was the same last shout of hundreds of Frenchmen as they staggered forward through the swamps, dawn, and fog of Savannah on October 9, 1779.

From Savannah to Yorktown

Benjamin Lincoln returned with the American forces to South Carolina. Seven months later he was trapped by a British siege at Charleston and surrendered the remaining southern army of around five thousand. For the moment the British commanded the entire South, except for hit-and-run efforts by the likes of the "Swamp Fox," Francis Marion.

On October 19, 1781, however, in a complete reversal of fortune, it was Lincoln who was chosen by Washington to accept the English sword of surrender at Yorktown, Virginia. (He politely touched it, but declined accepting it.) The surrender terms of Lord Cornwallis were hammered out by two Savannah veterans, John Laurens and Louis-Marie de Noailles. In remembering the harsh way the British handled the surrender at Charleston, Laurens required the British to duplicate the humiliating ceremony. In protest, the British marched out playing a popular comic tune, now in a context of chagrin and irony, called *The World Turned Upside Down: If buttercups buzzed after the bee, boats were on land and churches on sea, summer were spring, and t'other way round, then all the world would be upside down.*

This world-tilting event had been a long climb back for the Americans, with landmark battles like Cowpens, Guilford Court House, King's Mountain, Hobkirk Hill, and Eutaw Springs on the way to the Yorktown victory. The whole South was now on the brink of liberation; for Savannah it officially occurred on July 11, 1782.

Liberation of Savannah, 1782

The overall southern commander, Rhode Islander Nathanael Greene, detached a force of around five hundred men to retake Savannah. He put them under fearless "Mad" Anthony Wayne of Pennsylvania, sent south by Washington to help Greene in the liberation of Georgia. After retaking Augusta, Ebenezer, and Midway, Wayne and his subordinate, Colonel James Jackson, encircled Savannah. In January, Governor Wright nervously wrote that *a party of Continental Horse have Shewd themselves at Different times and Places for 2 or 3 days Past within 8 or 10 miles of Savannah & now all our Posts are Broke up & Called in, & we Expect every day to hear of the Main Body of the Rebel Army etc. having crossed Savannah River.*

With the tides of war now reversed on the British, Wayne could afford to wait them out. First he cut off all Indian aid and supplies to Savannah, trying to force a fight outside the city. Soldiers in Savannah

Francis Marion, the *Swamp Fox,* from a nineteenth-century print by Alonzo Chappel. A survivor of the debacle at Savannah, guerilla efforts like his were the only semblance of resistance against complete British dominance of the South.

Mad Anthony Wayne of Pennsylvania was sent south to mop up the remaining British after Yorktown. (Courtesy of V. and J. Duncan Antique Maps and Prints, Savannah.)

John Laurens, son of Henry Laurens of South Carolina. Heroic at Savannah in all of his undertakings, Laurens was a favorite aide of Washington. (Courtesy of Independence Hall National Park, Philadelphia.)

Fiery James Jackson, *the brawling pygmy,* who was given the honor of liberating Savannah by Anthony Wayne. The namesake of Fort Jackson, he fought, some say, twenty-three duels, mainly related to his pursuit of corrupt politicians in the Yazoo land fraud.

began to desert, especially the Hessians, who blended into their German stock in nearby New Ebenezer. Wayne sent feelers to Savannah offering two hogs, two hundred acres, and a cow to anyone wishing to switch sides. Nearly a hundred soldiers reversed their red English or green Loyalist coats to join the Americans. Several hundred more would desert by the time the British left.

Wayne encamped near Bethesda Orphanage in a rather relaxed posture, and was almost overrun by a surprise night attack of Loyalist Creek Indians. The sentry whom the Indians killed, before their war whoops gave the assault away, was the last death of the Revolution in Georgia. Another wasted fatality of those closing days was John Laurens, killed in a meaningless skirmish on a plantation near Charleston a month after the recapture of Savannah. Having tried unsuccessfully, early in the war, to free South Carolina slaves for service in the Continental Army, historians bemoan that our country will never know what more this honorable and able twenty-eight-year-old American might have done to alter the southern fabric that was rent asunder in the next century.

With the military stick gone after Yorktown, the British Parliament began negotiating its way out of her American enterprise, sending word to Wright in Savannah to evacuate. Not personally inclined, he nevertheless followed orders to avoid needless bloodshed. Earlier Wright had requested a cessation of hostilities from Mad Anthony, who refused. Loyalists withdrew to Tybee Island to await ships for England. Unsheltered from the sun, and swatting insects while their property was being seized and redistributed in Savannah, the Loyalists sat for weeks with their slaves. Within a few years 4,381 land grants composed of 250-acre parcels of the Loyalists' prior holdings would lure diverse revolutionary veterans to Georgia. Among them would be Nathanael Greene and Anthony Wayne, who wound up as neighbors on adjoining plantations.

On July 11, twenty-five-year-old James Jackson and his Georgia legion, *in consideration of his severe and fatiguing service,* were given the honor of first entering deserted Savannah streets to receive the keys to the city. They were uniformed in *Deer Skin dressed and turned up with what little blue cloth I could procure,* wrote Jackson. According to Wayne's instructions for reoccupation under military Governor Jackson, *the troops will take care to be provided with a clean shift of linen, and to make themselves as respectable as possible for the occasion. . . . Marauders may assure themselves of the most severe and exemplary punishment. . . . No goods or merchandise of any kind whatever are to be removed, secreted or sold . . . until the public and army are first served.*

It is a miracle that the valuable colonial records survived all the confusion. They had been on quite a trip, first fleeing fallen Savannah in

1778 under the flapping wing of Governor John Houstoun. Under a succession of rebel governors—George Walton, Nathan Brownson, and John Martin—the records stayed fleetingly at Ebenezer, Augusta, Charleston, New Bern, North Carolina, and, finally, Maryland to sit out the war. (Too confusing to sort out here, the war period was crazily the time of "three governors" of Georgia. Loyalist Wright was in Savannah while two rebel governments warred with Wright and each other up-country.) By 1783 the records came back to Savannah under Governor Lyman Hall, who returned to practice medicine.

As the *Georgia Gazette* reported on May 1, 1783, Savannah celebrated the news of the war-ending Treaty of Paris. *His Honour the Governor* was received by *respectable Strangers*, and the governor *then reviewed the troops, who had for that purpose marched to their former position, and fired a "feu de joie"* [musket salute]. *The behaviour of the Regulars was admirable, and the appearance of the Virginia line thought equal to that of the most disciplined and veteran Europeans.* In the parade was the *Chatham Regiment of Militia.*

This militia endures today as the Chatham Artillery, equally famous for its Chatham Artillery Punch, a revered drink enjoyed by fearless Savannahians. It is not recorded if this punch was used for the thirteen official toasts—toasts not to these thirteen new United States. Instead, amid *the huzzas of the populace* a confusing array of toasts went to Holland, the kings of Spain and France, recent English opponents George III and Charles Fox, George Washington, and *The American ladies.* This may well be the first recorded account of the disorienting effect of Chatham Artillery Punch.

Among the first in London to receive John Adams, America's first ambassador to the Court of St. James's, was a man who was eighty-seven years of age. Long retired as the senior ranking officer of the British army, the elderly man was now a man of letters, a member of the Royal Society, an intimate of Samuel Johnson, and a participant in the founding of the British Museum. Boswell sought to write his biography. Judging from a sketch done of him as he scanned a book from Dr. Johnson's estate sale, he was stooped, wrinkled, and toothless, but still with hawkish nose and long flowing wig. His name was James Edward Oglethorpe.

Oglethorpe died a few months after his meeting with Adams, and was buried next to his wife near her properties in tiny Cranham, in the Essex district of England. (One hundred forty years later his remains were almost removed to Georgia, almost followed brick for brick in 1976 by his Westbrook Estate in Godalming, Surrey.) Rest in peace, Father Oglethorpe.

What happened to those major participants in Georgia's transition? Noble Wymberley Jones stayed in Savannah and in 1804 became the

Elderly James Oglethorpe at the estate sale of his intimate English friend, Dr. Samuel Johnson. (Courtesy of V. and J. Duncan Antique Maps and Prints, Savannah.)

first president of the Georgia Medical Society; one of the nation's oldest, the society was founded and remains in Savannah. Joseph Habersham, the Liberty Boy who arrested Governor Wright in 1775, was appointed postmaster general by Washington in 1795 and served for three terms. Wright is buried in Westminster Abbey. Many of the Liberty Boys would be future governors of Georgia.

Lachlan McIntosh, Edwin Telfair, and John Houstoun composed the delegation to resolve the Georgia-Carolina border disputes once and for all. This was no humdrum mission, since during the war and after it, Carolina made serious attempts to annex Georgia out of existence. After the political smoke cleared, Georgia remained—and is still—the largest state east of the Mississippi River.

Fiery James Jackson became governor and ultimately U.S. Senator. He died in newly-named Washington of the cumulative effects of his many duels (some say twenty-three.) George Walton repeated Jackson's ascent, first governor and then U.S. senator. In between, Judge Walton would be horse-whipped—*well laid on*, he testified—by the son of McIntosh in a legacy of the duel and lingering feud over the killing of Button Gwinnett. Today Gwinnett, Bulloch, McIntosh, Clay, Samuel Elbert, John Berrien, James Johnson, Loyalist James Habersham, and his three patriot sons lie within yards of each other in Colonial Park Cemetery on Oglethorpe Avenue.

Another patriot interred at Colonial Park Cemetery (for 115 years) is Nathanael Greene, acclaimed by historians as Washington's most capable commander. As a war prize Greene received Mulberry Grove Plantation and moved to Savannah. The previous owner had been Lieutenant Governor John Graham, who left Tybee with Wright in 1782. Walking around Savannah's rice fields in 1786, Greene, at a hearty forty-four years of age, died of *Sunstroke*. Treatment was to *blister the temples and take blood freely*, which was futile in stopping Greene's three-day progressive coma. Wrote his new neighbor and old comrade, Anthony Wayne: *Pardon this scrawl; my feelings are too much affected because I have seen a great and good man die . . . immaculate as a friend*. Wayne would return to Pennsylvania to fight Indians a decade after Greene was buried with full military honors in the Graham vault in Colonial Park Cemetery. Ironically it was the same vault his Scottish counterpart, Colonel John Maitland, was buried in seven years earlier.

By 1786 the former Loyalist Anglican Church was so threadbare that no clergyman was available to perform Greene's funeral service. It was conducted by Judge William Stephens, *with tremulous voice, with thirteen discharges from the* [Chatham] *artillery and three from the musketry . . . the band playing the solemn Dead March in Saul*. Biscuits and punch were served along the funeral route to Greene's resting place.

It is most odd that the burial place of one so famous was lost for

General Nathanael Greene, by Charles Willson Peale. Given the Loyalist plantation of Mulberry Grove as a war prize, he was able to enjoy it only three years before he died of sunstroke. (Courtesy of Independence Hall National Park, Philadelphia.)

more than a century. In 1902 his remains would finally be found. The remains of Greene and his son, George Washington Greene, were exhumed and moved to Johnson Square, where they are interred beneath the monument erected in Nathanael Greene's honor.

POST-REVOLUTION

The War for American Independence was over. Savannah was no longer an English colonial city, but was the capital city of Georgia—until the capital was switched to Augusta in 1786. The parish system was changed, and Christ Church Parish was renamed Chatham County, after William Pitt, earl of Chatham; it was he who had said before the war, *I rejoice that America resisted.*

A city government was established after the Revolution, and Savannah became a municipality on December 23, 1789, under Governor Telfair. John Houstoun was the first mayor. Commerce grew, which was essential for establishing a sound economic base, since neither the crown nor the Trustees were around to bail out the city. Later, pounds, shillings, and pence were changed to dollars, dimes, and cents. Soon exports exceeded $300,000.

Social life revived. A dancing school opened, and on September 27, 1783, the *Georgia Gazette* recorded a traveling play put on at the Filature, the old silk factory on Reynolds Square. The title sounded rather steamy—*"The Fair Penitent," to which will be added an entertainment, "Miss in her Teens; or the Medley of Lovers."* The doors would open at half past five, the play to start *precisely at seven—no gentleman will be admitted behind the Scenes on any pretence.* It must have been a hit. By 1802 the Baptist minister, Henry Holcombe, complained of a playhouse not fifty yards from the Baptist meetinghouse: *I had to encounter a detachment of his Satanic majesty's forces called "Stage Players."*

William Pitt the Elder, earl of Chatham and namesake of the county. When he exalted *I rejoice that America resisted* the 1765 Stamp Act to the British Parliament, he gained undying Savannah respect.

Washington's Visit, 1791
"He Comes, the Hero Comes!"

In 1791 Savannah welcomed her most important visitor ever—President George Washington. The city pulled out all the stops in greeting the fifty-nine-year-old icon. *He Comes, the Hero Comes* was the popular song played and sung as Washington stepped onto the wharf on May 12 for a four-day visit. In the official greeting party were old Liberty Boys Joseph Habersham, Noble W. Jones, John Houstoun, Joseph Clay, and Lachlan McIntosh. Anthony Wayne was there as the president of the Georgia Society of the Cincinnati, an hereditary society founded in 1783 of American and French officers who had fought in the Revolution. Washington was the soci-

President George Washington, after a 1794 portrait by Adolph Wertmuller, giving him an uncommonly animated expression compared to his more famous dour, consciously cruel, images by Gilbert Stuart. The artist even painted in the white wig powder on Washington's collar.

ety's first president-general. (The Georgia Society still meets annually in Savannah, recently acquiring the Alida Harper Fowlkes mansion on Orleans Square. It was left by her to use as their headquarters.) James Jackson introduced President Washington to the mayor, Thomas Gibbons. (Little did any of them realize then that Jackson and Gibbons would fight a duel the next year.) After a gala parade, Washington was escorted to his lodgings in an inn at the corner of State and Barnard streets before he began his crushing schedule of countless ceremonies and endless tributes.

First was a dinner at Brown's Coffee House on Bay Street with dignitaries of every size and civic stripe. Following fifteen toasts, Washington understandably retired after a long day.

It is presumed the food was good at Brown's Coffee House, since Washington would dine there twice more, again with the Cincinnati and finally with the Freemasons. In between, he got a pleasant break from the constant male bonding with a ball in his honor at the Filature. There was, Washington wrote, *a dancing Assembly at which there was about 100 well dressed handsome ladies.* Washington was personally presented to ninety-six of them; perhaps he miscounted in the delirium of female companionship. *After a few minuets were moved, and one country dance,* Washington departed at 11 o'clock. (He had already been through fifteen toasts at the late lunch with the Cincinnati.) At midnight, dinner was served to the remaining throng, and the tipsy guests dined and danced until 3 o'clock in the morning.

Washington was wise to get some sleep. After a meal and more toasts with the Freemasons at the Coffee House the next day, he was again addressed with lengthy tributes. The one given by John Earnst Bergman for the Salzburgers was completely in Latin, beginning *Permittas, quaeso, Illustrissime Washington!* Around two hundred words later it ended with *ad Deum benignissimum, pro totius populi Americani salute.*

Washington then requested to see what remained of the battlefield from 1779. As he wrote in his diary: *I visited the City, and the attack & defence of it in the year 1779. . . . To form an opinion of the attack at this distance of time, and the change which has taken place in the appearance of the ground by the cutting away of the woods, &c. is hardly to be done with justice to the subject; especially as there is remaining scarcely any of the defences.*

Fortunately a survivor of the bloodbath was there; Lachlan McIntosh filled in the details from his own experience. Washington was described as listening long and pensively.

That evening there was an outdoor affair, a dinner *with a number of the Citizens (not less than 200) in an elegant Bower erected for the occasion on the Bank of the River below the Town . . . there was a tolerable good display of fireworks.* The Chatham Artillery later received Washington's present—two brass cannon used at Yorktown, which now sit in sheltered reverence on Bay Street near City Hall.

Upon leaving, Washington wrote a Savannah sketch in his diary, reflecting his usually keen interest in commerce: *Savanna stands upon what may be called high ground for this Country—It is extremely sandy wch makes the walking very disagreeable; & the houses uncomfortable in warm & windy weather, as they are filled with dust whenever these happen.—The town on 3 sides is surrounded with cultivated Rice fields which have a rich and luxuriant appearance. On the 4th or backside it is a fine sand.—The harbour is said to be very good, & often filled with square rigged vessels, but there is a bar below. . . . Rice & Tobacco (the last of*

The Washington guns, gifts of the president to the Chatham Artillery after his 1791 visit.

wch. is greatly increasing) are the principal Exports—Lumber & Indigo are also Exported, but the latter is on the decline, and it is supposed by Hemp & Cotton.

CATY GREENE—VAMP OF SAVANNAH

Although Nathanael Greene was now dead, he left a vibrant thirty-three-year-old widow, Catherine, who would become an important Savannahian in her own right. Upon Greene's death, "Caty" assumed responsibility for running Mulberry Grove, a large plantation where she raised her four young children. During his 1791 visit to Savannah, Washington recorded in his diary: *Called upon Mrs. Green the widow of the deceased Genl. Green, (at a place called Mulberry Grove) and asked her how she did.*

Caty, or Catherine Littlefield Greene Miller, from her early nineteenth-century portrait, attributed to James Frothingham. Her benign later-life appearance belies a spark that drove men—married, single, or not sure which—mad in her presence. (Courtesy of the Telfair Academy of Arts and Sciences, Savannah.)

Oarsmen in light blue silk jackets, black satin breeches, and white silk stockings rowed a barge with Washington and Savannah's welcoming delegation to her landing. Washington embraced Caty with memories sixteen years long, to the time when Caty told him she would name her firstborn male after him. She had. There was also a daughter named Martha. Obviously Washington was as enchanted with Catherine Greene as she was with him. As even her husband recorded of *a little dance* in 1779, *His Excellency* [Washington] *and Mrs. Greene danced upwards of three hours without once sitting down.* Besides Washington, her other constant dancing partner was Anthony Wayne. Washington again visited Caty on his way out of Savannah, far from the madding crowd. *A delightful sojourn here of a few hours* was Washington's final impression of Savannah.

Washington had offered to give his namesake *as good an education as this country . . . will afford . . . at my own cost and charge.* But he was not the only one to be captivated by Caty. The Marquis de Lafayette made the same offer. Instead of living at Mount Vernon, young George Washington Greene wound up in France during the French Revolution. (George Washington Greene would drown at Mulberry Grove a few years after returning from France, being buried with his father in the Graham vault in Colonial Park Cemetery.) As Lafayette wrote Henry Knox to help persuade Caty, *Whatever she and you bid me to do shall be done.*

These proper crushes, however, were only sideshows for the first vamp of Savannah. There was Anthony Wayne next door, footloose as ever while his estranged wife remained in Philadelphia. (In Savannah, another diversion of Wayne's was young Mary Maxwell.) There was Caty's lawyer in Savannah, Nathanael Pendleton, Jr., whose wife became progressively jealous. Acting as ventriloquist, "Nat" brazenly used his dog, Edmund, to "speak" to "Greenie" in thinly disguised amour. Later, a local French marquis made a serious swoop at her. And then there was Jeremiah Wadsworth in New York, who almost left his wife for Caty. Finally, there was the caretaker of Mulberry Grove, Phineas Miller. Ten years her junior, but with time on his side, Miller patiently waited while the gaggle of sometime suitors stumbled past. He eventually ended up Caty's second and last husband.

Meanwhile Caty was anxiously pleading her case before Congress. Requesting compensation for the considerable role her dead husband played in the war, she fervently begged for help with her debts. Excerpts of letters only touch on the sweeping emotions of this draining period. Between flirtations, fleeting obsessions, and lovers' quarrels, hot and cold passions darted through a busy, infant postal service.

Soon after arriving in the North, Caty had a letter from Wayne: *I endeavored to restrain every tender emotion. . . . The effort was too great. . . . My feelings were tremendously alive for the safety of an object never absent from my mind.* Later: *I pledge the honor of a soldier that I will repay you with compound interest upon your personal demand, in any Quarter of the Globe.* Still later, after a spat: *I am confident that my lips wou'd not have opened to give utterances to professions which my heart did not assent to—when made to you.*

Once, when up north, Caty wrote to married Jeremiah Wadsworth: *I cannot help running out to the Stage every time it passes in hopes of seeing you . . . which god knows I have done in too many instances in my life but I have almost done with hope now.* Later, after secretly spending the night together in New York, *You say you are unhappy because you never expected to see me again. I told you before I left you, that it depended on yourself alone. . . . Did you for one moment of your life think of coming to Georgia to see me. . . . You have no reason for the jealousy you mention—I give you my word.* After Wadsworth's jealousy castigated his rival, young Phineas Miller back in Savannah, Caty shot back: *[He] was very much hirt and I confess I think he had some reason for it. He is young—without friends and without fortune—he has an honest heart and a proud one.* Later, in writing to Wadsworth of her new widowed suitor in Savannah, the Marquis de Montalet: *I believe I forgot to mention my noble lover to you, the Marquis of ——, (I forget what) but he made very cerious propositions.*

Caty to Nat Pendleton: *You take care to Mention [the baby] that is just Born without ever saying a word of Edmond who I am so much interested in—dose he remember Greeney—I long to see the Dear little dog. . . . Give my love to Mrs. P. . . . I have never received a line from her or Genl Wayne since I left you.* Later: *I know not whether I ought to send my love to Mrs. Pendleton—she dose not treat me well. . . . Give my love to Edmond who I long to see—Tho I care nothing about the rest of you."*

Pendleton to Caty: *Edmund is in excellent health and a most amusing little dog. He frequently calls you, particularly when handsome ladies are in the room. But I asked him if he loved Greenie and he said "Greenie damn bitch."*

Caty to Pendleton: *I have been reflecting some time to determine what I shall write you or whether I shall write at all. . . . It is now two oclock and I have not been in bed yet—the strongest wish I have at this moment is that you were here in my room—we should have an uninterrupted tate a tate. . . . I should look disdainfully at you—I should quarrel with you—perhaps complain a little—No, that I would not do—but where am I rambling.*

On studying Caty's matronly, later-life portrait in the Telfair Academy, one thinks more of Martha Washington than a world-class femme fatale. What was her fatal attraction? According to several observers, male and female, she was very much a refreshingly liberated woman. She possessed honesty, candor, and bravery. Above all, she did not possess hypocrisy or pretense. She got much of this honestly; her mother went to the altar six months pregnant. Isaac Briggs, a Georgia politician, once had an unvarnished discourse with Caty over a local fallen woman, called by her former friends *an impudent, vile hussy, strumpet whore!* To Briggs's amazement, Caty alone wondered about the inner emotions of the outcast victim. Briggs wrote of Caty: *A lady who is superior to the little foibles of her sex, who disdains affectations, who thinks & acts as she pleases, within the limits of virtue and good sense, without consulting the world about it, is generally an object of envy and distraction.—Such is Lady Greene.—She confesses she has passions & propensities & that if she has any virtue 'tis in resisting and keeping them within due bounds. . . . She has an infinite fund of vivacity, the world calls it levity. She possesses an unbounded benevolence, . . . the world calls it imprudence. In short she is honest & unaffected enough to confess that she is a woman, & it seems to me the world dislikes her for nothing else.*

ELI WHITNEY AND THE COTTON GIN, 1793
"I INVOLUNTARILY HAPPENED TO BE THINKING ON THE SUBJECT"

In 1793 a breakthrough occurred on Caty's plantation that would have profound consequences for the South. The story began when an aspiring twenty-seven-year-old schoolteacher named Eli Whitney stepped off a ship from New Haven, Connecticut. He had come to Savannah to accept a teaching post, but when the position fell through, it was fine with Whitney. The job had been his father's idea, and Whitney had shuddered at the prospect.

Caty, however, persuaded the unemployed young man to stay on at Mulberry Grove. There Whitney could help tutor the children and, in general, tinker around. In his spare time Caty suggested that he might even study law under her, uh, good friend, Nat Pendleton. That flame was now dead, but Whitney marveled at the open relationship between

Eli Whitney, whose role in refining the cotton gin revolutionized the Deep South's economy, only momentarily interrupted by the Civil War.

Phineas Miller and Caty. (Whitney did not know that Caty and Phineas had drawn up a prospective marriage contract the year before.) Whitney wrote home: *I find myself in a new natural world and as for the moral world I believe it does not extend so far south.*

Since Yankee Whitney wouldn't have known a cotton boll if one bit him, Caty and a few friends pushed him in the direction of one of the Neanderthal cotton gins of the day. With his own inventive curiosity, the rest is history—sort of. As Whitney wrote home to his parents: *I heard much said of the extreme difficulty of ginning cotton, that is, separating it from its seeds. I involuntarily happened to be thinking on the Subject, and struck out a plan of a machine with which one man will clean ten times as much cotton as he can in any other way before known and also cleanse it much better than the usual mode. One man and a horse will be more than fifty men with the old machine.*

Working in an upstairs bedroom at Mulberry Grove, too engrossed to even eat regularly, Whitney came up with a working model within ten days. Finally he came downstairs and, rather despondently, laid a rotating barrel-like cylinder on the dining table. It was a brilliant innovation, but the machine clogged almost instantly when cotton and seeds became caught in its crude teeth. Whitney was mystified. Then Caty got an inspiration. According to the legend, Caty went over to the fireplace, grabbed the hearth brush, and exclaimed, *What! Allow such a trifle as that to worry you? Trust to a woman's wit for the cure, and turn the cylinder!* As Whitney excitedly turned the cylinder, while Caty held the brush over the teeth . . . not that much happened. But Whitney got the idea—that is, Caty's idea. *Thank you for the hint. I have it now!* he—by tradition—said. In a short time he really did, and the result *is* history. It was Caty's initiation, refinement—and most importantly—her complete and secret financial support that established the new company of Whitney and Miller. A litany of setbacks followed—the company lost her seed money in the Yazoo Company land fraud, a fire interrupted production in Whitney's New Haven workshop, and there were the inevitable illegal patent copiers. Although turning a profit, Whitney and Miller did not make their deserved killing.

"COTTON! COTTON! COTTON! COTTON!"

Certainly the cotton gin transformed Savannah. In 1790 cotton exports were one thousand bales; by 1820 they were ninety thousand bales a year. In 1794 Savannah's population was two thousand with export revenues under $500,000. By 1819 she was America's sixteenth largest city with exports exceeding $14,000,000. As early as 1802 one of the first branches of the U.S. Bank in Philadelphia opened in Savannah to handle all the money.

Prerevolutionary high society again appeared, as touched on by socialite Robert MacKay in 1801: *Savannah has been quite alive for this fortnight past. We all dined with Caig on Turtle in the Evening, there was a Wedding at Waynes & party after party has been the consequence almost every day since—but as usual in this place, pleasure and dissipation are either crammed down our throats or there is a total stagnation & we all become as dull as stockfish—there has been no less than three balls at this most charming of all Seasons. . . . There was a fiddle but unfortunately some of our quests liked the wine better than the dancing. . . . More Jelly, Pyes & Tarts than served us for two days dessert, though we had the Sweet Tooth Gentry to help us destroy them.*

Of course the cotton gin didn't print money per se, but depended on the growing raw material, as yawned at by John Davis in 1800: *There was a large party at supper, composed principally of cotton manufacturers from Manchester* [England], *whose conversation operated on me like a dose of opium. Cotton! Cotton! Cotton! Cotton! was their never-ceasing topic; . . . for my part, I fell asleep, and nodded till a negro offered to light me to my room.*

A generation later George Lewis recorded the pervasive trend: *Nothing was attended to but the rearing of cotton and slaves. The more cotton the more slaves, and the more slaves the more cotton.* In the same vein, visitor James Stirling wrote: *What capital they save, and that is not much, they lay out in niggers. Niggers and cotton—cotton and niggers: these are the law and prophets to the men of the South.* Cotton had become king and would continue to dominate Savannah for the rest of the century.

Light and Dark—1819, 1820

Historically it is impossible to describe two more diametrically opposed years in Savannah than 1819 and 1820. As if from some Old Testament chapter of feast and famine, 1819 was a year marked by enduring beauty and worldwide accomplishment; 1820 was a year of fire and pestilence. Coming together in a bright sunburst were the visit of President James Monroe to one of William Jay's architectural masterpieces and the christening of the first steamship to cross an ocean. Yet eight months later, two-thirds of Savannah would be wiped out by flames, and shortly thereafter a tenth of her people would be lying in graveyards—the victims of yellow fever.

William Jay

In 1818, after completing his training in London, twenty-three-year-old architect William Jay arrived in Savannah from Bath, his own architectural jewel of a hometown in England. Bright and charming, Jay's connections with the Bolton family in Savannah

The Scarbrough House on Martin Luther King, Jr., Boulevard, completed by William Jay in 1819, just in time to receive President James Monroe. Its existence mirrors that of Savannah— short boom, long bust, and recent restoration.

soon had him rubbing elbows with the same society who sought to outdo each other by means of Jay's houses. Money was of little object, even in the face of President Monroe's new protective tariffs that pinched cotton profits. The nouveau riche were wide open to any style that Jay might dream up—the grander, the better.

Jay stayed in Savannah seven years before returning to England. The buildings that he designed are Savannah's most elegant architectural masterpieces—the Richardson-Owens-Thomas House, the Scarbrough House, and the Telfair Academy of Arts and Sciences. Others, such as a bank, a theater, and several homes, would be destroyed over the years. Architectural historians debate over whether his hand was in on a few other Savannah structures, such as the now deteriorating building at 21 West Bay Street, formerly the old City Hotel.

William and Julia Scarbrough were delighted when Jay put the finishing touches on their new home on West Broad Street. He completed his work by May 8, 1819, the day President James Monroe walked up the classic porch stairs past Doric columns into Regency-style grandeur. This christening party would be only one of the many Scarbrough *blowouts*, as Julia called her galas. She loved giving parties, as demonstrated by inveterate party-goer Robert MacKay's description of one in her former home: *Last even'g we had a grand ball at Scarbrough's, we danced upstairs & Madam's bed was taken down to make room for us.* A woman visitor to the city wrote: *We hear ladies with families of small children boast of having been out to parties 10 nights in succession until after midnight, and sometimes until 3 o'clock in the morning; and that they had not seen their husbands for a week. Mrs. Scarbrough lately sent out*

William Scarbrough, well-off merchant who headed the S.S. *Savannah* adventure, the first steamship to cross any ocean. (Courtesy of the Georgia Department of Archives and History.)

Print of the S.S. *Savannah,* first sailing ship to add a steam-boat paddle. (Courtesy of V. and J. Duncan Antique Maps and Prints, Savannah.)

cards of invitation to five hundred persons. Three hundred attended. Every room in a large house was newly furnished for the occasion, the beds etc sent out; refreshments handed round from garret to cellar through the night.

S.S. SAVANNAH, 1819
"SUCCESS TO HER"

William Scarbrough was a wealthy, English-educated merchant. Along with twenty-one others, they had a new toy and glints in their eyes. They had something called a steamship. It was not the first boat powered by steam *(the steamboat)*, but it would be the first such vessel to make an ocean crossing.

Since Robert Fulton had showed the potential of steam with "Fulton's Folly" (the *Clermont* in 1807), other steamboats followed. In fact, the *Charleston* ran between that city and Savannah regularly. Moses Rogers, the future captain of the S.S. *Savannah,* the pride of the Savannah Steamship Company, even arrived in town propelled by steam. But the S.S. *Savannah* was different from those earlier vessels. Rogers had induced Scarbrough and associates to buy a brand new hybrid built in New York, a conventional sailing ship with auxiliary paddle-wheel, steam power.

The new *Savannah* was a beauty—thirty-five tons, 110 feet long, with three majestic sailing masts. On each side of the hull were fifteen-foot-diameter paddle wheels. Unlike the few predecessors, these could fold up like the huge arms of a Japanese fan for easy on-deck repairs. The Savannah newspaper didn't quite know how to advertise her. They had an illustration of a sailing ship and another of a steamboat. The paper ended up printing both, leaving the reader to imagine the merger.

Even before giving a president of the United States a ride, the owners just *had* to try it out. Why not scorch up to Charleston! Away they went, getting there in a dizzy eleven hours. As they proudly puffed around Charleston harbor—yes—even Charlestonians were impressed. The *Charleston City Gazette* wrote: *This novel spectacle drew a large concourse of spectators to the wharves, who cheered as she passed the city.* Sighed a Savannahian on board: *As a native, I confess that a glow of pride animates my heart. . . . While other ships were becalmed and lifeless . . . we glided quickly and majestically before the city . . . with the ease and facility of a dolphin.* When President Monroe rode back and forth to Tybee on May 11, it was the hit of the considerable spectacle Savannah put on for him. Also aboard was Secretary of War John C. Calhoun; as a Carolina native perhaps his considerable eyebrows glowered even more than usual, out of sheer envy.

Back in Savannah, President Monroe was met by saluting cannon, two of which were Washington's gift to the Chatham Artillery. He then attended the consecration of the beautiful new Independent Presbyterian Church on Bull Street. Designed by John H. Green, the plans had been inspired by the imposing Church of St. Martin-in-the-Fields in London. At the consecration the paper reported *an immense congregation so large a portion of which was formed of female beauty; . . . the performance of the vocal music tended to elevate the soul to sublime and heavenly musings.* Monroe's visit ended with a grand civic blowout in Johnson Square, in a special pavilion built by Jay for the occasion.

The S.S. *Savannah* barely waited for the celebration to die down before she left port on May 22, 1819. Destination: Liverpool, England. A world-beating twenty-nine days and eleven hours later her log recorded: *at 6 p.m. come to anchor off Liverpool.* She had used her steam engine only eighty hours. In England, Captain Moses Rogers was *greeted like Columbus*—although a few feared the project was a scheme to rescue Napoleon from exile on Saint Helena Island.

The trip over was not without its understandable ironies. In the Atlantic several concerned ships thought the *Savannah* was on fire and sinking. Off the coast of Ireland the king's cutter *Kite* chased the *Savannah* all day trying to rescue her, thinking she was aflame. Earlier in mid-Atlantic a Captain Livingston raced to the rescue only to discover *she went faster with fire and smoke than we possibly could with all sails set . . . a proud moment of Yankee skill and enterprise. Success to her.* As she glided by the *Pluto*, that ship's captain recorded: *She passed us at the rate of 9 or 10 knots . . . and the greatest compliment we could bestow was to give her three cheers.* As the crowds lin-

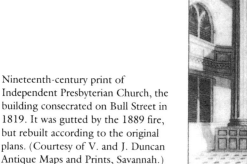

Nineteenth-century print of Independent Presbyterian Church, the building consecrated on Bull Street in 1819. It was gutted by the 1889 fire, but rebuilt according to the original plans. (Courtesy of V. and J. Duncan Antique Maps and Prints, Savannah.)

ing the Mersey River to Liverpool marveled, she cruised by *belching forth smoke and fire, yet uninjured.*

After Liverpool, the *Savannah* steamed up to Scotland, then over to Stockholm, and finally to St. Petersburg, Russia. The paper there reported: *This frigate is the first steam ship to cross the Atlantic Ocean. . . . There is perfection in every part.* Although Czar Alexander didn't purchase the *Savannah* as the owners had hoped, he presented Captain Rogers with an iron bench, presently at the Richardson-Owens-Thomas House. The S.S. *Savannah* returned home on November 30, beating her own twenty-nine-day record by four days. According to the log, *At 5 AM saw Tybee light . . . firl'd sails . . . got underway with steam and went up . . . and anchored off the town.*

Two years later, in 1821, the S.S. *Savannah* was pounded to pieces in a gale on the shores of Long Island.

1820 FIRE
"HUNDREDS OF FAMILIES ARE LITERALLY NAKED IN THE STREETS"

In Savannah it was a new year, and the beginning was not auspicious. Between one and two o'clock in the morning on January 11, 1820, a fire broke out in Boon's livery stable behind Mrs. Platt's boarding house off Bryan Street. A high northwest wind quickly spread it into adjacent Franklin Square. There it almost burned itself out, but managed to rekindle and turn down Bay Street, destroying businesses before it hit the City Market in Ellis Square. There, illegal gunpowder was stored; the massive explosion blew the fire all over town and totally demoralized the fire fighters. By 2 o'clock the next afternoon, Savannah was ashes from Bay to Broughton and Jefferson

The annual blessing of the tartans of the Scottish St. Andrew's Society in Independent Presbyterian Church, 1989.

to Abercorn. Two-thirds of Savannahians were burnt out of their homes.

It wasn't the first time the mainly wooden houses of Savannah went up in smoke; nearly the same area had burned in 1796. Then 229 of Savannah's four hundred structures were destroyed, leaving four hundred families homeless and Christ Church destroyed. Fear of fire was so acute that, only four months before the 1820 holocaust, wells had been dug in the middle of squares to provide closer access to water. Still, with at least six engines, two local fire companies unsuccessfully fought the 1820 blaze.

Thieving arsonists were suspected. Two Spaniards from Florida were said to have later confessed, but with no recorded verification. Gone now were 463 buildings, including the U.S. Bank, the public market, and the police station. Wrote one observer: *The town presents a most wretched picture. There is not a hardware store, Saddler's shop, apothecary's shop, or scarcely a dry goods store left. There is no estimating the loss—it is immense.* The estimate of damage was $5,000,000. The paper reported: *Many hundreds of families are literally naked in the streets; not even clothing was saved.* Evincing the struggling spirit of make-do, William Craig advertised that he *Informs his friends and cash customers, that an explosion has blown him from Johnson's Square to the southwest corner of the Exchange, with the remnant of his stock of WINES, LIQUORS and GROCERIES, which escaped the late fire.*

Under the able leadership of Mayor Thomas U. P. Charlton, the city struggled back. Donations poured in from around the state and entire nation, eventually exceeding $99,000. In an ugly harbinger of divisive regionalism, the $12,000 from New York was returned. North and South were in the first violent arguments of the Missouri Compromise over whether new states would be admitted with or without slavery. Thus the generous donation from the people of New York contained an insulting stipulation that funds be *applied exclusively to the relief of all indigent persons, without distinction of color.* Since there was no basis locally to support this slur of racism or profiteering, the city council voted to demand that Mayor Charlton reject New York's donation. Newspapers across the country chose sides in bitter editorials, further splitting North and South.

Four months later, in May, the revived Savannah newspaper heralded: *Our city—rising like a Phoenix from its ashes, may she continue to rise until she rivals in splendor her sister cities of the north.* The Savannah Volunteer Guards went ahead with their annual May festival.

Mayor Thomas U. P. Charlton, who helped raise national donations to restore Savannah after the 1820 fire. (Courtesy of Walter Charlton Hartridge, Savannah.)

1820 YELLOW FEVER EPIDEMIC

In that same spring month, Dr. William R. Waring recorded three deaths in the northeast quadrant of the city. The Washington Square area harbored many Irish immigrants, most having arrived in Savannah only the year before. Hundreds of more deaths would occur in their part of town.

In the words of Waring, the symptoms were most familiar and ghastly: *black emissions from the stomach . . . violence and consequent intercurrence of paroxysms* [fevers] *. . . neck and shoulders suffused with a dingy yellow* [jaundice] *. . . discharges of bile . . . sometimes haemorrhages took place from the nose, gums, kidneys, stomach and intestines, ears, uterus, from wounds, and . . . the urine being transparent, or turbid and red . . . sometimes the cheeks and lips, in women particularly, were flushed with a beautiful glow, sometimes the tongue was covered with a long or short fur . . . sometimes the mind was affected with stupor, delirium or fury . . . sometimes with an apathy to everything, so as to look* *on death, not only with indifference, but even cheerfulness . . . almost universally mortal, where black matter was ejected from the stomach. A Mechanic was attacked with Continued fever, . . . and died on the fourth day, with haemorrhages from the nose and bowels, with a spongy state of the gums.* The next case, Mr. Patrick Stanton, started with fever, *which terminated in black vomit and death.* The results of Waring's autopsies led him to believe *the stomach seemed to have been the constant, and perhaps universal, seat of disease.*

Waring grimly continued his tabulations. By June, 14 more died; in July, 39; August, 111; September, 241. In October, 263 more. By December, when the slaughter had subsided, 666 Savannahians—over one tenth of her population—were dead from yellow fever.

For those who hadn't fled the city—seventy percent had—the sight and sound of carts filled with bodies being carried to the cemetery were Dantesque. The streets were virtually deserted. The few citizens visible, primarily physicians and clergy, occasionally gave their own lives in helpless attendance of a plague for which they had no comprehension. As Waring so starkly described: *The scene of sickness, misery, and ruin was awful, shocking, and well-fitted to inspire a melancholy sentiment of the shortness, uncertainty, and insignificance of life.*

In Savannah's memory, 1820 is etched the Year of the Yellow Fever, but it was not the first or last time. In a seventy-eight-page official report to the city council, Waring estimated around four thousand had died from the same disease since 1807. If accurate (few records were kept before 1820), Savannah's general population of five thousand was numerically wiped out in fourteen-year cycles. Over ten percent of the colonists died of *the ague* in their first summer of 1733. (Fifty of the 114 original colonists on the *Anne* were dead by their second year in 1734, but not all from yellow fever.) Nine more epidemics would follow 1820. In 1854, 560 souls perished. In 1876 the nation's centennial July Fourth was interrupted by the shock of Custer's last stand in Montana—250 died. In Savannah in that same year, 1,066 died of yellow fever, from an estimated ten thousand cases.

Doctor James J. Waring, son of William R. Waring. The father fought the 1820 yellow fever epidemic, and the son battled the one in 1876. (Courtesy of the Georgia Historical Society and Dr. William W. Waring, New Orleans.)

In his report Waring deductively recorded the temperatures, rainfall, winds, and other factors leading to the prevailing theory that *miasma* (deadly vapors in capricious eastern winds caused by a combination of things, including *the decomposition of substances . . . of animal and vegetable matter*) caused the epidemics. To Waring, the recent fire helped further expose these factors by leaving open vaults and cellars. Wind patterns, even less than half a mile apart, must have pushed the miasmas heavily into the Washington Square area, while largely sparing the northwest Yamacraw quadrant. This, combined

Plaque in Colonial Park Cemetery, remembering victims of one of several major yellow fever epidemics in Savannah. Around ten percent of the population died in each epidemic.

Silhouette of revolutionary veteran Sheftall Sheftall, called *Cocked Hat* Sheftall. The hat is still in possession of his descendants, along with the original drawing. (From George White's *Historical Collections of Georgia*. Courtesy of Chatham-Effingham-Liberty Regional Library and Marion A. Levy, Savannah.)

with the classical pattern of mild winter, early spring, heavy rainfall, and humid summer, led to the deadly miasma. If there were additional factors, *I have yet to learn what they are.*

Since the colonial period, one time-honored preventative was to drink water with tar in it. Now black smoke from tar barrels burning in the squares added to the hellish scene. Others examined with alarm any mold on the new ballast stones from ships or on roof shingles. Tree trunks were whitewashed. Waring resisted the move by others to cut all of the city's trees down, although he advocated removing large branches for better air circulation. He soon noticed that doses of turpentine often made things worse. *My mind is not so entirely made up . . . I shall never administer it again.* Despite eight *recoveries, in many cases it increased the distressing sensations of the stomach . . . to make matters worse than they had been.* Indeed, all remedies—castor oil, mercury, blood letting, snake root, bark, blistering, pepper, sugar of lead, brandy—*are as ineffectual as a bull-rush against the Nile . . . mere trash.*

Strangers—especially off ships—were avoided, literally like the plague. According to the then prevailing *New York doctrine*, the ague was contagious, especially from ship passengers. Against current dogma, Waring stated: *I have not heard of one instance of it being communicated from one person to another.* Understandably nobody listened. A common vision of charity was a basket of sustenance left at the front gate of the victims, the benefactor fleeing down the road in terror and torment.

Wittingly, not unwittingly, Waring was meticulously chronicling the reservoirs of miasmic death—standing water. *What is there to prevent it?* [The rice canals] *can be easily drained & can be preserved as free from collections of water.* Now, 170 years later, one is tempted to clutch at Waring's fading report in the Georgia Historical Society, straining to respectfully tap him on the shoulder. *Sir, you're so close— it's the mosquitoes!* Tears seem the only response of this impossible attempt—tears for his professional bravery and visceral deduction amid nightmarish futility. So close, so far beyond his time. Yet it would be another eighty years before Dr. Walter Reed, some of his team also martyrs in the long search, proved yellow fever was transmitted by one particular species of mosquito—the *Aëdes aegypti.* In 1883, seventeen years before Reed, a Cuban physician, Carlos Finlay, had identified the same likely culprit; but his findings were dismissed. After all, the mosquito had always been with us.

During the 1854 epidemic the Savannah Young Men's Benevolent Association was founded, and during the 1876 epidemic the organization would contribute over $100,000 for relief of victims. It was estimated that one-third of Savannah's entire population was under the care of the association at that time. Still active, the group recently raised funds to aid Charleston after the devastation of Hurricane Hugo in 1989.

During the 1876 epidemic, William R. Waring's son, James J. Waring, was also a physician who proposed clearing the local drains of standing water.

The Marquis de Lafayette in his sixties, as he appeared when he visited Savannah in 1825. The print is based on his favorite portrait of himself.

LAFAYETTE'S VISIT, 1825
"AH, I REMEMBER . . ."

On March 19, 1825, a former sufferer of yellow fever was the distinguished guest of Savannah. His name was Marie Joseph Paul Yves Roch Gilbert du Motier, Marquis de Lafayette. He had contracted the disease when he was twenty-four years of age, helping Washington put the finishing touches on Lord Cornwallis at Yorktown in 1781. Now, at sixty-eight years of age, "Gilbert," as his Savannah friends knew him, returned to dedicate the monument in Johnson Square to his revolutionary friend, Nathanael Greene.

Like Washington and Monroe before, he arrived by boat from Charleston; he was greeted by Governor George Troup and the *Marseillaise*. Troup's greeting *evidently affected* Lafayette's emotions by revealing his *sea of troubles* and imprisonment during the French Revolution: *No more of dungeons, no more of Frowns of Tyrants. . . . But enough: welcome General, welcome; thrice welcome to the State of Georgia.* Amid the official delegation were Savannah's revolutionary veterans, including Sheftall Sheftall, wearing his enormous revolutionary tricorn hat (still in possession of a family member, Marion A. Levy). Over forty years after the Revolution he was known to all as *Cocked-Hat Sheftall*, religiously drilling in his old continental uniform up and down his porch until the boards had a regimented rut tramped in them. At the nostalgic reunion of these old warriors, a Captain Rees *proceeded to narrate some trifling incidents* of a brief meeting in Philadelphia nearly fifty years before. Lafayette replied: *"Ah, I remember!" and taking Capt. Rees hand between both of his, the eyes of each glistening with pleasure, they stood for a few moments apparently absorbed in recollections of the days of their youth.*

Lafayette was a special guest of Anthony Wayne's old paramour, Mary Maxwell. From her boarding house, now the Richardson-Owens-Thomas House, Lafayette reviewed Savannah's colorful militia as they trooped past the still-standing Greek revival balcony by William Jay. The parade was described as *more glorious than Rome in the days of her greatest splendor and power.* When the Savannah Volunteer Guards marched by, Lafayette exclaimed, *Ah! quels beaux soldats!* [The painting by Preston Russell reproduced on the cover of this book commemorates this event.]

The remaining festivities had a deja vu quality, echoing the visits of

Georgia Governor George Troup, namesake of Troup Square, who eloquently welcomed Lafayette to Savannah. (From George White's *Historical Collections of Georgia* Courtesy of the Chatham-Effingham-Liberty Regional Library.)

Famous balcony of the Richardson-Owens-Thomas House, where by tradition Lafayette received the adulation of nostalgic Savannah citizens. To this day the unanswered question at the museum is—Was his address in French or English? (Courtesy of Hank Ramsey, Savannah.)

Washington and Monroe. The first night, there was a crushing banquet—with the gauntlet of endless patriotic speeches and toasts. As with Washington and Monroe, the guest of honor slipped off before midnight to live to fight another day. *Volunteer toasts* and merriment continued—without Washington/Monroe/Lafayette—for several more hours. In the case of Lafayette, he made it through thirteen official toasts, as many monologues, and then retired after the thirty-first toast, given in memory of General Samuel Elbert. Twenty-one volunteer toasts followed his departure, winding down to such immortal sentiments as *to the civic arrangements of the day . . . to the present interesting festival.*

The next morning Lafayette made his presumably leaden way to the Johnson Square dedication of the Greene monument, while *500 school children, each carrying a basket of flowers, threw the blossoms in*

Lafayette's path. Many speeches and specially composed music greeted their arrival, and the scene was repeated at the site of Pulaski's memorial [then in Chippewa Square]. Lafayette related *having had the honour on the arrival of the gallant Pulawski on this shore, to introduce him to our American Army, and its commander-in-chief* [Washington].

After a 3 o'clock Masonic banquet, which included thirty-four toasts, the party escaped onto a boat to Augusta—and another forty-eight hours of unstinted ceremony. Lafayette's family motto, *Cur non* ("Why not") was never put more to the test. After his Georgia visits, his secretary noted with due alarm that he *suffered a fatigue which caused us a momentary inquietude.* Small wonder. Why not.

He fell in a Duel on the 16th of January, 1815, by the hand of a man who, a short time ago, would have been friendless but for him. . . . By his untimely death the prop of a Mother's age is broken: The hope and consolation of Sisters is destroyed, the pride of Brothers humbled in the dust and a whole Family, happy until then, overwhelmed with affliction.

This 1815 epitaph in Colonial Park Cemetery for young U.S. officer James Wilde was typical of an avoidable tragic story of too much "honor" running around Savannah. Wilde had been killed by his friend, Captain Robert P. Johnson, with a shot through the heart on the fourth exchange. Wilde's brother, Richard Henry Wilde, was moved to write a poem on the matter with a very famous first line:

> *My life is like the Summer Rose*
> *That opens to the morning sky;*
> *But ere the shades of evening close*
> *Is scattered on the ground—to die.*

The 1815 headstone of James Wilde in Colonial Park Cemetery. Wilde was killed in a duel by a fellow officer and friend. The blunt eloquence of the eulogy is the ultimate retort to the excesses of personal honor.

Another epitaph from 1831, describing the dueling death of Odrey Miller, has the name of the alleged *politician* who killed him chiseled out by parties unknown. Thus the contradictory complexity of the nineteenth-century understanding of honor and chivalry.

The first recorded dueling death in Savannah was in 1740, as Peter Grant was killed by a Mr. Shenton, using swords. Two more of Oglethorpe's officers died at the hands of their fellow officers in 1740 and 1741. In old age Oglethorpe was quoted by Samuel Johnson's biographer, James Boswell, as asserting, *Undoubtedly a man has a right to defend his honor.* According to Boswell, this set off a long discourse by Oglethorpe's dinner partner, Samuel Johnson. He, in general, disagreed on moral and Christian grounds with the excessive result of formally defending one's self in duels; but Johnson concluded, *A man may shoot the man who invades his character.*

During the next century few Savannahians disagreed with Oglethorpe's articulation of honor. After all, he had not invented the ritual of the centuries-old Code Duello. Even those who declined a duel, and it was not usually out of cowardice, still defended themselves if attacked by an enraged challenger. Under those circumstances, the attacker was *an assassin*, not an honorable opponent. In 1796 James Jackson was attacked and nearly killed in the streets by Robert Watkins, who was armed with *a bayonet*. Jackson fought him off, despite a near-fatal stab in the chest, to fight Watkins later with pistols—twice. In the same year Jackson turned down a challenge by Jacob Waldburger. The challenger then posted Jackson in the paper: *I therefore pronounce General James Jackson an ASSASSIN of reputation AND A COWARD.* Such postings were not unusual, but the following in 1798 are the most baldly expressed:

> *For the assertion of repeated falsehoods, and the highest provocations, I thought proper to send a message to John Miller, . . . requesting him to meet me, and give me that satisfaction I was entitled to demand. I therefore proclaim to the world, that the same John Miller, refusing to accept my said message, has envinced himself a lyar, a scoundrel, and a cowardly assassin.*
> *6th June, 1798*   *Richard Henry Leake.*

> *Attention*
> *I DO proclaim RICHARD HENRY LEAKE, Attorney-at Law, to be an infamous LIAR AND VILE DEFAMER. Fathers of families, if you value the reputation of your daughters, suffer him not to enter your doors.*
>   *John Miller.*

General Nathanael Greene, in refusing a duel in 1785 with Captain James Gunn, still warned him: *I always wear pistols and will defend myself.* It is generally believed that the same James Gunn, later a senator, fought James Jackson with pistols. Jackson engaged in most of his duels during his exposure of the notorious Yazoo land fraud beginning in 1795, in which Gunn was a prime mover. Jackson was the avenging angel that voided the swindle of 35 million acres in west Georgia, "legally" bought at 1.5 cents an acre, often by corrupt politicians. English born and short, Jackson was described as a *brawling pygmy* by a political opponent. He hounded many involved in the swindle into their graves or out of the state. Some books say that Jackson fought twenty-three duels, although Thomas Gamble recorded less than half that number. Jackson's appropriate epitaph in Washington's Congressional Cemetery reads: *The scourge and terror of corruption at home.*

Most of the duels recorded in Thomas Gamble's book, *Savannah Duels and Duelists, 1733–1877*, weren't fatal, for a variety of reasons. Some duelists were merely wounded and seconds interceded, as in Savannah's most famous duel between Gwinnett and McIntosh (Gwinnett technically died of a wound infection, which was a common occurrence before antibiotics). Others weren't physically able to last until the coup de grace. During the Revolution, John McIntosh and a Captain Elholm both cut each other up with swords to the point of mutual collapse. Both recovered.

Some, at the moment of destiny, fired their pistols in the air and shook hands. Others appear simply to have missed and declined another shot. Such was the case in 1778, when General Robert Howe, Savannah's commander when she fell to the British in the same year, shot off the tip of Christopher Gadsen's ear. Even at the traditional ten to twelve paces Gadsen had missed outright. A British officer, Major John Andre, wrote a humorous poem on the nonfatal encounter: *H. missed his mark but not his aim/The shot was well directed;/It saved them both from hurt and shame,/What more could be expected?*

Smooth-bore pistols were accurate up to fifty-yards, but there were occasional misfires. In 1814 the paper recorded that Samuel H. Bryan *was killed at the second fire [shot] without having firing at all, his pistol having missed fire twice.* From the large number of leg wounds—Gwinnett, McIntosh, and Jackson—one must wonder if at the last instant there was occasional psychological block against shooting to kill. In 1792 Jackson and Mayor Thomas Gibbons missed each other cleanly three times. This wasn't Jackson's usual record; in 1780 he killed George Wells outright with one shot. In 1866 there was a quite understandable reason why the shooting never commenced. The challenger dropped his weapon on the brink of *Are you ready?* Faced off at Tybee Island, the challenged had *fully* exercised his right to choose the weapons—double-barreled shotguns loaded with fifteen slugs at twenty yards. The challenger appears to have had second thoughts.

By 1826 Savannah had formed an Anti-Dueling Association. Its first chairman was George Jones, son of Liberty Boy Noble W. Jones. The group wasn't always effective in stopping duels, but it was progressively successful in curbing a custom established since colonial days.

In 1827 the society persuaded Robert W. Pooler to back down by writing him: *It has been intimated that there exists a difference between yourself and Mr. George Millen, which it is apprehended may lead to serious results. . . . The committee will be happy to hear from you in reply. . . . We believe you will receive this in the spirit which dictates it, and not as an officious interference.* By 1836 the society's message to Dr. Richard D. Arnold advising him against dueling Thomas Bourke was much more direct: *The committee then resolved to make one more effort to prevent A FASHIONABLE MURDER. . . . The quarrel was settled in a manner honorable to both parties.* Arnold was a member of the society, and, according to folklore, was said to have fought several duels.

During the seven years after the society's formation, few recorded duels occurred. In August 1832, however, the paper noted: *James Jones Starke . . . was shot at the City Hotel, by Dr. Philip Minis, through the breast, and almost instantaneously expired.* Put on trial, Minis was acquitted after the jury deliberated for two hours. There were four lawyers for the prosecution and six for the defense.

Because of mounting legal consequences, Savannahians tended to row over to Screvens Ferry, South Carolina. Carolinians in turn came over to Georgia's Tybee Island to fight it out near the old lighthouse. Before such caution, locals fought duels traditionally on *the Strand* at the east end of River Street by Fort Wayne, around Sheftall Cemetery, behind Colonial Park Cemetery, or over on Hutchinson Island.

The last duels recorded by Gamble occurred in the 1870's at Brampton Plantation, three miles outside of Savannah. In 1870 Ludlow Cohen was killed by Richardson F. Aiken on the fifth exchange— shot in the right side, the bullet *passing through the abdomen, cutting the intestines.* Although Aiken was an experienced marksman, Cohen was not. Still, Cohen denied nervousness before the fatal fifth exchange. *Nervous? Not a bit* were his last words as he twirled his pistol into the air and caught it by the barrel. He died in horrible agony the same afternoon. Both proud owners of sailboats and former friends, Cohen had been accused of cheating in a sailboat race. The coroner's jury found Aiken guilty of murder *whilst fighting a duel, contrary to the laws of Georgia.* Later a grand jury failed to bring an indictment, but the public was further aroused when Cohen's many friends made a great display of his funeral.

Six years later, during the 1876 yellow fever epidemic, Dr. James J. Waring almost got his head handed to him by the son of Mayor Edward C. Anderson. Amid the trying horrors for all, Waring accused the mayor of *supineness and indifference . . . [being] a professional office holder and politician.* In retort, the mayor's son demanded *the personal satisfaction customary among gentlemen.* Waring quickly backed off, explaining, *I cannot recognize your right to make the demand.* After all, it was with the father, not the son, that Waring foolishly picked his fight. Waring had previously been mediated out of a duel in 1868, when he challenged the editor of the Savannah *Advertiser,* Captain S. Yates Levy, over a hot political editorial that Waring took personally.

In 1877 the last recorded pistol shots snapped across Brampton Plantation. Outside the courtroom two young lawyers were extending the altercation of their bitter case. One had written offensive remarks in a brief, beyond the "normal" adversarial language. The duel was at dusk because the challenger was late, having lost his way. After a harmless first exchange, the physician of the challenged interceded: *This must be settled, or we must have another shot promptly. It is getting dark and my man is nearsighted. It is not fair to him to further delay.* Darkness fell on Savannah's recorded dueling era. Both men became cordial friends until natural death separated them forty-six years later.

"BORN OR TO BE BORN—ABSOLUTE SLAVES"
1755–1860

Slavery in the post-revolutionary era was an established institution. One of the first things the new government of 1755 did was to put a slave code in writing. The preamble was crushing in its hopeless inhumanity, rendered almost banal by its matter-of-fact legal language: *All Negroes . . . mulattos or mestizos who are now or shall hereafter be in this province and all their issue and offspring Born or to be Born shall be and they are hereby declared to be and remain hereafter absolute slaves and shall follow the condition of the mother and shall be deemed in law to be chattels personal in the hands of their owners and possessors.*

By the code, slaves could not be taught to read or write; there was a £15 penalty to any who tried. The fine for working a slave more than sixteen hours a day was only £3. If a slave left a plantation without written permission, a maximum of twenty lashes could result. Crimes punishable by death were murder, rape, arson, and poisoning a white person. A bounty could be paid to the Indians for any scalp of a slave who ran away. No ownership of property, renting, trading for profit, or learning a trade was allowed. Some instruction in Christianity was selectively permitted as *salutary.* However, despite the law that no more than seven slaves could assemble without the presence of a white person, a quarter century later groups of slaves would gather on Yamacraw bluff, reading, writing, and praying.

In fact, over the years more than one northern visitor would echo the words of a Congregationalist minister from Massachusetts, Nehemiah Adams, in 1854: *A better-looking, happier, more courteous set of people I had never seen than those colored men, women and children I met in Savannah. A visitor is made to feel that good and kind treatment of the slaves is the common law.* By contrast, in 1852 Charles

Slaves picking cotton near Savannah, 1858.

Parsons, a Maine physician, wrote from Savannah that slaveholders were a cruel and heartless people and Georgia was a *land of bolts and chains.*

As Mills B. Lane points out in his fine book, *Savannah Revisited* (1969): "These two views of slavery were more complementary than contradictory: Parsons had traveled overland to Savannah and seen slavery on the plantations, where life was often nasty, brutish and short, while Adams had taken a steamship to Savannah and seen primarily the indulgent, rather comfortable life of domestic servants and skilled laborers in the city."

By the nineteenth century in Savannah, blacks were allowed to congregate in their own quarter of the city. They were an amalgam of runaways, freedmen, and idle drifters with no place else to go. They had to be off the street, however, by 8 P.M., when the bell rang in the old City Exchange on Bay Street. (Sailors too were traditionally fined if on the streets after the bell.) Blacks could not buy or sell liquor, watch a parade, or own a dog. Such "laws" were selectively enforced, as blacks had long had the opportunity of free religious assembly. There many were openly taught to read and write—still technically against the law.

African Baptist Church, 1788
"Beloved Brother Andrew"

Andrew Bryan, David George, and George Liele: the names of these revolutionary-era slaves were the genesis of the African Baptist Church in Savannah, the oldest black church in America. David George was a runaway slave from Virginia who hid out with the Indians until a chief, King Jack, sold him to a Georgia plantation owner. George fled to the British side when they captured Savannah in 1778. Liele (pronounced Lyle) also was a Virginia slave, brought to Georgia by his master. Like George, Liele finally won freedom during the British occupation in 1778. Both would leave Savannah with the British in 1782. George relocated to Nova Scotia for ten years until hostility there forced him to West Africa, where he became one of the founding fathers of Sierra Leone. Liele sailed with the British to Jamaica to set up a black congregation numbering over three hundred.

It was these two men, while in Savannah, who inspired a forty-one-year-old slave named Andrew Bryan. Bryan and his wife, Hannah, were baptized by Liele in 1782. Nine months after Liele and George left, Bryan assumed their ministry. He first began by preaching to small groups on Yamacraw bluff. His owner, Jonathan Bryan (slaves often adopted the last name of their masters), felt his influence on the slaves *salutary* and encouraged him. A few whites began attending his sermons as well. However, when these outdoor meetings graduated to a local shack, hostile whites *artfully dispossessed* him. Andrew and his brother Sampson were forced to tend their flock in the local swamps.

On January 20, 1788, white Baptist minister Abraham Marshall and black minister Jesse Peter formally certified *the Ethiopian Church of Jesus Christ* and ordained *beloved Brother Andrew to the work of the ministry . . . to preach the Gospel, and administer the ordinances, as God in his providence may call.* This was too much for Savannah's slave masters, who forbade their slaves to attend. As Marshall recorded by 1790: *The whites grew more and more inveterate; taking numbers of them before magistrates [about fifty including Sampson]—they were imprisoned and whipped . . . particularly Andrew, who was cut and bled abundantly . . . he held up his hand, and told his persecutors that he rejoiced not only to be whipped, but would freely suffer death for the cause of Jesus Christ.*

On protest by his owner, Jonathan Bryan, Andrew was released. He moved his congregation to a barn on Bryan's Brampton Plantation, three miles from Savannah. By 1791, 350 slaves had been converted, but were prevented by their masters from being baptized; Christianity was now not so salutary. Still Andrew Bryan persisted, and by 1792 he had appointed four deacons, with his brother Sampson as assistant preacher. Fifty members of the congregation could read, and three could write.

Having bought his own freedom for £50 the year before, Bryan in 1794 raised enough money to erect a house of prayer. By 1800 he wrote to a white Baptist colleague: *With much pleasure, I inform you, dear sir, that I enjoy good health, and am strong in body, tho' 63 years old, and am blessed with a pious wife, whose freedom I have obtained,*

The First African Baptist Church on Franklin Square memorializes two of its ministers in stained-glass splendor. At the top is Andrew Bryan, founder of America's oldest black congregation in 1788. At the bottom is Andrew Marshall, prominent minister from 1812 to 1856.

The two low, rectangular graves in the foreground hold Andrew Bryan and his brother, Samson, in Laurel Grove Cemetery South. The crypt next to them holds the Reverend Andrew Marshall.

and an only daughter and child, who is married to a free man, tho' she, and consequently, under our laws, her seven children, five sons and two daughters, are slaves. By a kind Providence I am well provided for, as to worldly comforts, (tho' I have had very little given to me as a minister) having a house and a lot in this city, besides the land on which several buildings stand, for which I receive a small rent, and a fifty-six acre tract of land, with all necessary buildings, four miles in the country.

By the time Bryan died in 1812 at the age of seventy-five, his congregation had *gotten too unwieldy for one body;* second and third African Baptist churches were also now in Savannah.

The flickering ray of enlightenment embodied in the founding of the African Baptist Church was still engulfed by the overwhelming darkness of timeless slavery. King Cotton was impossible without it. Even the 1788 U.S. Constitution—for representation purposes only—considered slaves three-fifths of a *person.* Yet this human property, if for economic reasons alone, was in general not treated inhumanely. A healthy slave was worth $500 to $1,000 in the nineteenth century.

In 1831 the bloody Nat Turner slave insurrection in Virginia sent a shudder of terror throughout the nation. By 1833 the Georgia penal code again enforced laws against the teaching of blacks, or even allowing them to work around printing presses. Yet, amid all of this oppression a free Haitian named Julian Troumontaine operated a clandestine school for blacks in Savannah until 1844.

According to the 1860 census, Georgia had over 465,000 blacks, 3,500 of them free persons. This was more than ten percent of the total American black population, of which ninety percent were still in slavery. Five years later over 180,000 blacks had fought for the North, comprising ten percent of its army and twenty percent of its navy.

In his book *Major Butler's Legacy* Savannahian Malcolm Bell follows five generations of regional slaveowners and records the selling of 463 slaves owned by Pierce Butler in 1859. Newly poor because of bad investments, Butler recouped $300,205 from the sale. It occurred three miles west of Savannah where the *property* were brought in railroad cars and kept in racehorse stables. The transactions took place over two days in the pouring rain. Each slave sold for an average of $716 a head—well above the anticipated appraisal of $572.47 per slave, but, according to the *Savannah Republican* paper, a somewhat lower and disappointing first day average of $660.

Horace Greeley of the *New York Tribune* had sent his ace reporter, Mortimer Neal Thomson, known as *Doesticks* in the trade, to cover the sale. Somewhere between reality and an *Uncle Tom's Cabin* bias, the incognito *Doesticks* reported: *The negroes were examined with as little consideration as if they had been brutes indeed; the buyers pulling*

Slave auction, from the *London Illustrated Weekly*. (Courtesy of Willis Hakim Jones, Savannah.)

their mouths open to see their teeth, pinching their limbs to find how muscular they were, walking them up and down to detect any signs of lameness, making them stoop and bend in different ways that they might be certain there was no concealed rupture or wound; and in addition to all this treatment, asking them scores of questions relative to their qualifications and accomplishments. All these humiliations were submitted to without a murmur, and in some instances with good-natured cheerfulness—where the slave liked the appearance of the proposed buyer, and fancied that he might prove a kind "Mas'r."

Little had changed since a visitor in 1838 witnessed a slave sale in front of the Savannah Courthouse: *Saw fifty-four men, women and children sold as chattels, but not without emotion, to see the serious look, the falling tear, and the submissive will. There are three auctioneers selling at the same time. Sometimes one man is up for sale, sometimes three or more. Sometimes a woman and children, called "an interesting family of negroes." Now, a plantation—now, a gun—now, an old man, wife and daughter—now, a young man, etc, etc. The time for this traffic in slaves, and the souls of men, is the first Monday in each month.*

The South moved toward Civil War.

CIVIL WAR

1860: Savannah on the brink. She was a beautiful old city of around fourteen thousand, not including more than eight thousand slaves working the plantations of her prosperity. Antebellum homes stretched majestically to Gaston Street, met by Forsyth Park with its flowing fountain. *A tranquil old city,* English novelist William Make-

Civil War–era print looking west on Liberty Street, showing the bustle of a thriving little city. (Courtesy of the Thomas Gamble Collection, Chatham-Effingham-Liberty Regional Library.)

peace Thackeray called it, *wide-streeted, tree-planted, with a few cows and carriages toiling through the sandy road, a few happy negroes sauntering here and there, a red river with a tranquil little fleet of merchantmen taking in cargo, and tranquil ware-houses barricaded with packs of cotton—no row, no tearing Northern bustle, no ceaseless hotel racket, no crowds, drinking at bars.* The cows described by Thackeray's bucolic prose were there by city ordinance, an attempt to eat up the tall grass in Savannah's unpaved streets.

Three railroads terminated in Savannah, dumping King Cotton and lumber into her lap. Multiple cotton compresses, sawmills, and shipyards worked their alchemy to turn these products into export gold. Cotton merchants paced the ramps of Bay Street's Factor's Walk, nodding their bids as they inspected the produce amid the majestic sidewalks and catacombs of ships' ballast stones. *I glory in the prosperity of Savannah*, wrote a returning visitor. Seven years earlier the new Forsyth Park that greeted this same visitor had been the wooded area of Oglethorpe's time.

"LET IT COME NOW"

At a political rally, a voice rose, echoing shuttering opposition to the prospect of a gangly threat named Lincoln—just growing his first beard and running for the presidency. Lawyer Francis S. Bartow was working his usual magic on the audience: *If any man is to peril life, fortune and honor in defense of our rights, I claim to be one of those men. Let it come now, I am ready for it. Put it not off until tomorrow, or next day, we shall not be stronger by waiting. . . . I would peril all, ALL, before I will abandon our rights in the Union or submit to be governed by an unprincipled majority.*

Bust of Francis Bartow in Forsyth Park.

Confederate Memorial Day reminds Savannah each April that it is the Deep South. Reenactment cannon crews perform in Forsyth Park with the 1875 Confederate monument in the background.

Bartow would indeed risk all and die at Bull Run ten months later. He was buried in Laurel Grove Cemetery, where his body was carried in a hearse drawn by four gray horses—*the most solemn and imposing spectacle we have ever witnessed in Savannah,* reported the *Morning News.*

Other voices emerged, such as Dr. Richard Arnold, who four years later would be the mayor to surrender the city to General William Tecumseh Sherman: *We are ready for war to the knife and the knife to the handle. . . . It is a practical question with us, not only as to existence and prosperity, but whether we are to [be] disfranchised of our liberties and subjugated to domination of the Black Race.*

Later, Georgian Alexander H. Stephens, then vice-president of the Confederacy, made his famous *Cornerstone Speech* in Savannah to the largest crowd ever assembled at the Athenaeum on Bull Street: *The cornerstone . . . rests upon the great truth, that the negro is not equal to the white man; that slavery—subordination to the superior race—is his natural and normal condition.*

Lincoln and his *Black Republicans* threatened all this. *With the exception of eight or ten citizens here, all are in favor of secession,* wrote a *New York Times* correspondent. But feelings were mixed. The rector of St. John's Church shuddered at the prospect of secession: *We will sing the requiem of these United States.* Bishop Augustin Verot, however, over at the nearby Catholic church, prayed for secession, blaming northern Protestant abolitionists for bringing on *the deplorable state of things.*

In December, when word reached Savannah that South Carolina had become the first state to secede from the Union, the whole town was

Marching off to war in faraway Virginia and bloody Bull Run, troops pass the 1854 Pulaski monument in Monterey Square. (Coutesy of the Thomas Gamble Collection, Chatham-Effingham-Liberty Regional Library.)

illuminated. Crowds filled the streets wearing secession rosettes and badges. A rally in Johnson Square sported a banner with a design resurrected from Georgia's revolutionary days—a coiled snake with the motto *Don't Tread on Me*

To Arms—"We Are a Miniature Sparta"

Savannah's established militia units exchanged their Napoleonic-inspired uniforms for field-practical gray. The Chatham Artillery, the oldest of the city's militia units, paraded with the Irish Jasper Greens, the Republican Blues, the Oglethorpe Light Infantry, the Georgia Hussars, the Pulaski Guards, and with the *beaux soldats*—as Lafayette had called them in 1825—of the Savannah Volunteer Guards.

Colonel Alexander R. Lawton headed a parade of fourteen such companies, over one thousand strong. *The most imposing and gratifying military display we have seen in Savannah*, recorded the local paper. The Chatham Artillery proudly displayed their two Yorktown cannons given them by President Washington in 1791. *We are a miniature Sparta and every man is a soldier*, wrote George A. Mercer. *Our drill rooms are open nightly; companies drill every afternoon; three corps were on the parade ground last night exercising by moonlight.*

Over two hundred of those same Savannahians would lie casualties in the moonlight on their first battlefield, Bull Run. Six of them had been mates in Sunday school and would be reunited at their funeral in Independent Presbyterian Church on Bull Street.

Fort Pulaski
"I Yield My Sword,
But I Trust I Have Not Disgraced It"

Savannah was aroused. Something must be done about impregnable Fort Pulaski at the mouth of the river. Construction began on this defensive legacy in 1831, the first assignment of a twenty-three-year-old military engineer, Robert Edward Lee. Now, thirty years later, it would be seized by Confederates—the first belligerent act of the rebellious South—three months before Charleston fired on Fort Sumter on April 16, 1861. Led by Charles Olmstead, on January 3, 1861, 134 members of the Chatham Artillery, the Oglethorpe Light Infantry, and the Savannah Volunteer Guards embarked by steamer for the fort. They found it defended by an ordinance sergeant and a caretaker. As the troops entered beneath the magnificent brick arches, the sun broke through the clouds, considered by one soldier *an auspicious omen.* Years later Olmstead recorded his unopposed entry: *I can shut my eyes and see it all now, the proud step of officers and men, the colors snapping in the strong breeze from the ocean; the bright sunlight of the parade as we emerged from the shadow of the archway; the first glimpse of a gun through an open casemate door: one and all they were photographed on my mind.*

Over a year later, the day before the firing on Fort Pulaski commenced, Olmstead remained confident of the fort's impregnability. He coolly responded to the Yankees' demand for surrender: *In reply, I can only say that I am here to defend the Fort, not to surrender it.*

Like Olmstead, Robert E. Lee was also convinced of the fort's impregnability. As the new inspector of southern coastal defenses, he visited Savannah in 1861, renewing acquaintances from his youthful engineering days thirty years before. Wrote one defender at Pulaski: *We were visited the other day by Gens Lee, Lawton, and Mercer and a good many other little puffs. Gen Lee was dressed very plainly while his inferiors were dressed within an inch of their lives.* After inspecting Fort Pulaski, Lee gazed at Goat Point on Tybee over 1,700 yards away and concluded: *They will make it pretty hot for you with shells, but they cannot breach your walls at that distance.* On April 11, 1862, however, Olmstead would surrender this supposedly invincible bastion to the rifled cannon of Union General Quincy A. Gilmore, firing from nearly two thousand yards away on deserted Tybee Island. Over five thousand shells later and thirty hours after firing commenced, most of Fort Pulaski's cannons were knocked out and a gaping breech opened in the seven-foot-thick walls, exposing the powder magazine. Wrote a correspondent for the *New York Herald*, the wall seemed *to have the small pox . . . blotches appearing all over it.*

Contemplating the needless loss of 385 defenders inside, Olmstead conceded: *I yield my sword, but I trust I have not disgraced it.*

When George A. Mercer learned of this *mortifying and stunning blow* back in Savannah, he grasped its impact for the future. *The whole system of warfare is revolutionized. Brick is no longer of any avail.* With rifled cannon, the tactics of war had *leaped a century forward and all are behind the age.*

Even Gilmore, the instant Union hero, was astounded by the leveling success of his new rifled cannon against Fort Pulaski. *Had we possessed our present knowledge of their power, the eight weeks of laborious preparations for its reduction could have been curtailed to one week.*

To this day in Savannah, however, a few diehards still echo the sentiments of Mayor Charles C. Jones, Jr. He wrote at the time: *Never did man or officer have a better opportunity of giving a name to History and honor to his country than did Olmstead.* Jones would have fought to the bitter end—*then blown the whole concern to atoms.*

But Olmstead did not delay. By two o'clock on the afternoon of the eleventh, the Confederate flag came down and Fort Pulaski was surrendered.

Colonel Charles Olmstead, who was criticized for giving up Fort Pulaski too easily. (Courtesy of the Fort Pulaski National Monument.)

Union General Quincy A. Gilmore. Even he was surprised at the leveling impact of new rifled cannon against previously impregnable thick masonry.

Fort Pulaski after thirty hours of shelling. (Courtesy of Fort Pulaski National Monument.)

THE GEORGIA NAVY—"ABSURD ABORTION"

With the fall of Fort Pulaski, only minor batteries out on the islands and old Fort Jackson on the river a mile below town were left. They were not impressive defenses. A Union commander accurately termed Fort Jackson *a little old brick fort that would have been knocked down by half a dozen heavy shells.* Fortunately it didn't come to that, and Fort Jackson today remains a favorite setting for Savannahians' beloved oyster roasts.*

After the capture of Pulaski, the city's confidence was shattered. Only one day after the surrender, an observer wrote: *Women are leaving and property of all kinds is being sent off.* Furthermore, the "Georgia Navy" offered scant comfort. This euphemism covered exactly four vessels—two converted paddle-wheel steamers and two old tugboats with a cannon thrown aboard. The side-wheelers had their engines and boilers well above deck, ready to blow sky high with one minor hit. At least they were anointed with formidable names: the *Savannah,* the *Huntress,* the *Samson,* and the *Resolute.* On assuming command of the *Savannah,* John Newland Maffitt grimaced: *A more absurd abortion for a man of war was rarely witnessed.* More resolute was the armada's commodore, sixty-five-year-old Josiah Tattnall, son of Governor Tattnall from Savannah. Serving the Stars and Stripes since the War of 1812, the commodore's most lasting legacy is the phrase *Blood is thicker than water,* uttered in Chinese waters in 1859.

---

*Philip Thicknesse, a Savannah resident in 1736, recorded what may be the first notation of that beloved tradition peculiar to Savannah: *I have often in the River and Creeks of Savanna, made Fires, at low Water, on Oyster Islands, and roasted enough to feed an Hundred Men. . . . The Indians . . . make fires at low water on the Islands of oysters, which are then left high and dry, and roast the greatest part of an Island at once.*

He was alleged to have *often made holy vows that he will yet sink each and all those d—d old tubs off the bar.* A friend wrote: *I suppose no officer of his rank and quality was ever doomed to the indignity of such an inefficient command.*

Meanwhile out at Fort Pulaski, Union troops from New York regiments drilled away the tedium of occupation. The huge field inside the fort's walls was ideal for the new national diversion, baseball. The game's traditional (but debatable) inventor was Captain Abner Doubleday, the Union officer who fired the first shot in defense of Fort Sumter the year before. Doubtless the first recorded baseball score in Georgia was on January 3, 1863. The Forty-eighth New York downed the Forty-seventh New York by a score of twenty to seven.

The Union Blockade
"I Will Cork Up Savannah"

In between band concerts, plays, photo taking, fishing, and duck hunting, the fort's garrison managed to partially throttle the Confederate blockade runners coming in from Bermuda and Nassau. The blockade by the Union fleet, under Admiral Samuel Francis DuPont, had begun the year before the fall of Fort Pulaski. When DuPont captured nearby Port Royal and Hilton Head as a base of operations, he vowed: *I will cork up Savannah like a bottle by placing a frigate in the roads opposite Tybee.* By December 1861 he declared: *Savannah is completely bottled up.*

Not quite. Three weeks before, the *Fingal* had arrived in the port of Savannah, where she was greeted by delirious crowds. Her cap-

Panic in Johnson Square, titled *Indiscriminate Flight of the Inhabitants,* on hearing news that the Yankees were occupying home shores only miles away. (Courtesy of V. and J. Duncan Antique Maps and Prints, Savannah.)

A Union regiment formally poses for its portrait in occupied Fort Pulaski. In the background an example of real life is inadvertently recorded for perhaps the first time—baseball. (Courtesy of the Fort Pulaski National Monument.)

tain, Edward C. Anderson, was an instant hero, receiving three cheers from the throng. And why not? Aboard from England were 18,500 firearms, a quarter million cartridges, and seventeen thousand pounds of gunpowder. The *Fingal* was not the only ship to evade DuPont's blockade. A few days before the *Fingal's* arrival, the *Bermuda*, loaded down with cotton, had slipped out of Savannah for English ports. She had just delivered from Liverpool 6,500 Enfield rifles, *24,000 pairs of blankets, 50,000 pairs of shoes, 20 Rifled cannon, shot shell & powder, a lot of pants, coats, drawers & shirts made up.*

Obviously England was not much honoring Uncle Sam's blockade. Indeed, Savannahians were convinced that England would join the Confederates any week now—as soon as she missed her southern cotton. Mrs. H. J. Wayne predicted: *Certainly if the President insists upon blockading our Ports England and France will interfere. They cannot do without our cotton and rice.*

Of course this was not to be. The fate of the *Fingal* when she left Savannah with her load of cotton would become the new reality. Trying to slip out a back waterway, she met Union gunboats at Thunderbolt and turned back. James D. Bulloch reported at the time: *I consider the port of Savannah as completely closed to commerce for an indefinite time.*

In addition to Union guns, the shallow waterways around Savannah were a major problem. The *Jupiter*, the *Alliance*, the *Glide*, the *Evening Star*, the *Persis*, the *Arletta*, the *Oconee*, the *Admiral*, the *Cheshire*, and the *Lodona* were just some of the ships either run aground or surrendered to Union gunboats—usually in that order.

The Forty-eighth New York Regimental Band, circa 1863, at Fort Pulaski. (Courtesy of the Fort Pulaski National Monument.)

STRANGULATION
"IT TAKES A GREAT DEAL OF CONFEDERATE MONEY TO BUY LITTLE OR NOTHING"

The pinch of the blockade had a telling effect on Savannah's economy. *Our commerce is perfectly prostrated. Many are closing up business,* reported a merchant in 1861. In the first half of 1862 the customhouse collected no export duties at all; import duties had dropped ninety percent from the year before. In 1861 the *Bermuda* ran the blockades loaded with 1,800 bales of cotton. By comparison, in 1863 the *Persis* and *Evening Star* were captured with twenty-two and seven bales respectively.

Charles Olmstead returned to Savannah in late 1862 to find commerce *dead* and the few stores open having *depleted stocks and many empty shelves.* A visitor also described the ghost town atmosphere: *A strange, mysterious, weird quietude reigns perpetually. Stagnation and paralysis obstruct the channels where business briskly flowed . . . the whole town—every thing—seems to have halted in the precise attitude of one who, with respiration suspended, is listening all agape for some undefined announcement to be made.*

It takes a great deal of Confederate money to buy little or nothing, wrote another Savannahian. A standing joke, according to Olmstead, was that a housewife needed her market basket to carry her money; the palm of her free hand sufficed to hold the purchases. *Paper is so high, I have written between the lines,* Mrs. Josephine C. Habersham wrote in her diary in 1863. She continued: *$58.00 for a* *summer muslin . . . $195.00 for a dress I could have got two years ago for just $9.00 . . . Sixty dollars for a straw bonnet—untrimmed!* Lieutenant Henry Graves made $80 a month. A pair of boots cost two and a half times that—*I am almost persuaded to get married here and go and live with the girl's father.* The *Morning News* even made the *sensible suggestion* that Georgia go into the wooden shoe business. A popular poem by Carrie Bell Sinclair reflected both Savannah distress and spunk:

> *The homespun dress is plain, I know,*
> *My hat's palmetto, too;*
> *But then it shows what Southern girls*
> *For Southern rights will do.*

But inflation and profiteering only increased; eggs went to three times their normal price of fifty cents in one year, and flour went from $40 a barrel to $125. In 1864 Colonel Anderson paid $30 for four forlorn fish that once cost fifty cents. Mayor Richard Arnold wrote General Beauregard in Charleston that the end was near; for a whole week hardly a household had a supply of—gasp—grits. They too had tripled in price. Soon boiled shrimp became the breakfast staple of Savannah. In 1864 a mob of armed women marched through streets demanding food. The riot ended with the ring leaders put in jail.

It looks to me like the Confederate States is compelled to starve in a short time, wrote a Union private from Thunderbolt in 1864. He did not care *how soon the starving commenced, if it would begin on the right ones.*

THE TAKING OF THE *WATER WITCH*
"WE ARE REBELS! . . . THREE CHEERS AND BOARD HER!"

The blockade put Savannah and the Union at a standoff; one result was monumental boredom. *Blockading was desperately tedious work, make the best one could of it. Day after day, roll, roll,* wrote a Union officer on the U.S.S. *Cimmaron* in Wassaw Sound in 1863. Union Admiral J. A. G. Dahlgren commented: *As far as the eye can reach, not a living soul is to be seen for months that looks like an enemy.* The only hostile fire the C.S.S. *Savannah* ever took were careless potshots by pickets from her own side as she occasionally lumbered down the river at a sluggish six knots. Such absurd incidents infuriated her captain. Adding to his irritation was the fact that the ship couldn't go up the river against the current; for that, towboats were needed. At least the Union in their tedium knew that the blockade was bottling up the enemy. They also had the incentive of winning prize money for seized vessels.

In Savannah no one chafed in frustration more than Thomas Postell Pelot, a Confederate officer on the C.S.S. *Georgia*. This vessel was so slow that, in essence, it was a floating battery towed sluggishly around Fort Jackson. Pelot's daily excitation was to watch the raising and lowering of the Stars and Stripes over captured Fort Pulaski, until he decided to do something about the situation. Rounding up around 125 crew members from blockaded Confederate vessels, he vowed to capture a Union ship the old-fashioned way—like pirates—scampering over the rigging with cutlass in teeth.

The first night's foray around Beaulieu turned up no targets; *the bird had flown*, concluded Pelot. But the next night was different. In a moonless and squally dark, the Confederates spotted the U.S.S. *Water Witch* anchored in Ossabaw Sound near Bradley's Creek.

We rowed quietly along with muffled oars, recalled Arthur C. Freeman, and around 2 A.M. the Confederates approached the Union vessel.

Boat ahoy! Who goes there? challenged the watch.

Runaway negroes, responded a black pilot, Moses Dallas.

Silently the Confederates drifted to the side of the *Water Witch*.

Then suddenly Pelot shouted, *We are rebels! Give way, boys! Three cheers and board her!*

Bellowing like fiends, the boarders cut through the protective netting and swarmed onto the deck. Lightning flashes illuminated the wild melee from stem to stern. Rain dampened the gunpowder; cutlasses and pikes were the main weapons used.

Many Union sailors were caught below deck, their courage perhaps dampened by Tom Muller's shout down the hatchway: *Stay down there, or I'll cut your damned noses off.* The bravest defender was a black seaman in charge of the small-arms rack. He fired revolver after revolver until he fell dead, with six or eight bullets in his body.

After twenty minutes of bloody fury, the U.S.S. *Water Witch* was a captured vessel. Pelot lay dead on the deck, shot through the heart. The *Water Witch* remained stranded in the Vernon River, unable to even reach Savannah proper because of the strong Union blockade, but its capture gave a momentary morale boost to the comically impotent Confederate navy.

CONFEDERATE OCCUPATION
"IF A LADY HAS AN ESCORT, IT WEARS A UNIFORM"
Unfortunately for the Confederates, most dreams of action like Pelot's

The Republican Blues, from *Frank Leslie's Illustrated Newspaper,* 1860. They were only one of many resplendent Savannah militia units who evolved in the nineteenth century. (Courtesy of the Thomas Gamble Collection, Chatham-Effingham-Liberty Regional Library.)

were seldom fulfilled. The city abounded with soldiers, but the relentless blockade continued.

According to historian Alexander A. Lawrence, there probably were never more than fourteen thousand troops at one time in Savannah, but the turnover and variety were eye-catching. In the words of war correspondent Felix Gregory De Fontaine: *Probably there is no city in the Confederacy where you would be so struck by the military air that pervades everything as here. In the Park, if a lady has an escort, it wears a uniform. . . . These regiments are made up of all degrees of humanity from the wealthiest to the poorest and from the white haired veteran to the boy of thirteen. Their garments represent every hue that the scriptural Joseph ever dreamed of in contemplating his own historic coat; some wear patched bed quilts that look like dilapidated rag carpets; some have hats without vizors; some red shirts, some white; (a few almost none at all); some wear coats, some don't.*

George Mercer, now on the staff of his father, General Hugh W. Mercer (descendant of revolutionary hero General Hugh Mercer, and ancestor of world-famous Savannah songwriter Johnny Mercer), recorded: *Our low country men are tall, boney, swarthy fellows; they are more useful than showy—strong, hardy, and seasoned, daring and resolute, and soldiers by instinct and habit. Every man of them is familiar with horse, gun, exposure, and hardship.* In typical Savannah fashion, Mercer added that they were *no respecters of persons, and have little reverence for uniform or rank.*

Even among officers, irreverence got out of hand. According to later charges, Major O. C. Myers, on official business to Colonel E. W. Chastain, was greeted with these words screamed in front of God and everybody: *Go to Hell, God damn you, Dont speak to me. I hate you.*

Troops rotating in from all over the South often didn't find Savannah as hospitable as "back home." It was too hot, and the sulfurous drinking water was not as sweet. To a soldier named Wood the suburbs were *filthy.* Seventeen-year-old Thomas Barrow cursed the same thing Washington and British soldiers did in the Revolution—the sandy streets were about a foot deep. Barrow also found the inhabitants *a set of stuck up know nothing fools.* A lonely Louisiana soldier complained: *We came here as strangers and strangers we have remained . . . the greater portion of us do not know the name of a man, woman or child in Savannah. The ladies down here are the poorest apologies for beauty I ever saw,* added Thomas Barrow, *not one to compare with Miss Livie or Helen* back home in Athens.

And the bugs! Sand flies could be heard *all over the regiment cussing the fleas.* Concluded a soldier: *I had pretty near as live [leave] fight the Yankees as the fleas.* Out on Skidaway Island, William W. Gordon recorded: *I took a bath this morning & attempted to rub some stuff on the red bugs to kill them but the sand flies on my naked body almost drove me crazy. I fairly hollered.*

The mosquitoes, especially (and still) around Fort Jackson, were *thick as rice and large as humming birds.* Too often those mosquitoes *literally stung into a fever.* Among the Volunteer Guards on the Savannah River, every man came down with yellow fever except their commander, Major William S. Basinger. In 1862 the account book of a cabinetmaker showed twelve *stained & trimmed coffins ($12 each)* for deceased members of the Thirty-second Georgia Regiment.

Measles were also epidemic and occasionally fatal. Private James H. Espey progressively wrote home that he had been *fiting the measles . . . got them conquerd,* but had not *fuly gained* his *former strength yet.* Later a friend wrote that Espey was *verry low with pneumonia fever.* He eventually died with a smile on his face as *he saw Jesus standing with his arms open and inviting him to come declaring that all was piece with him on earth.*

William Washington Gordon, II, in his Confederate uniform was only one of gray and blue alike who were devoured by insects during the long standoff. (Courtesy of the Juliette Gordon Low Girl Scout National Center.)

SAVANNAH LADIES
"YOU WOMEN ARE THE TOUGHEST SET I EVER KNEW"

In the city the ladies of Savannah tirelessly applied their hands to the war effort. Sewing circles abounded, among them the Ladies' Knitting Society, the Monterey Square Knitting Society, and the Rebel Sock Society. Additional groups employed their skills to make munitions. Recorded George Mercer: *Only this morning I was in our drill room assisting a number of ladies to make cartridges; among them were my sweet-heart, my sister and six cousins; there they were patiently cleaning the greased balls, filling the paper caps with powder, and tieing up the missles of death.* The ladies who met at the home of Mrs. Emma P. Hopkins turned out more than four thousand cartridges in five days.

As Alexander Lawrence described: "When it came to hatred, the Confederate female was probably more ardent than the male. She hated with a passion mere man can not always muster. Her letters abound with references to 'vile creatures' and 'vile wretches.' If that particular adjective had been a deadly missile, the struggle would have ended soon in Southern victory."

You women are the toughest set I ever knew, William T. Sherman is reputed to have said after he took Savannah. *The men would have given up long ago but for you. I believe you would have kept up this war for thirty years.* Another exchange with a woman revealed a razor's edge. When accosted on a Savannah street by *General, you may con-*

Confederate Major William S. Basinger, the only one in his command who did not contract yellow fever, often fatal. (Courtesy of Colonel Walter Wright, Savannah.)

Portrait of Nelly Gordon, northern-born wife of Confederate officer William Washington Gordon, II. (Courtesy of the Juliette Gordon Low Girl Scout National Center.)

quer, but you can't subjugate us, Sherman shot back: *I don't want to subjugate you; I mean to kill you, the whole of you, if you don't stop this rebellion.*

To the northern-born wife of Confederate William W. Gordon, a Savannah woman said, *I hear, Mrs. Gordon, that your brother is an officer in the Union Army, and all I have to say is, that I hope the first shot fired will kill him dead.* Mrs. Gordon's only reply was, *Thank you.* According to Gordon family tradition, Mrs. Gordon later was said to have remarked to this same woman: *I hear that your brother has been shot in the back; mine is doing very well, thank you.*

Beneath these incredible barbs of the tongue, however, was a resilience of the soul too often put to the ultimate test. According to Episcopal Bishop Stephen Elliott's description, the Savannah woman's daily language was: *He perished for his country. I would not have it otherwise, but I should like to have given the dying boy my blessing, the expiring husband my last kiss of affection, the bleeding lover the comfort of knowing that I knelt beside him.*

Certainly no better example of the southern woman's strength can be found than in the words of Mrs. Josephine C. Habersham—she of the between-the-lines diary. When being consoled on the death of her two sons, Joseph and Willie, who were killed on the same day, she replied: *God is wise and just and good—infinitely good. . . . Believe me, young friend, that the true secret of Life's happiness is to be able to say "Thy Will, not mine, be done!"*

SORROW AND LOSS
"WILLIE AND I ARE WELL"

So many Savannahians were far away, fighting or fallen. When Francis Bartow was killed at Bull Run, President Jefferson Davis' wife traveled to Savannah to break the news to his widow. Turning away wordlessly, Mrs. Bartow later revealed: *As soon as I saw Mrs. Davis's face . . . I knew it all. . . . I knew it before I wrapped the shawl about my head.* Among the Savannahians killed in that same first battle were the six Sunday school mates at Independent Presbyterian Church—Bryan Morel, Thomas Purse, George M. Butler, John L. Branch, Julius A. Ferrill, and William H. Crane.

Before one skirmish near Atlanta on July 21, 1864, Lieutenant Joseph C. Habersham scribbled to his mother: *Willie and I are well.* Both he and his brother, William N. Habersham, would be dead within an hour of each other. For their mother—*Thy will . . . be done.* In addition to the Habershams, General Hugh W. Mercer's brigade suffered 168 casualties around Atlanta in a single day.

Joseph McLeod Turner of the Georgia Hussars was killed in 1863 at Kelly's Ford, Virginia. Firing his pistol against a Union attack, he

Young Joseph C. Habersham *(left)* and William N. Habersham *(right),* brothers killed on the same day in the battle of Atlanta. (Courtesy of the Georgia Historical Society.)

was struck in the forehead as he fired his last shot. Midshipman Edward Maffitt Anderson was captured when the famed Confederate raider, *Alabama,* was sunk by the U.S.S. *Kearsage* off Cherbourg, France, in 1864. *My heart has sunk within me, for my fears tell me that my darling boy is lost,* wrote his father (mercifully not correct).

In other distant fields, G. Moxley Sorrel was a hero at the Wilderness in 1864. By the same year, artilleryman Robert Falligant was a hero at both Sharpsburg and Cold Harbor. Meanwhile Lieutenant Robert Saussy was doing his duty in the far-off Pennsylvania campaign. Twenty-three-year-old Edward S. Willis was lost as the brightest of Stonewall Jackson's staff at Mechanicsville—*shot down, mortally wounded—the gallant, fair-headed, white-skinned slight young colonel . . . valiantly leading the brigade,* wrote Sorrel. Both had grown up on Harris Street in Savannah. Sorrel would be twice wounded after he wrote this lament for his childhood friend. At the very sight of Sorrel toward the last of the war, the Twelfth Virginia took off their hats amid shouts of *Lead us, Sorrel! Lead us as you did in the Wilderness!*

SHERMAN COMES

"YOU MAY HEAR ME CURSED AND INSULTED"

The invincible Union army, however, continued to march. In his definitive book on this period in Savannah, *A Present for Mr. Lincoln,* Alexander Lawrence has the reader imagine: "Had it been possible to look down over Georgia from a great height in late November, 1864, the hypothetical observer would have seen what appeared as four gigantic blue caterpillars, crawling slowly on innumerable legs across the country in the direction of the sea."

Over 120,000 legs to be precise, two per each bluecoat of the army that had just crushed Atlanta. General John Bell Hood and the southern remnants fled north to Tennessee, soon to be crushed at Franklin. As they left Georgia they sang a popular song of unrequited love, *Lorena,* a tune so heartbreaking that it caused desertions even before the South's swan song.

At Savannah by the sea, around nine thousand gray coats waited under General William J. Hardee. The Union, under William Tecumseh Sherman, would get there in less than a month after burning Atlanta.

Prophetically, in terms of southern memory, Sherman had written his wife before leaving Atlanta: *Long before this war is over, much as you hear me praised now, you may hear me cursed and insulted.* It was Sherman, after all, who later pronounced, *War is hell.* (In context, what he actually said to a group of idealistic youth fifteen years after

General William T. Sherman, the name still most vilified in the South.

the war: *There is many a boy here today who looks on war as all glory, but, boys, it is all hell.*) Abhorrent at needless blood spilled in war, Sherman shrugged at the curious fact that a general who destroyed property was looked upon as a greater brute than one who fought terrible battles.

Slithering toward the sea, little groups of blue legs—*Sherman's Bummers*—would break off from those massive caterpillars and spread out to cut a path of destruction sixty miles wide through the heart of Georgia. They lived off the fat of the land they did not destroy. It was *one big picnick,* according to Colonel Charles Ewing. *Turkies chickens ducks and sweet potatoes at every meal,* wrote General Henry W. Slocum.

We are giving georgey one of the gratest rakings ever it got, recorded an Indiana soldier. *We cut off all the raleroads and burnt as we went.* The iron rails were heated and bent around trees. *Sherman's neckties,* as these twisted rails were called, became a sign of the Yankee soldiers' passage.

As those blue forms crept closer to Savannah, tentative brown tails began to grow, the result of thousands of slaves following behind in a desperate grasp at "freedom." Sherman would be called on the carpet for their partial amputation when he reached Savannah.

By December 11, a Wisconsin soldier wrote that the army was *now within sight of the spires of Savannah (i.e. we would see them if there were not so many trees in the way.)*

Amazingly, the fat-of-the-land marauders were getting hunger pangs, having now consumed the thousands of cows that they had driven along on their march to the sea. Nothing remained in tidewater country but rice for the men and rice straw for the horses. *How the Chinese and Japanese get along with it* was a puzzle to another Wisconsin soldier. Sherman needed to link up with his navy in order to refurbish his supplies. The navy was also carrying twenty tons of accumulated mail for the *Lost Army.* After Atlanta, Sherman and his men had disappeared, even from President Lincoln.

FORT MCALLISTER—"LIKE A LION AT BAY"

Sherman's way, however, was barred—*in plain view . . . sullen and silent, like a great lion at bay, stood Fort McAllister.* The earthwork fort on the Ogeechee River blocked Sherman from his navy. It had survived seven attacks in the preceding two years. (The fort, meticulously restored, is now a state park at Richmond Hill.) Inside the fort was Confederate commander George W. Anderson with 150

The storming of Fort McAllister. (Courtesy of the Thomas Gamble Collection, Chatham-Effingham-Liberty Regional Library.)

defenders, a number of them mere boys. At sunset on December 13, 1864, 1,500 Union veterans would charge over them. In fifteen minutes half of the Confederate defenders would be casualties, but they would dispatch over twice their number among the attackers. Both sides showed exceptional valor in what Sherman described as *the handsomest thing I have seen in this war*.

Even if the battle at Fort McAllister was not of the magnitude of Gettysburg, the swift violent scene bears remembering. From the diary of Union Major George Ward Nichols: *General Sherman walked nervously to and fro, turning quickly now and then from viewing the scene of conflict to observe the sun sinking slowly behind the treetops. No longer willing to bear the suspense, he said: "Signal General Hazen that he must carry the fort by assault—tonight, if possible."*

The little flag waved and fluttered in the evening air, and the answer came: "I am ready, and will assault at once."

The words had hardly passed when from out the encircling woods there came a long line of blue coats and bright bayonets, and the dear old flag was there, waving proudly in the breeze. Then the fort seemed alive with flame—quick, thick jets of fire shooting out from all its sides, while the white smoke . . . covered the place and then rolled away. . . .

The line of blue moved steadily on; too slowly, as it seemed to us, for we exclaimed, "Why don't they dash forward?" But their measured step was unfaltering.

Now the flag goes down, but the line does not halt. A moment longer and the banner gleams again in the front. We, the lookers-on, clutched one another's arms convulsively, and scarcely breathed in the eager intensity of our gaze.

Sherman stood watching with anxious air, awaiting the decisive moment. Then the enemy's fire redoubled in rapidity and violence. The darting streams of fire alone told the position of the fort. The line of blue entered the enshrouding folds of smoke. The flag was at last dimly seen, and then it went out of sight altogether.

"They have been repulsed!" said one of the group of officers who was watching the fight.

"No, by Heaven!" said another. "There is not a man in retreat—not a straggler in all the glorious line!"

The firing ceased. The wind lifted the smoke. Crowds of men were visible on the parapets, fiercely fighting—but our flag was planted there.

There were a few scattering musket shots, and then the sounds of battle ceased. Then the bombproofs and parapets were alive with crowding swarms of gallant men, who fired their pieces in the air as a feu de joie. Victory! The fort was won.

Then all of us who witnessed the strife . . . grasped each the other's hand, embraced, and were glad; and some of us found the water in our eyes.

I never saw General Sherman in as good spirits as that night, recorded Colonel William E. Strong, relating how Sherman joined in the chorus of many a familiar song. Sherman also joined captured Major Anderson for dinner. When Anderson went to offer Sherman a Havana cigar in salute, Sherman responded with a smile, *Thank you, but I have some very good ones here. Permit me,* handing Anderson one of his own cigars, just captured. The joking gallantry did not stop Sherman from using Anderson's captured troops to clear out the Confederate defensive mine fields around Fort McAllister— the fields that had been so deadly to Sherman's troops. Anderson howled in protest at this abuse of prisoners of war.

SAVANNAH EVACUATED—"PLAYED OUT! PLAYED OUT!"

Once Sherman was resupplied by his navy via the Ogeechee River, *Savannah is doomed,* prophesied a Union officer. The enemy, he said, *might as well "git up and dust."* In Savannah, General Hardee was thinking the same thing.

Hardee asked advice from his superior, General P. G. T. Beauregard, in Charleston. Beauregard visited Hardee twice, but their evaluations of the situation differed greatly. On site for three weeks, Hardee perceived that a Union army of seventy thousand was beginning to cut off every avenue of escape from Savannah.

Beauregard did not sense the same threat, as he retorted: *My God, Harry! what has come over you? You did not used to be so nervous! General Bragg telegraphs me from Augusta that Sherman has not more than twenty-one thousand men with him . . . and is making a hasty retreat for his gunboats, either across Sister's Ferry to Port Royal, or to Ossabaw.*

By the second visit Beauregard was more in tune with Hardee's concern, giving him personal discretion for the defense of Savannah. Since no reinforcements were available, Hardee began building a massive pontoon bridge over the river to South Carolina. More than a thousand slaves were driven to build a span linking Savannah with Hutchinson Island and onward to the Carolina side of the river.

None too soon. On December 17 Hardee received the surrender demand written in Sherman's own hand. Sherman warned that he possessed guns that *can cast heavy and destructive shot as far as the heart of your city* and that he now *controlled every avenue by which Savannah can be supplied.*

On December 20 troops and wagons loaded with Confederate baggage began to cross the pontoon bridges toward Hardeeville,

Sherman and his generals, with Savannah in the background completing his famous march to the sea that broke the back of the Confederacy. (Courtesy of V. and J. Duncan Antique Maps and Prints, Savannah.)

South Carolina. Huge fires lit up the river as the Confederate navy yard and war vessels were burned to avoid capture.

Honorable old Josiah Tattnall's *mosquito fleet* had largely been knocked out of action by this time—except for the C.S.S. *Savannah.* Her last engagement was to fire on Fort Jackson as the Stars and Stripes were raised there. This would be the only hostile fire the fort would receive in her history. Then, with all avenues of escape closed by Union gunboats, the *Savannah* itself was blown up on December 21. The explosion rattled windows as far away as Hilton Head. To Robert Watson, a member of the crew, the explosion lit the skies so brightly he *could see to pick up a pin* eight miles away. Union correspondent David Conyngham described: *First came a flash of light; then, as if from the crater of a volcano, an immense volume of flame shot up, illumining the heavens for miles; then came the fearful report, and the rebel ram "Savannah" was no more. The concussion was fearful, rocking the city.*

Amid the evacuation a Confederate band attempted a forlorn rendition of "Dixie." Union pickets called back across the lines: *Played out! Played out!*

SHERMAN ENTERS SAVANNAH

Savannah Ga. Dec 22, 1864
To his Excellency,
    President Lincoln.
Dear Sir,
I beg to present you as a Christmas Gift, the
City of Savannah with 150 heavy guns and plenty of
ammunition; and also about 25,000 bales of Cotton.
          W. T. Sherman
          Maj Genl.

This telegraph was received in Washington on Christmas eve. Lincoln responded: *Many, many thanks for your Christmas gift—the capture of Savannah. When you were about leaving Atlanta for the Atlantic Coast, I was anxious, if not fearful; but feeling that you were the better judge, and remembering that "nothing risked, nothing gained," I did not interfere. . . . But what next? I suppose it will be safe if I leave General Grant and yourself to decide.*

In the coming days Sherman would be lionized by Congress, his feat eclipsing the past glories of Grant, who was now bogged down against Lee before Richmond and Petersburg. Certain offers of adulation suggested high promotion for Sherman, perhaps equal, if not superior, to Grant.

Sherman demurred, *I will accept no commission that would tend to create a rivalry with Grant.* He then added his second most remembered quote: *He stood by me when I was crazy, and I stood by him when he was drunk. And now, by thunder, we stand by each other!*

Mayor Richard Arnold surrendered Savannah to Sherman's representative, General John W. Geary. When Geary proudly marched into Savannah as military governor, there were mixed feelings. Women peered out from behind window curtains in shock, but various responsible citizens greeted the Union army with relief, heartened that looting would be squelched—which it was.

Looting was a serious concern. Citizen William T. Hodgson guarded the Telfair mansion (now the Telfair Academy of Arts and Sciences) on Telfair Square. Retreating Confederates only made off with a horse and three mules belonging to the Telfairs. Some of the worst offenders were Joe Wheeler's parting cavalry, who had *stolen and destroyed more than the enemy . . . the meanest set of men that ever lived,* remembered one Savannahian. Another blamed the *white scum of the city which came out of their dens like nocturnal beasts to the work of pillage.* According to the *New York Herald,* mobs of *Irish and Dutch women, negroes and the thievish [Confederate] soldiers* were responsible for the night of chaos. In fact, city officials walked out the old Augusta Road to meet their conquerors; Wheeler's men had stolen their carriage horses.

Richard D. Arnold, physician, historian, and five-time mayor of Savannah, who surrendered the city to Sherman. It befell him to also preside over Savannah's meeting to voluntarily rejoin the Union. (Portrait on loan to the Georgia Medical Society from the Georgia Historical Society.)

The famous message in Sherman's own hand presenting Savannah as *a Christmas Gift* to President Lincoln. (Courtesy of V. and J. Duncan Antique Maps and Prints, Savannah.)

Sherman's headquarters at the Charles Green house on Madison Square, now little changed as the parish house of St. John's Episcopal Church. (Courtesy of the Chatham-Effingham-Liberty Regional Library.)

General Geary quickly sent patrols throughout the city to stop looting. Among other places, he put guards at the Masonic Lodge, saving valuable city mementos. At the City Exchange on Bay Street, Geary raised the Stars and Stripes and made *a fine speech* complimenting his troops. During the ceremony a Union sergeant walked into a store and exited with a fireman's hat as a souvenir. After Geary's speech, another Union officer walked over to the sergeant and ripped off his stripes.

Sherman entered Savannah the morning after the occupation. He was first billeted at the Pulaski Hotel on Bryan Street, where he had stayed years before as a young lieutenant. Soon he was offered alternate accommodations. Charles Green, a prosperous Englishman, proposed Sherman use his own expansive house on Madison Square as his headquarters. Sherman promptly accepted the courtly offer. Romantics accept Green's expressed motives that he would spare any native Savannahian the humiliation of giving up his home to Sherman. Cynics, however, believe that Green was protecting the considerable cotton stores for export to England.

Many British flags flew over Savannah buildings. Sherman soon surmised they "diplomatically" sheltered export cotton for England. Sherman seized it all in the name of Uncle Sam. Sherman had underestimated the *25,000 bales of Cotton* in his telegraph to Lincoln; it turned out to be over 38,000 bales.

Her British Majesty Victoria's Savannah consul got a rough lesson in bluffing when he violently protested the seizure to Sherman. As voices rose in retorts over who the cotton legally belonged to, Sherman topped the argument by threatening to go to England's Bahama Islands capital, Nassau—a haven for southern blockade run-

Sherman reviews his triumphant troops parading down Bay Street, with the columned 1852 custom-house in the background. (Drawing by A. R. Waud. Courtesy of the Library of Congress.)

ners. Sherman thundered: *I'll take with me a quantity of picks and shovels, and throw that cursed sand hill into the sea, sir. You may tell "that" to your government. . . . Good day, sir!*

OCCUPATION
"SONNY, I AM GENERAL SHERMAN, BUT THAT NEED NOT FRIGHTEN YOU"

On this, Sherman's second visit to Savannah, he commented that he was pleased to see again *the large yards, ornamented with shrubbery and flowers.* The streets and parks were lined with live oak, *the handsomest shade trees* he had ever ridden under. Sherman recorded: *It was estimated that there were about twenty thousand inhabitants in Savannah, all of whom had participated more or less in the war and had no special claims to our favor, but . . . I concluded to give them the option to remain or to join their friends in Charleston or Augusta, and so announced in general orders. . . . The great bulk of the inhabitants chose to remain in Savannah, generally behaved with propriety; and good social relations at once arose between them and the army. . . . The guard-mountings and parades, as well as the greater reviews, became the daily resort of the ladies, to hear the music of our excellent bands. Schools were opened, and the churches every Sunday were well filled with most devout and respectful congregations. Stores were reopened, and markets for provisions, meat, wood, etc., were established.*

The occupation was a model of order, even occasional pleasantry, with both sides generally behaving like ladies and gentlemen. Gentleman to gentleman, British subject Edmund Molyneux surprised the renowned "Christian General" O. O. Howard by presenting him a $11,000 bill for damages. Molyneux's home on Bull Street (presently

Young Juliette Gordon at the age she used to defy Sherman's conquest to the point of inducing his laughter. (Courtesy of the Juliette Gordon Low Girl Scout National Center.)

the Oglethorpe Club) had been taken over by Howard and his staff. Much of the library and all of the expensive wine and brandy were missing after they departed. A Union subordinate later confessed to "finding" the missing items at headquarters, much to Howard's embarrassment. In a letter allowed to pass between the lines, Confederate Edward Anderson assessed Sherman's actions to his wife: *I am rejoiced to hear that Genl Shermans policy toward our people is marked with humanity and kindness. After so brilliant a campaign as he has made he cannot afford to stain it with an unsoldierly course.*

Sherman loved children and particularly enjoyed playing with Savannah's young. At the Green mansion, Major George W. Nichols recorded: *His headquarters and private room became the playground of hosts of little ones, upon whom the door was never closed, no matter what business was pending.* Some were quite hesitant, like thirteen-year-old George Pritchard. When greeted in the garden by a lean redheaded officer who announced, *Sonny, I am General Sherman, but that need not frighten you,* Pritchard later confessed, *I flew home.* Another less hesitant five-year-old girl brought roars from Sherman with her Confederate sympathies when he frequently visited her family's home on Bull Street. On seeing the missing arm of General O. O. Howard, Juliette Gordon exclaimed: *I shouldn't wonder if my papa "did it." He has shot lots of Yankees!* Forty-seven years later, Juliette Gordon Low would found the Girl Scouts of America.

Tragically while in Savannah, Sherman received word that he had lost his own second child to illness. *All spoke of him as so bright and fair,* he wrote his wife, Ellen, *that I hoped he would be spared us to fill the great void in our hearts left by Willy. . . . Oh, that Willy were living. How his eyes would brighten and his bosom swell with honest pride.* To his brother, John, he wrote: *I have now lost Willy and the baby without seeing him . . . I should insist upon a little rest. As it is, I must go on.*

William B. Hodgson began to find Sherman's character that of *innate benevolence,* his mind *quickly perceptive,* and his manner *genial.* As the mayor and city council were kept in their normal capacity, Richard Arnold also began referring to the Union military governor as *The Noble Geary.* Yankee and rebel soon mingled freely at the Freemason's Lodge on Bull Street, in the centuries-old fraternal tradition of Masonry. Responding to a petition from fifty Savannahians, Arnold called a public meeting only four days after surrender. *Burying bygones in the grave of the past,* more than seven hundred citizens voted to submit to national authority under the Constitution. Savannah, if not Georgia, was officially at peace with the United States.

Augusta, by contrasting apoplexy, was livid. The city's paper

Savannah ladies swallow their pride to stand in food-ration lines provided by Sherman's occupying forces. (Courtesy of the Thomas Gamble Collection, Chatham-Effingham-Liberty Regional Library.)

called Savannahians *miserable Sycophants. If there is one sink lower than any other in the abyss of degradation the people of Savannah have reached it.*

In general, Savannah's women remained the most resentful, refusing to walk beneath the American flag. According to Mary Wragg Bond, one of the *many things that seemed hard for us to bear was the suspending of flags across the streets so as to compel us to walk beneath.* Nellie K. Gordon smiled at herself, remembering the first days of occupation. She had carried a small concealed pistol when walking down Bull Street, just in case of *sass.* The soldiers most politely stepped out of her way.

Consorting with the enemy—flirtation—was scorned, especially by the all-seeing eye of Fanny Cohen, a bright, talkative, young Jewish woman who lived on Lafayette Square. She vowed, *I shall never do it as long as I live*—befriend a Yankee, that is. Other Savannahians made the best of the situation. Mrs. Basinger and her daughter, Elizabeth, took in five Union boarders, who honorably paid their rent, but skipped town without paying their gas bill. In spite of constant overtures at conversation by the lonely soldiers, the Basingers maintained a hostile posture, remaining so stone silent at meals that the soldiers quit showing up at the dinner table altogether. As Elizabeth wrote: *I do not remember the names of the men, we were only too glad to forget all of them. If we had been sociable with them I have no doubt they would have provided much better; but our pride could not come down to that.*

Thus nature took its course. *I am on duty every other day,* wrote a Pennsylvania soldier, *but the reason of it is because there are so many hore houses in town which must have a sentinel at each door for to keep them straight.* Another soldier wrote: *There is the most hoars here that I saw in my life both black and white. I thought that Washington had enough but this beats that.* Presumably this was an exaggeration; Washington, D. C., had more than four hundred houses of prostitution during the war.

Union sightseeing was also the order of the day, after a little Union housekeeping was implemented. The complaints that *Fences are broken down, sidewalks and wharves are going to ruin and Sherman's dead horses are laying about the streets by the dozen* were rectified. In two months 568 carcasses of animals and 7,200 loads of manure were removed. The warehouses on Bay Street were whitewashed. According to the proud cleanup officer, Albert Stearns, in one month 6,200 trees also were whitewashed, each up to a height of seven feet. Apparently Captain Stearns got carried away. The whitewashing of tree trunks, however, was still considered a preventative against yellow fever.

Our whole army has fallen in love with this city . . . every mark of wealth, intelligence, refinement & aristocracy, wrote Major Connolly, an Indiana surgeon. *A vaery nice Place,* wrote a private, *the Buildings look Ancient and appear to be built after some other country stile than America.* However, a more laconic private sightseer from Ohio wrote: *See every thing that can be seen and return. Dont think much of the place.*

Popular with all ranks was the fountain in Forsyth Park, just as it had been with the occupying Confederate soldiers. A Union chaplain, however, found Nathanael Greene's monument in Johnson Square to be *a wretched execution . . . an unsightly pile of large, square stones.*

PULASKI LEGACY
"THREE CHEERS FOR SAVANNAH AND SHERMAN"

Opinions varied on Savannah's tributes to her past. An Illinois soldier wrote of being posted at *Don Pulaski's Monument* in Monterey Square. *The nicest thing I have seen yet. It is a wonder that the rebels have not disfigured it.* This international symbol to the Polish blood spilt in establishing the Union would have a practical emotional consequence for Savannah.

Drawn by Savannah's Polish ties, a Polish-American New Yorker, Julian Allen, arrived in Savannah shortly after Sherman. He quickly became a crusader for northern generosity. Returning to New York, he appealed for aid to relieve the hunger pangs of the city. *It would awaken pity in almost any one to see the pale emaciated faces of the women and children,* Allen declared. He enlisted the help of Edward Everett, the most renowned orator of his day.

It was Everett, former president of Harvard College, who had preceded Lincoln for two hours at Gettysburg before the president rose to give *a few remarks*. Amid some national criticism that Lincoln's Gettysburg Address was insultingly brief and inane, Everett wrote the president: *I should be glad to flatter myself that I came as near to the central idea of the occasion, in two hours as you did in two minutes.*

In what turned out to be the last speech of Everett's life—*one of the most touching which ever fell from his lips*—a Boston audience adjourned with *three cheers for Savannah and Sherman.* Several weeks later three ships from New York and Boston entered Savannah loaded with donated food supplies. This supplemented the rations furnished by Sherman to Savannah citizens, including captured stores left by retreating Confederates. Many women in Savannah, however, were too proud to accept this charity.

"JEFF DAVIS AND THE DEVIL NEED PRAYING FOR VERY MUCH"

Savannah's churches were particularly admired by the northerners. Union Chaplain George Pepper described Independent Presbyterian on Bull Street as easily the finest structure he had ever seen. Christ Church on Johnson Square was *a perfect gem.* The Reverend Pepper preached a sermon at St. John's Episcopal Church on Madison Square to General Sherman and his staff.

If local ministers happened not to include President Lincoln in their prayers, it was a definite cause for Union commotion. As the story goes, however, the coin was reversed when *a rebel Episcopal divine* asked Sherman for permission to include Confederate President Davis in his prayers. Sherman is said to have replied: *Pray for Jeff Davis, why certainly! You ought to pray for him every day, for Jeff. Davis and the devil need praying for very much.*

Including Lincoln and the Union in their prayers had never been a problem for Savannah's black churches. Nor had they neglected prayers for their liberator, Sherman. A freedman told the conquering general: *Been prayin' for you all long time, Sir, prayin' day and night for you, and now, bless God, you is come.* Charles Coffin of Boston described an assembly of several hundred blacks at Second African Baptist Church in Savannah. General Rufus Saxon was present to exclaim, *You are all free.* His announcement was met with a chorus of *Glory to God! Hallelujah! Amen! God bless General Sherman! Amen! that's so!*

St. John's Episcopal Church on Madison Square during the Civil War era. Its pulpit under Bishop Stephen Elliott decried secession. Union chaplains gave guest sermons there during Sherman's occupation. (Courtesy of the Thomas Gamble Collection, Chatham-Effingham-Liberty Regional Library.)

SHERMAN AND "INEVITABLE SAMBO"

Not all in the North, however, considered Sherman's motives or actions pure enough by liberal abolitionist standards. One of his officers, General Jefferson C. Davis (no relation to Confederate President Jefferson Davis), had already been involved in an ugly incident. He was accused of abandoning the thousands of blacks who had trailed Sherman's march. Now an old friend of Sherman's, General Henry Halleck warned Sherman of a visit by the stern secretary of war, Edwin M. Stanton. Halleck confided: *While almost everyone is praising your great march . . . there is a certain class having now great influence with the President . . . who are decidedly disposed to make a point against you—I mean in regard to "Inevitable Sambo." They say you have manifested an almost "criminal" dislike of the Negro, and that you are not willing to carry out the wishes of the Government in regard to him, but repulse him with contempt. They say you might have brought with you to Savannah more than 50,000, thus stripping Georgia of that number of laborers, and opening a road by which as many more could have escaped from their masters; but that, instead of this, you drove them from your ranks.*

Sherman responded privately: *If it be insisted that I shall so conduct my operations that the Negro alone is consulted . . . I shall be defeated, and then where will be Sambo? Don't military success imply the safety of Sambo, and vice versa? . . . The South deserves all she has got for her injustice to the Negro, but that is no reason why we should go to the other extreme. I do, and will do, the best I can for the Negroes, and feel sure that the problem is solving itself slowly and naturally. It needs nothing more than our fostering care.*

On January 11 Stanton stepped off a revenue cutter at Savannah. With the pinched, glowering appearance of Captain Ahab in *Moby Dick,* this Ohio abolitionist was the accusing personification of an Old Testament prophet, even to Lincoln. A meeting at the present Green-Meldrim House followed, attended by Sherman and his inquisitor, Stanton, who acted as his own recording secretary. The jury was composed of twenty black pastors, mostly Baptist and Methodist. The pastors chose the highly articulate Garrison Frazier as their spokesman. Frazier completely satisfied Stanton's general questions on enforcement of the Emancipation Proclamation passed one year before.

Up to this time I was present, said Sherman, *and on Mr. Stanton's intimating that he wanted to ask some questions affecting me, I withdrew.* Sherman paced the hall outside the closed door, grinding his teeth over being tried because *I had not loaded down my army by other hundreds of thousands of poor Negroes and was construed . . . as hostile to the black race.*

Inconveniently for Stanton, Frazier personally cleared Sherman: *His conduct and deportment toward us characterized him as a friend and a gentleman. We have confidence in General Sherman, and think that whatever concerns us could not be in better hands.* The group was less confident of the fair treatment of blacks by conquered southern citizens.

"We Can Punish South Carolina as She Deserves"

It was now time to leave Savannah and invade toppling South Carolina. By degrees, portions of the vast Union army crossed the Savannah River and headed north—in their mind's eye—toward the heart of sedition, Charleston. The fortunes of war would largely spare her, but not poor Columbia, which was flattened in Sherman's path. If the consuming fire there was accidental, the consuming emotion behind it is clear in Sherman's letter to Grant in Virginia: *With Savannah in our possession . . . we can punish South Carolina as she deserves, and as thousands of people in Georgia hope we will do. I do sincerely believe that the whole United States, North and South, would rejoice to have this army turned loose on South Carolina, to devastate that state in the manner we have done in Georgia, and it would have a direct and immediate bearing on your campaign in Virginia.*

"We Must Be Resigned to Necessity"

Grant would finally run Lee into the ground less than three months later. Lee would surrender at Appomattox Court House on April 9, 1865. The war was effectively over, except for the southern remnants under the command of Joseph E. Johnston. These forces would be surrendered to Sherman near Raleigh, North Carolina, on April 18. At their own initiative, Grant and Sherman gave humane terms in the spirit of Lincoln's *with malice toward none, with charity for all* inaugural address only months before. Sherman exceeded Grant in generosity, promising southerners return to protection under the U.S. Bill of Rights.

But what next?—to repeat Lincoln's telegraphed question to Sherman in Savannah four months before. What happened next was the most devastating event possible for the South. A single fatal shot exploded at Ford's Theatre in Washington on the evening of April 14. Breaking the news of President Lincoln's assassination to Johnston, Sherman noted the Confederate general's stricken reaction. *The perspiration came out in large drops on his forehead, and he did not attempt to conceal his distress. He denounced the act as a disgrace to the age, and hoped I did not charge it to the Confederate Government.*

Sherman's subordinate, General Jacob Cox, asked the unanswerable: *We puzzle our brains out in the vain effort to conjecture how the destiny of the country might have been modified if that horrible murder had not been committed.*

The South's greatest hope for mercy and sanity had been slain. The buffer of reason against Radical Republican plans for vengeance against the South had died with a bullet in the back of the head. Some Radical Republicans in Washington even celebrated Lincoln's assassination. The very act prompted moderate northerners to join the Radicals in their quest for retribution.

The new President Andrew Johnson and Secretary Stanton called a midnight cabinet meeting on April 21; they renounced Sherman's liberal conditions of surrender, in terms akin to treason. Grant intervened to save Sherman from being relieved of his command.

While Sherman's and Grant's armies made a last march toward Washington for one final glorious parade, a Confederate officer, J. P. Austin, described the parade of the South: *On the other hand, the shattered remnants of the Confederate army, with their bloodstained banners trailing in the dust; footsore, weary, and broken in spirits; without money and with scarcely sufficent clothing to shield them from the scorching rays of the summer sun . . . must scatter singly, or in groups, to make their way as best they could through a devastated country, to their distant and desolate homes. God, in his infinite wisdom, had decreed against them, and they were forced to bow in humble submission to this stern and immutable decree.*

By Lincoln's death, the stern and immutable course was set for Reconstruction. As Robert E. Lee wrote to a relative only days after the war: *We must be resigned to necessity, and submit ourselves in adversity to the will of a merciful God as cheerfully as in prosperity.*

RECONSTRUCTION

Savannah 1865: The moss still hangs from the oak trees; the squares are still green, but the landscape is beginning to look neglected. The old homes, former mansions of the rich, are becoming shabby. Vandalism and lack of repairs have taken their toll. Confederate money is worthless. Food is scarce. Carriages are rarely seen, and there are few horses. Jobless men wander the streets looking for work. Businesses are closed. The city is bankrupt. Genteel poverty is not so genteel. Complexions are sallow. Skinny legs, lusterless hair, and boils from malnutrition disfigure the children. Clothing is in tatters. Many women are in black. Smallpox is decimating the Negro population.

Four years of war have ravaged Savannah's beauty.

THE NEW SOUTH
"HOW CRUSHED AND SAD THE PEOPLE ARE"
"Reconstruction" is commonly considered by historians to be the

eleven years immediately following the surrender of the Confederate States at Appomattox in 1865, but in Savannah it began the moment Sherman's troops arrived four months before. Although city leaders kept their positions, they were now under the direction of the military governor, General John Geary. For Savannah, the war was over.

Charles Carleton Coffin, a correspondent for the *Boston Journal*, reported the new status quo of occupied Savannah: *Society in the South, and especially in Savannah, had undergone a great change. The extremes of social life were very wide apart before the war. They were no nearer the night before Sherman marched into the city. But the morning after, there was a convulsion, an upheaval, a shaking up and a settling down of all the discordant elements. The tread of that army of the West . . . was like a moral earthquake, overturning aristocratic pride, privilege, and power.*

On the night before Sherman entered the city, there were citizens who could enumerate their wealth by millions; at sunrise the next morning they were worth scarcely a dime. Their property had been in cotton, Negroes, houses, land, Confederate bonds and currency, railroad and bank stocks.

Government had seized their cotton, the Negroes had possession of their lands and had become freedmen, their houses were occupied by troops, Confederate bonds were wastepaper, their railroads were destroyed, and their banks were insolvent. They had not only lost wealth, but they had lost their cause.

Compared to the rest of the South, however, Savannah had a tolerable Reconstruction. Sherman had not burned the city, although a disastrous fire a month after surrender did destroy many buildings and increase hardships. The relationship between the citizens and their captors was generally tranquil. Once Savannah voted to submit to

Selling sweets to occupying Union troops was suddenly not beneath the dignity of some of Savannah's finest homes. (Courtesy of the Gamble Collection, Chatham-Effingham-Liberty Regional Library.)

national authority, the city could return to rebuilding the economy.

Times were still hard. Regardless of the civility between citizens and Union soldiers, Savannah was still a conquered domain. On her visit to Savannah in 1866, Frances Butler Leigh wrote: *I can hardly give a true idea of how crushed and sad the people are. You hear no bitterness towards the North; they are too sad to be bitter; their grief is overwhelming. . . . The women live in the past, and the men only in the daily present, trying, in a listless sort of way, to repair their ruined fortunes. . . . Politics are never mentioned.*

Another author adds human insight into this period. In *The Children of Pride* Robert Manson Myers has published an exhaustive collection of family letters of the Reverend Dr. Charles Colcock Jones. In a letter dated November 15, 1865, Charles C. Jones, Jr., recounts to his mother: *The more I see of Savannah, the more am I convinced that there is—for the present, at least—but little prospect for aught else than a living. If practicable, I must try and do more.* He concluded a few weeks later: *I find also in the depressed condition of affairs in Savannah that there is a chance there only for a bare subsistence.*

ECONOMIC PROGNOSIS
"RECUPERATIVE ENERGIES OF THE PEOPLE"

Like the rest of the South, the reestablishment of a sound economy was essential. At the end of the war there was only $2,000 in the city treasury—to offset almost $400,000 in debts. If Savannah was to regain economic stability, the port was of utmost importance. The first priority was to remove the defensive obstructions in the Savannah River—ship hulks left from both the Civil and Revolutionary wars, sunk to impede the use of the harbor by enemy vessels. Now the city would have to clean up the channel to allow peacetime shipping to resume.

Selling the cotton on hand was an expedient next step. Sherman concurred and in January 1865 permitted citizens who wanted to take the amnesty oath to do so. (The Proclamation of Amnesty of May 29, 1865, disfranchised many Confederates. The proclamation required loyalty oaths to the United States for reinstatement of voting rights, but prohibited many southerners—Confederate officers with the rank above major and those with over $20,000 in property—from being allowed to take the oath.) Sherman had confiscated over 38,000 bales of cotton, worth thirteen million dollars; but in other areas of Georgia—areas Sherman had not passed through—cotton had accumulated during the four years of war. A month after he enacted his field order resuming the cotton trade, bales began arriving in the city.

General Grant added his support. He ordered the commanding officers at Savannah and other cities *to give every facility for the marketing of cotton and other produce, to make no seizure of the private property or search for Confederate cotton.* He felt the entire nation would benefit from a swift return to the export market.

Back in business, the Savannah customhouse on Bay Street was reopened. But there were conditions attached to Sherman's edict. Savannahians were competitively hampered by only being allowed to ask 75 percent of the market price of cotton in New York; still, cotton was selling for over ten times its prewar price.

In 1860, 314,084 bales of cotton had been shipped out of Savannah. In 1865 over 250,000 bales were shipped, but these were the result of four years' accumulation due to the wartime blockade. By 1867 more than 500,000 bales were shipped, amazingly almost double prewar levels. By 1872 the Cotton Exchange would open on Bay Street. (The current Cotton Exchange Building was constructed in 1887, although cotton was then selling for as little as ten cents a pound.)

With these positive steps, prospects brightened. As Sidney Andrews, a northern journalist, wrote in December 1865: *Business in the city has been very brisk all the fall, and many a merchant has had all he could do who moaned last spring for the "good old days." . . . I have found no place in the South where early faith in the recuperative energies of the people has met with such large reward as here. Many men seem inclined to believe that the promise will not be kept, and are prophesying a dull season next year. Others are more hopeful and say that when the railroads connecting with Augusta, Macon, and Thomasville are repaired, the trade of the city will be fifty per cent greater than ever. This latter view seems to me to be the correct one.*

This was not to be. Compared to the hopefulness of 1865, 1866 was a year of stagnation. The railroads were not repaired as quickly as expected. There was little capital left in the South and fewer northerners than hoped invested in the southern states. Overriding all, political uncertainty continued to cloud the future.

Food was scarce. Few crops were being planted, and most of those did not come to harvest. Fortunately Savannah was on the coast and seafood was plentiful. Jobs were still difficult to find.

Southerners needed money, but Federal treasury agents—some diligent, some dishonest—had confiscated most movable property. Those southerners lucky enough to have salvaged their furniture and other personal possessions were in not much better shape than those who had lost all. They might have furniture to sit on, but if they needed to sell their possessions, neighbors were too poor to buy the goods. A Union officer, George Spencer Greer, wrote his impression of Savannah to his wife in June 1865: *The people down here are awfully poor, they have no money and what things they have they are obliged to sell in many cases for the necessities of life, so where there is so little money one with a very little can make more very fast.*

Land also could not be sold; there were no purchasers. Charles Jones, Jr., went north looking for work. He wrote to his mother from New York in early March 1867: *All reports we have from the South are gloomy. I have endeavored in vain to effect a sale of our real estate. Parties here do not wish to invest at the South when so many better lands, and at cheaper rates, are offered in the West.* In October the prospects were no better. *I have endeavored in vain to interest a single purchaser. Parties will not buy, and for very good reason. Who does wish to buy in a country in such an unhappy condition as that in which our beloved South now is, and in a climate far from healthy during the warm months of the summer? I must confess my heart is very heavy when I think of the present and the future of the South.*

Life was especially hard for southern women. The war had killed thousands of men, leaving their wives to carry on alone for the first time in their lives. But many had courage and made the best of a bad situation. A Scarlet O'Hara spirit was voiced by a Savannah lady, Jane Basinger, wife of Confederate officer William Starr Basinger: *Come, let us up and be doing! These Yankees all want something sweet and we want some greenbacks.* The basements of many fine residences became pastry shops. Some of Mrs. Basinger's trays of sweets were stolen by the drooling troops. Soldiers also told of an old Irish woman selling whiskey that was able to *kill in forty minutes at fifty yards.*

Charles C. Jones, Jr., recorded: *The disastrous influences of this recent war have wrought sad vicissitudes, and where peace and order and content once reigned there are little else than disquietude, turmoil, and desolation.*

His mother captured the feeling even more poignantly, recalling a rainy day in January 1867: *All is gloom without, and not much light within.*

Southerners may have been defeated by the overwhelming magnitude of the northern army, and Reconstruction might have been conceived to take vengeance on the vanquished, but southern convictions did not waver. Major William Starr Basinger, the former commander of the Savannah Volunteer Guards, continued to argue the point decades later: *I do not object to the Union, if it is made what it was intended to be. But if the Government at Washington is to go on as it has since the war . . . and if the Union is what both [political] parties pretend that it is, I am utterly opposed to it, and want to get rid of it—I regard it as an enemy to liberty. Georgia is my country and nothing but Georgia.*

Major William Starr Basinger, former commander of the Savannah Volunteer Guards, never regretted his allegiance to the Confederate cause, and was not particularly quiet about it for decades after. (Courtesy of Colonel Walter Wright, Savannah.)

"Conquered Province"

Immediately after the war, came the "reconstruction" period, and the reign of thieves and "carpet-baggers," William Basinger howled. There is little doubt that the revitalization of the southern states was hindered by the influx of northern adventurers. Although there were legitimate economic opportunities and humanitarian causes, many northerners came only to make quick profit. Since Radical politicians wanted the North to take vengeance on the South, they encouraged northern settlement in this "new land of opportunity."

Thaddeus Stevens, the most radical of the Radicals, propounded the "conquered-province" concept. This theory admitted that the South had once been part of the Union, but—having seceded—declared it was now a conquered territory without constitutional protection. The Radicals were determined to retain control over the South with carpetbaggers and their handmaidens—white southern Republicans, called scalawags.

Under Sherman's brief occupation, southerners were returned to the fold and once again had constitutional protection. With Stevens' conquered province doctrine, however, this protection was revoked. Most southerners lost their rights as American citizens.

The southern states were essentially placed under martial law. The governors of Georgia, Louisiana, Virginia, Mississippi, and Texas, along with local officials, were removed from office. *Loyal men*—carpetbaggers, Union army officers, or scalawags—supplanted the displaced southerners. Police forces were reorganized, and occupying troops patrolled the streets. The military dissolved the militia, suppressed newspapers, suspended laws, annulled court decrees, licensed public meetings, and forbade parades. Petty graft abounded locally, while massive graft engulfed state government.

Mail could not be received if one had not taken the amnesty oath. Even women over the age of eighteen had to take the loyalty oath in order to collect post. Mary Jones, widowed mother of Charles C. Jones, Jr., wrote in 1886: *Without an oath we cannot have a mail or a post office, a railroad conductor, express agent, or any civil officer. How long will this continue?* Many would not take the oath, setting up their own mail delivery. Letters were delivered by friends traveling from one town to another.

At the national level Radicals correctly surmised that if southern Negroes were given suffrage, they would vote the Republican ticket. Their opponent Democratic party would thus be further weakened. Since many former Confederates were not allowed to vote, the Negro vote would assure the preservation of the Radicals' power base. (The Fourteenth Amendment continued the disfranchisement of any Confederate who had once held federal office and taken a loyalty oath to the Constitution.)

Dedicated to registering the black voter, Union or Loyal leagues were organized in Georgia as early as the summer of 1866. By the fall election of 1867 there were over 85,000 members of the leagues in Georgia, two-thirds of them black. These groups registered voters by day, converting them to Republicans by night. Understandably, native southerners loathed the Radical Republicans and the carpetbaggers who represented them.

Conservative, aristocratic Savannah especially detested carpetbaggers. Even the idealistic young women who came from the North to teach in Negro schools were shunned. They found it difficult to secure board with white families, and often ended up living in the black community.

Despite the traditional ostracism of Yankees, not all southerners immediately spurned the arrival of the northerners. In 1865 Union officer George Greer wrote of Savannah to his wife: *At the place where I boarded the people were secessionists the same as all here, but they know the thing has played out and for that reason are ancious to treat every one from the North and especially an Officer, very kindly. In fact it is the nature of the Southern people to be hospitable. I like them and I know if you were down here you would like the people and make friends very fast. As for the climate I dont think you ever saw such evenings and sun sets as we have here. I dont wonder Southern people think there is no place like the South, I think so too.*

Other southerners welcomed the infusion of northern money and hoped that the Negroes would return to work on the plantations if they had northern bosses. But it did not happen.

"DELUDED"

Most freed slaves naively thought emancipation meant freedom from work. Mary Jones, a widow trying to manage a plantation on her own, lamented: *They [blacks] are perfectly deluded—will not contract or enter into any engagement for another year, and will not work now except as it pleases them. I know not from day to day if I will have one left about me or on the place. Several of them refuse positively to do any work.*

Yankee influence on the blacks did not help. With their assurances that in the coming year the government would give forty acres of confiscated land to each former slave, the Negroes were encouraged to await their award, and idled away their time until the government distributed their acreage.

Mary Jones concluded: *Such is the demoralized condition of the Negroes in Liberty that until half of them die of starvation they will not realize the necessity of earning their bread in the sweat of their brows.*

THE GLORIES, THE DIFFICULTIES OF FREEDOM

Freedom was no small thing, no matter how disruptive to white southerners. The emancipation of slaves was the result of four years of fighting, but there were many problems inherent in abrupt independence.

Although there have been many reminiscences written of the slavery era, unfortunately very few blacks recorded their reflections of the Reconstruction period. Their viewpoint is largely unheard. All we have is conjecture, and that conjecture recorded by the defeated, usually bitter, southern white. Yet a black culture did develop, mainly substantiated by results rather than the written word.

Most blacks left their rural homes and moved to the cities. According to Robert E. Perdue in his book, *The Negro in Savannah*, "The urbanization of the Negroes in the years since the Civil War has been second only to slavery in the impact it has had on their lives." Most slaves had never left the plantation where they were born, and the right to relocate was the most direct means of testing their new freedom. Although often worse off than had they remained, one old black woman expressed her reasons why she had left the old place: *What fur? Joy my freedom!*

Almost every town developed areas on the outskirts, where blacks lived together in rude huts or with no shelter at all. Little rental housing was available to blacks, except primitive outbuildings. Either they could not afford the rent or white owners refused to rent to blacks, fearing they would be unable to rent the same housing to white persons in the future. The limitations of housing in Savannah restricted normal family structure, since most "homes" housed non-family members.

In slavery there had been no legal marriages and the father had little authority over, or responsibility for, his children. Since their young children were often taken to be raised in plantation nurseries, mothers often had little knowledge of child care. With freedom, these practices ingrained by slavery would present problems. Although many blacks obtained marriage certificates from the Freedmen's Bureau, over one-quarter of the black families in 1870 and 1880 were headed by women. Despite encouragement by the Freedmen's Bureau and northern missionaries, it was difficult for the black male to adjust to the responsibilities of a stable family structure.

As black shanty areas grew in Savannah, disease became a major problem. Lack of sanitation soon spawned smallpox, which decimated the black community. Most blacks were hesitant to accept aid, and shunned the free physicians and medicine offered by the city, the Georgia Infirmary, and Lincoln Freedmen's Hospital.

Another difficulty was the care of dependent blacks—the old, the young, the helpless. The Freedmen's Bureau helped some, while others remained in their old homes and were taken care of by their former masters. Still more were left to the mercies of their peers.

The naiveté of the newly free also made them vulnerable to almost every con man that came their way. Flimflammers flourished as former slaves bought useless skin bleaches, hair straightener, or stakes for marking off their land—the forty acres the con artists assured them would be forthcoming.

Until 1865 most states had laws forbidding the teaching of reading and writing to slaves. Particularly in Savannah, some were taught in spite of the prohibition; but at the beginning of Reconstruction, more than ninety percent of blacks were still illiterate.

Actually, in the first years after the war, Negro children had more educational opportunities than poor white children, on account of the Freedmen's Bureau and northern philanthropic groups. In Savannah seventy-five percent of the 1,600 black children were soon in school, compared to less than one-third of the 2,000 white children. But northern teachers who had thought co-racial education a possibility soon found it would not work. White children refused to attend the Freedmen's schools. Most northern teachers left in frustration.

In 1866 Savannah set up a board of education and the Roman Catholic schools were incorporated into the public school system. Chartered in 1788 as a private institution, Chatham Academy became part of the public system in 1869. Public education, however, concentrated on the care of white children since the Freedmen's Bureau and other philanthropic organizations provided for the education of the blacks.

Prudent black leaders also established schools. The Savannah Educational Association opened two schools in January 1865, followed

Susie King Taylor served as a Union nurse. After the war she ran a school for black children in her South Broad Street home. (Courtesy of the New York Public Library.)

Undated photograph of black school children in Savannah with their teacher. (Courtesy of Willis Hakim Jones, Savannah.)

by Beach Institute in 1867 and the Georgia State Industrial College in 1891. Recently Beach Institute has been converted into a black studies center.

Although there were thirteen black schools in 1865, by 1870 only five were still functioning. Northern support had declined, and the majority of blacks were still illiterate. There was a shortage of classrooms and funds. The black community pressed the Chatham County Board of Education to establish black schools. Yet in 1869 the public school system continued to be for whites only because northern missionaries refused to give up their control of black education. Not until 1878 was the board's charter amended to include Negro education, but the basic root of the inadequate educational system of the South lay in the extreme poverty of the postwar era.

The Freedmen's Bureau had been set up in an attempt to help settle the newly uprooted blacks. Eventually its powers were extended to *control all matters relating to Negroes and refugees for one year after the war ended.* At first the bureau was conceived only as a means to redistribute confiscated Confederate lands to the blacks; but little land, in fact, became available, and it was generally worthless.

What the bureau actually replaced was the old plantation system as a means of caring for blacks. The bureau worked with philanthropic organizations; encouraged education; leased school buildings when teachers were furnished by other groups; encouraged blacks to work the land and make contracts. The bureau made valiant efforts, but the task was overwhelming.

There were also inherent problems with the setup. Many of the agents of the Freedmen's Bureau were incompetent or corrupt. Agents were paid on a fee basis, encouraging some to use their control over

Print entitled *The Freedmen's Bureau at Dr. Fuller's Plantation* shows a representative in animated explanation of new possibilities for former slaves. (Courtesy of the University of Georgia Library.)

the black labor market as a means of extortion. Bribes often greased their palms. Graft was widespread. According to historians William B. Hesseltine and David L. Smiley in their book, *The South in American History*, perhaps the greatest tragedy of the Freedmen's Bureau was teaching the freed slave to expect too much from the government.

Whereas the labor situation frustrated white southerners, they were not unsympathetic to the cataclysmic adjustment of blacks. Charles Jones expressed his hope for the former slave: *Time alone can impart the necessary intelligence; and the fear of the law, as well as kindness and instruction, must unite in compelling an appreciation and discharge of the novel duties and responsibilities resting upon him.*

BLACKS
"SEPARATE BUT EQUAL"

Surprisingly, the immediate social consequence of emancipation was not dramatic. Although Negroes at first were accused of "putting on airs," a general feeling of goodwill between whites and blacks remained. In the early years militant black leaders like Aaron Bradley failed to find fertile ground for a black power base. Negroes were free, but they were not assimilated into the white population, apparently by mutual consent. Garison Frazier, the black minister who spoke up for Sherman, advocated separate communities. Blacks developed their own areas, their own society. Black churches increased, as men like James Porter and James Simms joined Frazier in separatist leadership.

Life was not easy for the newly freed man. Blacks were now responsible for their support, their food, their housing. As Mrs. Mary Jones observed: *They often groan being burdened with freedom.*

Even within the black community a caste system developed. Mulattoes, those with white blood or light skin, were as racist as the white community toward the newly freed black slave. According to one black, the mulatto clique *considered black Negroes entitled to nothing but the vote.* Mulattoes often expressed contempt for blacks' bad morals and worse manners. E. Franklin Frazier, in his book, *Black Bourgeoisie*, reports one female mulatto's opinion of an ill-mannered Negro: *Well, if I have got to live with these niggers, I might as well accept this kind of behavior, and try to act like them.*

Mulattoes, with their aristocratic airs, obviously considered themselves above dark-skinned blacks. However, according to Robert E. Perdue's *The Negro in Savannah*, commonly education, not color, was the deciding factor of social acceptance. Those at the top were generally literate and relatively well-off.

Socially blacks established a life similar to that of the white southerner. Duels were even fought on Hutchinson Island and near the strand on Bay Street.

Undated photograph of members of the First African Baptist Church. (Courtesy of the First African Baptist Church Museum.)

Picnics, baseball games, and steamboat excursions were popular. Blacks celebrated Liberian Independence Day, Emancipation Day, Lincoln's Birthday, and the anniversaries of the Fourteenth and Fifteenth amendments. Saloons, gambling houses, and the city market on Saturday nights were frequented.

Bands such as the Skidmore Club and String Band and the Brahms String Band provided music for dances of the Ladies and Gents Social Club, the Union Coterie, the Social Club of Savannah, and the Committee of Nine. The oldest American musical group of blacks, Old Hundred, had been organized in 1817 and was still active in Savannah at the end of the war.

According to Perdue, four Masonic lodges and three Odd Fellows lodges were organized, holding frequent meetings and suppers. Even eight black militia units regularly drilled on the Forsyth Park Parade Ground and held shooting and riding contests.

The Young Man's Bible Literary Association and the Young Beginners Literary and Social Society were popular. The latter often held debates, deliberating such subjects as: (1) Who did the most in support of Protestant religion, Martin Luther or Queen Elizabeth? and (2) Which is the most helpful to the world of man, a box of matches or a spring of water?

Such organizations provided an escape from daily living, plus vital companionship. Men adrift in the city found moral support from the brotherhood that the clubs provided. Membership also granted a sense of dignity and status, fulfilling a desire for positions of leadership.

Several black newspapers were started. The *Freedmen's Standard*, earlier called the *Southern Radical and Freedmen's Journal*, was the first black newspaper in Savannah. It was edited by the Reverend James

Turn-of-the-century studio portrait of a black woman identified as Mitilda Beasley. (Courtesy of the Georgia Historical Society.)

Simms, who later became a legislator. *The Savannah Tribune,* the *Savannah Weekly Echo,* and the *Daily News and Herald* soon followed—all published by black journalists. John H. Deveaux, as editor of the *Savannah Tribune,* tried to teach blacks their duties as citizens and Christians, often publishing a sermon on the front page. But he also defended blacks from discrimination and kept them informed of social activities in the black community.

"I SHALL CEASE MY ANXIETIES FOR THE RACE"

Race relations, however, suffered as animosity against the despotism of the carpetbaggers grew. According to Savannahian William Harden in his book *Recollections of a Long and Satisfactory Life*, eventually southern whites began reorganizing antebellum militia groups in retaliation. Now illegal as such in the South, they were called "clubs"—the Oglethorpe Light Infantry *Club*, the Savannah Volunteer Guard *Club*—but were prepared to march with arms if a prearranged alarm signal was tolled on the Exchange Bell.

The tentative friendly relations between whites and Negroes began to deteriorate. The Negroes had expected the federal government to take care of them; and when it did not, stealing from whites soon became an accepted means of support. Encouraged by abolitionists, Negroes became impudent—a natural, if regrettable, assertion of their new equality. A Savannah woman in 1865 lamented: *It is almost impossible to walk the streets without meeting some negro with a segar stuck in his mouth, puffing its smoke in the faces of persons passing, whether they be ladies or gentlemen.*

As explained by historians Hesseltine and Smiley: "In a land where good manners had been an essential attribute of cultural achievement, bad manners were sins of great magnitude. Clashes between Negroes and the lower element of the whites became common. Among the better classes, the tendency to withdraw from their former kindly patronage of the Negro was marked . . . the prejudices of the poor whites became the dominant philosophy of the South. Perhaps this was the worst calamity of a 'tragic era.'"

At last even Mary Jones was fed up. She wrote her son after the desertion of yet another one of her laborers: *I shall cease my anxieties for the race. My life long (I mean since I had a home) I have been laboring and caring for them, and since the war have labored with all my*

Undated photograph of a black fraternal organization on West Broad Street. (Courtesy of Willis Hakim Jones, Savannah.)

might to supply their wants, and expended everything I had upon their
support, directly or indirectly; and this is their return.

"RAW HEAD AND BLOODY BONES"

Conditions were not as bearable in the rest of the state, or the rest of
the South, as in Savannah. In the summer of 1868 the seven southern
states that had ratified their new constitutions were restored to the
Union, their representatives legally returned to Congress. Only Virginia, Mississippi, and Texas were holdouts. The North still controlled
the South, but now by Radical governors instead of military generals.

Georgia had managed a less obnoxious new constitution than most,
as southern conservatives began their return to the state legislature.
Soon they were sufficient in numbers to rule that although the constitution gave Negroes the right to vote, it did not give them the right
to hold office. Georgia was remanded to military rule. Representation
in Washington was not restored until the middle of 1870.

State government under Radical Governor Rufus Bullock was run
with appalling corruption. Both taxes and state debt increased. New
money secured by railroad bonds went the way of bribery, with few
railroads started—much less completed. Personal graft was outrageous. One manager of a state-owned railroad glibly explained how
he amassed $30,000 on a salary of $3,000—*by the exercise of the most
rigid economy.*

The Radicals were determined to retain their lucrative control. Fab-
ricated accounts of southern atrocities were sent to Washington to jus-
tify the continued presence of the Radical government. Georgians,
irritated by the national image the Radicals portrayed of their state,
protested. An editorial satirizing those lies appeared in the *Atlanta
Constitution* on April 23, 1870, skewering Governor Bullock and the
boys in Washington:

> *Wanted—Ku Klux Outrages.*
> *Wanted, a liberal supply of Ku Klux outrages in Georgia.*
> *They must be as ferocious and blood-thirsty as possible. No*
> *regard need be paid to the truth. . . . Raw head and bloody*
> *bones, in every style can be served up to profit.*
> *The highest price paid. Apply to R. B. Bullock . . . or to the*
> *Reconstruction Committee, Washington, D.C.*

KU KLUX KLAN
"THE WHITE MAN'S REVOLT"

Since most southern white males were excluded from the polls and
from holding office due to disfranchisement, the corrupt administration of carpetbaggers and their generally trusting black supporters
could not be changed through legal means. Most black legislators

View of Savannah's riverfront in 1872, reflecting revived cotton exports after the war. (Courtesy of V. and J. Duncan Antique Maps and Prints, Savannah.)

were illiterate and unsophisticated. Because of their ignorance, blacks were manipulated by carpetbaggers into raising taxes, increasing state debt, often unaware of the unmanageable bribery taking place. In desperation, white southerners turned to extralegal means to rectify the situation—the Ku Klux Klan.

The Ku Klux Klan started in Tennessee, and fiery Confederate General Nathan Bedford Forrest was appointed as grand wizard in 1867. It was not the only such organization. Many lesser-known groups—such as the Knights of the White Camelia, the White League, and the Pale Faces—were also started by the disfranchised and overtaxed.

Social disorder increased in the years after 1867. In the first years whites were mostly concerned with getting the Negro to return to his former labor. In 1867 concern focused more on keeping the Negro aware of his inferior social status, regardless of the legal declaration of equality.

There was a rise in crime. In Savannah most of the lawlessness was due to the large number of Negro refugees who crowded the city. Commonly these men worked on the wharves, with much idle time. Citizens lamented: *The freedmen—nearly all of them—went to Savannah for their money; and though they need bread, almost all of them . . . bought either a musket, double-barreled gun, or revolver!*

Before the war most of the Negroes in Savannah had been domestic servants or free blacks. House servants were generally more learned than field hands and were accustomed to more freedom. The arrival of the rougher, rural plantation slaves tended to be an intimidating experience for urban Savannahians. Fear developed that the blacks would organize for open rebellion.

In the spring of 1868 friction intensified and Aaron Bradley, the militant Negro leader, was able to rouse Savannah's blacks. He urged them to hold meetings and stirred resentment with inflammatory speeches.

Later Bradley was accused of having served a sentence for felony in New York State and was expelled from the Georgia legislature.

At first the Klan relied on fear and the gullibility of the Negroes to control them, but once the blacks saw through the ruse, the Klan resorted to violence. There were lynchings and shootings in many parts of the state, but none recorded in Savannah. Other sources disagree and report that hangings and shootings of Negroes in Savannah were so commonplace as to be hardly spoken of.

Before the April elections of 1868, the Ku Klux Klan in the city posted warnings in an attempt to terrify the blacks. The blacks countered; the Loyal League retaliated with its own threats by way of a handbill:

Take
Notice
K. K. K.
And all BADMEN of the
City of Savannah, who now
THREATEN
the LIVES of all the LEADERS
and NOMINEES of the Republican Party, and the
President and Members of the Union League
of America. If you Strike a Blow, the
Man or Men will be followed, and the
house in which he or they takes shelter,
will be burned to the ground.
TAKE HEED! MARK WELL!!
Members of the Union.
Rally! Rally!! Rally!!!
For God, Life and Liberty!!!

Fortunately, as time passed racial tensions gradually lessened. By 1869 General Forrest had ordered the Klan's dissolution. The formal Klan organization was gone, but the pillaging and hazing continued. Poor whites refused to abandon their only avenue to establish superiority. Racial strife continued well into the next century.

Rebuilding Savannah's Economy
"Cotton Is Recrowned"

Back in the business world, Savannah continued its effort to expand the city's economy, primarily concentrating on the export of cotton. But times had changed; the plantation system had collapsed. Without slave labor, field hands were difficult to find; without field hands, cotton was impossible to produce. Learning to use the free Negro was a problem. Although some Negroes returned to the cotton fields, when they did, owners found management difficult.

Charles Jones believed: *The use of this free labor [the freedmen] is an absolute experiment; and while I hope that . . . we may be able to control it to at least a limited extent, I very much fear that for some time to come there will result but little profit from its employment. Poverty and severe legislation can alone render it available.* His mother was less optimistic. In her opinion: *If there was hope of improvement in the future, I could endure any temporary trials; but I am convinced the condition of things will grow worse and worse.*

White immigrant labor from the North was tried, but failed. According to the *Savannah News* (November 8, 1866), the importation of coolie labor for growing cotton and rice was considered, and actually tried, along the coast. The lack of a sufficient labor force made many planters consider leaving the area. Brazil even offered free passage in an effort to encourage immigration of disgruntled farmers.

Eventually conditions settled down. Faced with the necessity of steady work or starvation, many blacks reconciled themselves to work in the fields. Other planters solved the labor problem by parcelling out their land to tenant farmers in return for a share of the crop. This custom grew, and sharecropping soon became a common practice in the South. The fields were no longer fallow, and Savannah began her return to economic health.

Banking was in transition. Most of the banks in prewar Savannah had invested in Confederate bonds, and all banks but the banking division of the Central Railroad and Banking Company closed at the end of the war. Even that soon shut down. The South had lost its banking capital.

Yet, since postwar Savannah was soon making money again from cotton, banks were needed to handle the finances. New financial institutions responded to the improving fiscal climate. New banks with new capital, mainly supplied by the North, provided one of the few infusions of anticipated northern capital into the South. Merchants National Bank was chartered in 1866. Savannah Bank and Trust began in 1869, and was followed a year later by Southern Bank (later called Citizens & Southern Bank of Georgia, and now NationsBank).

One Confederate business did eventually make a comeback from the collapse of the prewar economy—the Central Railroad and Banking Company. Charles Jones astutely cautioned his mother not to sell her stock if she could possibly help it. In May 1866 he wrote: *I would be loath also, Mother, to part with that stock, the annual income from which you will need, and which is the very best security in Georgia.* He continued his cautions throughout the following months. *The Central Railroad and Banking Company of Georgia will, we are informed, declare a*

Post–Civil War photo of the 1858 Forsyth fountain, circa 1880's. As for Confederate and Union soldiers, it was and remains a social gathering spot for locals and visitors alike. (Courtesy of the Juliette Gordon Low Girl Scout National Center.)

dividend by the 15th prox. Do not part with that stock: it is the best investment we have. Hopefully she listened.

SOCIAL SAVANNAH DURING RECONSTRUCTION

Social life among the whites did not totally stagnate during these years. As economic conditions improved, society reappeared. Entertaining became popular again. The St. Andrew's Society, the Hibernian Society, Masonic lodges, the various Volunteer Guards, the Georgia Hussars, as well as other groups reinstituted their functions. New organizations were formed.

The Harmonie Club, Georgia's first Jewish social club, was founded in Savannah in 1865. Unlike its New York namesake, the Savannah club was more interested in sponsoring winter balls and other social events than in reading rooms. Soon they had purchased a downtown clubhouse on the corner of Bull and Jones. Although most popular as a recreational center for the Reformed Jewish community, the club included both Reformed and Orthodox congregations. By 1939 the group was popular enough to purchase additional property on Tybee Island.

The German Club, believed to be the third oldest dancing club in the United States, was first organized in 1817. Soon after the war, the club was once again meeting regularly. Today the Cotillion Club, as it is now known, remains a Savannah tradition where proud parents present their gowned debutante daughters to society.

Interest in golf returned. The Savannah Golf Club was organized sometime before 1796. An announcement in the September issue of the *Georgia Gazette* of that year stated: *Saturday, the first of October, being the anniversary of the Savannah Golf Club, the members are requested to attend at the Merchants and Planters coffee house for the purpose of electing officers for the ensuing 12 months.* The club is probably not the oldest in the nation, but certainly one of the first. Golfing activity revived shortly after the war, and Confederate bunkers were actually incorporated into the course.

The Savannah Yacht Club was also organized. Originally known as the Regatta Association of the State of Georgia, the yacht club was founded in Savannah on June 14, 1869. After several moves, it is now situated on the Wilmington River, the traditional hangout of Savannah's boating crowd.

In 1870 the Oglethorpe Club was established as a men's club by a group of Savannah's leading citizens. Now located in the Molyneux house on the corner of Bull and Gaston streets, it is still fashionable today.

Over two decades after the Oglethorpe Club's founding, a rival group with a sense of humor emerged. Calling itself the Tomochichi Club, the group mocked the gentile exclusiveness of the older club. It soon evolved back to the Savannah Volunteer Guards Club, reflecting the core of its membership.

The outstanding Savannah social occasion of this period, however, was the last visit of a southern icon.

LEE'S LAST HURRAH

"THAT SPOT OF SPOTS! THAT PLACE OF PLACES!! THAT CITY OF CITIES!!!" On the first of April 1870 a sixty-three-year-old man and his daughter stepped off the train into a pleasant Savannah evening. Thunderous cheers erupted from a waiting crowd so large that it spilled out onto West Broad Street. Dignitaries had difficulty clearing the way for the carriage of this private citizen on a personal vacation. Slowly the white-haired, bearded man, his face aged beyond his years, rose and made a wordless bow. The crowd parted. Robert Edward Lee, former soldier and president of tiny Washington College in Virginia, rode off into the evening.

The carriage proceeded to the corner of York and Lincoln streets, home of Lee's host, General Alexander R. Lawton. In his recollections over fifty years later, the proudest citizen in all Savannah was Lawton's eleven-year-old son, Alexander, Jr., seated erectly next to the carriage driver. Struggling through the cheering throng that surrounded Lawton's home, Lee and his daughter, Agnes, made their way inside, anxious for some peace and quiet. They would not get it. Outside, two brass bands played "Dixie," "The Bonnie Blue Flag," "Hail to the Chief," and other wartime songs into the night.

Unknown to the bands, Lee eventually was spirited out a back entrance. In search of a decent night's sleep, he departed for the

Young Robert Edward Lee, painted as a lieutenant of engineers in 1838 by William E. West. Lee's first assignment after West Point was to build Fort Pulaski. (Courtesy of Washington and Lee University.)

Eliza MacKay of Savannah, young "Bob" Lee's love interest before his Virginia marriage to the great-grand-daughter of Martha Washington. (Courtesy of the Juliette Gordon Low Girl Scout National Center.)

Andrew Low home on Lafayette Square. Before leaving, however, Lee paused to greet young Lawton's boyhood friends, a few who had secretly slipped in a side entrance. According to Lawton's most cherished memory, Lee took each of his awed young chums by the hand and talked to them *in his usual democratic way.*

Five years had passed since Appomattox, and Lee was prematurely aged by his failing heart. From Savannah he wrote his wife, Mary: *I perceive no change in the stricture in my chest. If I attempt to walk beyond a very slow gait, the pain is always there.* But he added in two stunning understatements: *The old soldiers have greeted me very cordially* and *I do not think traveling in this way procures me much quiet and repose.* Agnes' report to her mother was more comforting: *Papa has borne the journey and the crowds far better than I thought he would and seems stronger.*

Fans had deluged Lee for the entire journey. Along their train route Agnes had beheld lines of veterans and their wives with *the sweetest little children—dressed to their eyes.* Those too young to introduce themselves had *tiny cards in their fat little hands—with their names—often Robert E. Lee.* When they neared Savannah, a delegation of Lee's former officers stopped the train, entered his car, and escorted him into the city.

Lee certainly had a spiritual reason to feel stronger in Savannah. Here he could nostalgically reflect back forty years to his first engineering assignment after West Point—the construction of Fort Pulaski, sixteen miles east of the city. The site of the fort was a miserable marshy place on Cockspur Island, but Jack MacKay's home on Congress Street had been a pleasant oasis. Nearly forty years before his marriage to Mary Custis, the great-granddaughter of Martha Washington, Lieutenant Lee had been smitten by MacKay's daughter, Eliza. As one indication, before Lee departed Cockspur Island to return to Virginia for his prestigious marriage, he wrote Eliza: *It did grieve me to see the Boats coming down one after another, without any of those little comforts which are now so necessary to me. Oh me! . . . But you will send some sometimes, Will you not Sweet—? How I will besiege the P. Office.*

Over the years Lee kept up with all the MacKays, including Eliza. His youthful amour had developed into a long and lasting friendship. Eliza and her ensuing children visited Lee and his wife several times at Arlington, and Lee's career had often brought him back to the MacKay's home. Savannahian Hugh Mercer, Lee's West Point classmate, reported a festive dinner there after the Mexican War. *Bob Lee . . . I do not find him at all changed—he runs on just as he used to—He made me laugh very heartily and laughed himself until the tears ran down his face.* One must read much about one called *the*

Old comrades Robert E. Lee and Joseph Johnston. One of the last photos of Lee before his death, taken at Ryan's Studio in Savannah. (Courtesy of Paul Blatner and the Savannah History Museum.)

marble man before again encountering Bob *running on,* or Bob with face streaked by tears of merriment. Judging by Lee's own youthful words and Byronic punctuation, Savannah was unique. As Lee wrote to Jack MacKay: *That spot of spots! That place of places!! That city of cities!!!*

By 1870 Lee's visit was a time of peaceful veneration, although only a few years before, he had narrowly escaped a national trial for high treason. The Radicals in Washington had screamed for it, but the prosecution was ultimately thwarted by the personal intervention of the one who had finally worn Lee down—Ulysses S. Grant. Now in the Andrew Low house, Lee received the respectful visits of Savannah's Union and Confederate veterans alike.

Lee himself made a personal visit to 105 E. Oglethorpe Avenue, despite his regular complaint of *pain in my chest, along the heart bone, is ever present when I walk or make any exertion.* The address was the home of a prospering insurance executive, Joseph E. Johnston. Johnston had commanded the Confederate army before being twice wounded as he recklessly led his troops near Richmond in 1862. It happened under the eyes of President Jefferson Davis and his chief advisor, Lee. Previously snickered at as *Granny* because of excessive caution, Lee was given Johnston's post. If anyone ever called him anything but *General Lee* after that, it was his own soldiers, who whispered—or shouted in the face of death—*Marse Robert.* Marse—the Master!

It is not recorded what these two old comrades discussed. The meeting may have been awkward; already southern image makers were sculpting Lee from merely extraordinary to the olympian marble man—at the expense of his valiant fellow officers, including Johnston. Whatever the chat was about would have been drowned out by those persistent brass bands that followed Lee to Johnston's home. Lee again beat a masterly retreat to the rear of the house, leaving Johnston on the porch to receive an ovation of *three rousing cheers and a tiger* for both of them.

Although Lee and Johnston shunned further glorification, they were somehow cajoled to show up at a local photography studio. The photograph of two bearded old men sitting erectly across a table is wonderfully described by author Charles B. Flood as "two old grey lions, their faces looking as if they were enjoying tales of long-ago cadet days."

Lee would be dead five months later. In rising to give the dinner blessing at his home in Virginia, he awkwardly sat down with a silent look of resignation that his family had never before seen. He lapsed into a coma. His last delirious words were remembered by his wife as *he wandered to those dreadful battlefields.* Toward the last he cried out: *Tell Hill he must come up!*

It is unlikely that the city officials or any among the throngs of citizens were ever privy to the private side of Bob Lee, who had *run on just as he used to* about his *city of cities!!!* But upon news of his death, Savannah was the first city in the nation to declare his birthday a public holiday on January 19, 1871. In equally short order Washington College was renamed Washington and Lee.

Reconstruction Ends With a Whimper

At the same time Reconstruction in Georgia was nearing its tiresome end. In 1871 Democrats won the majority in the legislature; Rufus Bullock—Georgia's corrupt Radical governor—was impeached. By

1872 the state elected a Democratic governor, James M. Smith; there was not even Republican opposition in the special election.

A major reason conservatives were able to displace the Radical regime was the growing discontent of the Negroes with their so-called advocates; most powerful or well-paying positions were taken by carpetbaggers and scalawags. Blacks were no longer the naive men and women who had left the plantations. At the same time the Negroes were beginning to rebel, even many of the white scalawags—themselves susceptible to graft—were becoming repulsed by the even more monumental corruption of the northern Radicals.

Reconstruction's demise, however, would not have been imminent without equal outrage in the North over such corruption. Even Horace Greeley, the news mogul who once championed northern *colonies in the South,* had by 1871 concluded that the carpetbaggers must go. Further scandals rocked the North under the notorious Grant administration. The country was primed to renounce all Radical rule.

The presidential election of 1876 was the contested climax. Samuel J. Tilden, the Democratic candidate, overwhelmingly received more popular votes than Rutherford B. Hayes, the Republican candidate. Effectively Reconstruction ended on February 28, 1877, when some of Hayes's northern friends met with southern leaders for an electoral swap-off. If southerners, including stern John B. Gordon of Georgia, would "help out" Hayes's closed-door election, the new president would promise to withdraw the remaining troops from the South. Never mind the lurid details of easily the most corrupt presidential election in American history. They did. He did.

POST-RECONSTRUCTION

From the end of Reconstruction to the middle of the twentieth century, Savannah was a paradox of development. The period saw significant change, but Savannah made progress more through luck than effort. It was still an ultraconservative town, relying on cotton. In 1872 the Cotton Exchange was built on Bay Street, when export revenue was $40 million; by the 1880's the area was known as *the Wall Street of the South.* The introduction of naval stores (turpentine and rosin) created new exports in 1870, rivaling cotton's revenue by 1883. The new exports were by-products of lumber, another long-term staple since revolutionary times. But Savannah did not search out new sources of revenue. King Cotton was a mixed blessing, beguiling the city into complacency.

Savannah was still the largest city in Georgia at the end of Reconstruction, but Atlanta was the Georgia city on the move—becoming the new capitol in 1868. This did not ruffle Savannahians, as Thomas

Even in 1935, the bustle of the Cotton Exchange reflects that cotton was still hanging on as a mainstay of Savannah's sagging economy. (Courtesy of the Georgia Historical Society.)

Gamble reflected on the local mentality of the 1880's: *To tell the truth, Atlanta was still regarded as a sort of parvenu, whose pretentions Savannah smiled at indulgently or repudiated scornfully. . . . Caustic critics at that time referred to Savannah's sister city of the Piedmont section as a boastful town whose homes were plastered with mortgages and whose women wore unbleached underwear.*

Savannah was too insular, too complacent, too content to rest on her colonial laurels. Blissfully perched on a cotton bale, she only halfheartedly sought out new opportunities. Even in 1912, A. C. Laut's comment in the *Saturday Evening Post* captured Savannah's conservative posture: *She is a city that has never had a boom and has never had a bank failure!*

THE RAVAGES OF NATURE

Savannah endured a litany of natural disasters in the last half of the nineteenth century. A bad fire in 1876 destroyed much of the waterfront. Yellow fever also returned the same year, claiming over a thousand lives. In 1883 another fire destroyed the Yamacraw ghetto area, leaving eight dead and 1,200 homeless. In 1886 Savannah experienced a lesser version of the major earthquake that hit Charleston. Terrified families slept in the open squares for weeks. In 1889 three major fires occurred, the largest destroying the exquisite Independent Presbyterian Church (rebuilt according to the original 1819 plan). In 1893 and 1896 large hurricanes hit, damaging a

Today the 1888 Cotton Exchange no longer crackles with the sharp bidding of factors, but the building remains as a reminder of cotton's influence on Savannah's history.

thousand buildings, wrecking thirty ships, and killing dozens. The hurricanes were followed by two destructive cyclones in 1898. Savannah was constantly rebuilding and repairing; perhaps she did not have the energy to explore new fields.

From such pain, however, progress was made. The yellow fever epidemic hastened drainage of lowlands, under a system devised by Dr. James J. Waring. A sanitary department was established in 1876, with a sewer system, garbage disposal, and series of artisan wells.

Aftermath of the 1889 fire, with the Telfair Academy spared by a shifting wind. The vertical ruins to the right are the remains of the Odd Fellows Hall, built on the site where Washington had stayed in 1791. (Courtesy of the Georgia Historical Society.)

In the winter of 1879 General Ulysses S. Grant visited the city and was well received; he was actually invited. Georgia's 150th birthday followed in 1883, and preparations in the original colonial city spurred more progress; two hundred electric street lights dotted the city for the first time, replacing gas lighting from the 1850's. The former vice-president of the Confederacy, Governor Alexander Stephens, attended. It was an unfortunate decision. He became ill while in Savannah and died soon after his return to Atlanta. In the same year President Chester A. Arthur visited his relative Henry Botts in his still elegant home on Monterey Square. Several blocks up Bull Street the towering monument to William Washington Gordon was unveiled. Built to honor the former president of the Central of Georgia Railroad, the memorial was probably placed right over Tomochichi's 1739 grave site in Wright Square. The 1880's continued monumentally. In 1888 the exquisite statue of dying revolutionary hero William Jasper was unveiled in Madision Square; President Grover Cleveland arrived in town on the same day, staying less than two hours for the occasion before hopping a train for Florida.

TOWARD THE TURN OF THE CENTURY

The city was growing—if grudgingly. In 1870 the fourth "new" city market was built in Ellis Square. On New Year's Day of 1890 the elegant De Soto Hotel opened. (A reception there in 1897 introduced the long-distance phone, as guests excitedly shouted at the receiver to relatives in far-off Brunswick and Jacksonville.) The residential area expanded south of Gaston Street, the city's traditional edge; the Victorian District, with its "gingerbread" architecture, delightfully added another period style to Savannah's persona. Other

The Telfair Academy of Arts and Sciences, Mary Telfair's visionary intent from 1875, continues to be an important center of the Savannah cultural scene. (Courtesy of Hank Ramsey, Savannah.)

homes, destroyed by fire and storms, were replaced with equal Victorian grandeur. In 1875 the Telfair Academy of Arts and Sciences was established through the will of Mary Telfair. Her combined generosity also resulted in the present building of the Georgia Historical Society on Whitaker Street. Named for her brother-in-law, William B. Hodgson, it overlooks Forsyth Park, Hodgson's inspiration for the city in 1851.

Electric streetcars appeared in 1890, on streets beginning to be paved to cover the ankle-deep sand. Yet, by 1893 still only twenty percent of the streets had been surfaced. When the streetcar fare was reduced from five cents to one cent, citizens responded with nearly fifty thousand rides a day, approximating Savannah's population. The fare soon swelled back to three cents. As a way to reach the sea breezes and to escape the summer heat, a railroad to Tybee Beach was started in 1886, followed by the Tybee Hotel in 1887. The railroad's developer, Daniel G. Purse, was thought to have lost his mind. But as he wrote three years later: *It was freely predicted . . . the attempt . . . would meet its Waterloo in the sinking out of sight of the first locomotive.* Instead, he beamed to the stockholders, *Tybee can be reached in forty minutes is now the admiration.* The 1893 hurricane wiped out the line, but it was rebuilt. Band concerts in Forsyth Park, plays at William Jay's old theater on Chippewa Square, as well as yacht and horse races were civilized Victorian diversions. The Savannah Brewing Company opened in 1889, and thousands showed up for an introductory free sample.

After the river channel was dredged in 1898 to nearly twice its

In 1898 Savannah was a major port of embarkation for the Spanish-American War. This statue in Forsyth Park salutes the men who served their country in that now forgotten conflict.

Born in 1855, Richard Robert Wright, Sr., was influenced by the Freedmen's Bureau as a youth, becoming Savannah State College's founding president in 1891. He served for thirty years. In his sixties he took up banking—quite successfully. (Courtesy of Clyde W. Hall.)

previous depth, Savannah became the major port of embarkation for the Spanish-American War. One legacy of those heady days is the little-noticed elegant statue of a typical soldier in the south end of Forsyth Park. The city council sent Mayor Peter W. Meldrim to Washington to negotiate for a U.S. military camp in the area, spending $6,500 in the quest. President McKinley and his cabinet later visited, followed by the hero of Manila Bay, Admiral George Dewey. General Fitzhugh Lee, Robert E. Lee's nephew, gave a splendid review with sixteen thousand troops of his Seventh Army Corp before leaving for Cuba. This wartime attention to military facilities started a trend that would grow to be a major contribution to Savannah's future economy.

The year 1899 also marked the end of another ancient economy; the export house of Harris and Habersham was closed. Beginning over 150 years before, at the same Bay Street locale, its life span and rice exports mirrored each other.

Based on two timeworn connections, cotton and its port, Savannah was thriving at the close of the century. Typical for the entire 1890's, cotton exports were around a million bales, with total port revenues over $100 million. From 1,200 to 1,400 vessels a year cleared the customhouse on Bay Street. Since the earliest days of the colony, the port was important because of Savannah's location on the Atlantic coast. It is here that the coast curves inland, or westward, to position the harbor closer to the cotton fields than any other port. Even today, with the cost of overland transport a major consideration, Savannah's western-most port on the Atlantic seaboard makes her the most cost-effective port for inland-bound products.

Cotton, however, would not remain the port's faithful staple. Within two decades a small grey-beaked beetle—the boll weevil— began to decimate cotton production. Described by hapless cotton farmers as *a cross between a termite and a tank,* this beasty had the same decimating effect on the city's sleepy prosperity. In the early 1920's the boll weevil destroyed half of Georgia's cotton, already declining because of exhausted soil.

Interest in social reform emerged at the turn of the century. There was some improvement in education, prison reform, and child labor laws. Racially, *separate but equal* was entrenched, but as Edward Chan Sieg observed in his book on Savannah, *Eden on the Marsh,* "this seemed progressive indeed." In 1878 the first public school for Negroes was established by the board of education, itself formed in 1866. Jay's magnificent Scarbrough House was turned into a school. In 1891 the Georgia Industrial College for blacks was founded. Today, renamed Savannah State, it is part of the University of Georgia system.

Habersham and Harris on Bay Street, an icon of trade since 1749, when the firm shipped the first cotton to England. It closed in 1899. (Courtesy of the Georgia Historical Society.)

Blacks were making some progress, but their jobs were mostly limited to menial or manual labor. Black slums grew. The Negro Civic Improvement League soon formed to try to clean up the slums. In an effort to escape their wretched situation, a few blacks formed their own businesses. One such example was the Wage Earner's Bank, which was started with $102. By 1915 the bank complex occupied an entire downtown block. Although racial tension was evident in the rest of the state, as shown by the Atlanta race riot in 1906, it was not as intense in Savannah.

THE TWENTIETH CENTURY

In the first decade of the new century, an anomaly occurred in Savannah. Three grand prix auto races took place between 1908 and 1911, drawing worldwide attention and 100,000 spectators. In pursuit of the Vanderbilt Cup, the Holy Grail of racing, fourteen teams from Italy, France, and Germany roared into Savannah. Six teams from the United States rounded out the competition, as they all sprinted four hundred miles around a twenty-five-mile-long course sixteen times. At the average speed of sixty-five miles per hour, the international daredevils zoomed—and on occasion, crashed—around the south of town and the Isle of Hope, starting and finishing on the great straightaway of Victory Drive. As lovingly detailed by Savannahian Dr. Julian Quattlebaum, Sr., in *The Great Savannah Races,* Italian Fiats, French Renaults, and German Benzs (costing up to $25,000) usually beat early American car makes, including a Buick. The young

The Vanderbilt Cup races between 1908 and 1911, at the start-finish line on present Victory Drive. (Courtesy of the Thomas Gamble Collection, Chatham-Effingham-Liberty Regional Library.)

engineer Louis Chevrolet made his last race in Savannah and retired to spend more time on the engineering of cars. The overflow crowds were such that the president of Michelin Tire Company was put up in the county jail—not to complain. The hospitality was so warm that he and his assistants *were tempted to commit a misdemeanor so they might remain in this wonderful city a few days longer.*

A truly public library was established in 1903. In 1901 Savannah, in her insular way, had refused a Carnegie grant to build a library, but eventually accepted Carnegie's help. For a period the library shared Hodgson Hall on Whitaker Street with the Georgia Historical Society. In his reports of 1904 and 1906 George A. Mercer, the president of the combined institutions, had mixed feelings about Savannah's reading habits. On one hand, he reported there were nearly thirty thousand visitors a year, a thirty percent increase in attendance. On the other hand, the growing allure was not historical tomes, but fiction and romantic novels. In 1904 Mercer was philosophical: *One of the prime purposes of a public library is the cultivation of a taste for and habit of reading, which, certainly at first begins with sweets, and only later develops into desire for less alluring and more nourishing aliment.* By 1906, however, he gloomily stated: *I expressed the former opinion . . . that any reading not actually bad was better than no reading at all. I am now inclined to question the correctness of this opinion. The very large percentage of fiction that is called for is discouraging, and the character of most of this fiction is to the thoughtful—depressing.*

A new City Hall was constructed in 1906, along with the other large buildings near it that still define the city's skyline. Industry was promoted, but not assertively. Cotton was momentarily still Old

Today Hodgson Hall remains the Savannah headquarters of the Georgia Historical Society.

Charming shot of Oglethorpe Avenue in 1909, recording the visit of President Taft, in front carriage in top hat. (Courtesy of the Juliette Gordon Low Girl Scout National Center.)

Reliable, although some important new businesses like Dixie Crystals Sugar had started in Savannah.

According to Savannah historian William Harden, the year before World War I the city bustled with seventy thousand citizens, optimistic about the future. Her manner was still essentially English and definitely nineteenth century.

World War I dramatically changed that tranquil complexion. Nationally inflation increased, but the price of cotton rose from seven cents per pound five fold to ride the tide; exports in 1913 were nearly two million bales. The city once again prospered as a major war port, although much black labor was lured to the industrial North in search of higher wages and better jobs. At one dramatic point seven trains of the Pennsylvania Railroad left Savannah packed with black laborers. Henry Ford, a Savannah visitor during the glamorous auto races, would be one of the industrialists to swallow them up to his new factories.

THE DEPRESSION—1930's

The Depression, when it hit after the 1929 stock market crash, effected Savannah like everywhere else. Real estate values declined; property extensively changed hands; business stagnated. The poorer population moved into the downtown area. The once magnificent townhouses were cut up into apartments, renting for as little as eight dollars a month. Charity food lines appeared for the first time since Sherman's occupation.

Amid such gloom Georgia celebrated her two hundredth anniversary in 1933. President Franklin Roosevelt attended, entertained by

The Armstrong mansion (1920) was the last large home built in the downtown historic district. In 1935 it became the home of Armstrong Junior College and remained a college until 1962. It is now occupied by a law firm.

Mayor Thomas Gamble, Savannah's most prolific amateur historian. With one loving eye always on his city's past, Gamble had urged the restoration of the old City Exchange (built in 1799) on Bay Street, instead of replacing it with present City Hall in 1906.

Roosevelt's New Deal was at first resisted out of haughty pride; but grudgingly, then gratefully, Savannah welcomed the vital new jobs created by programs like the W.P.A., C.C.C., and the Army Corp of Engineers. Seeds sown from such hands-on labor would result in Fort Pulaski being restored as a National Park. In 1935 another source of "Yankee" aid descended on Savannah—the Union Bag and Paper Company. The now bygone rice plantations were sold and parcelled into industrial complexes, such as this mammoth industry located on the site of the Hermitage Plantation. Union Bag provided nearly six hundred jobs and a whopping Depression-era payroll of one million dollars. Now renamed Union Camp, Savannah's largest industry has around 3,500 employees, with an estimated community impact of $400 million.

Also in 1935, Mayor Gamble proudly opened his dream, the first institute of higher learning for whites, Armstrong Junior College. It was located in the Armstrong House on the corner of Bull and Gaston streets, the last massive downtown mansion built in 1920.

WORLD WAR II

Along with Union Bag, World War II helped end the Depression in Savannah. As in World War I, the military buildup saved the economy. Fort Stewart was established not far away, with Hunter Field just outside the city. From there enormous bombers of the famed

Eighth Air Force were ferried off to reduce Hitler's forces in Europe. Shipbuilding was reestablished, employing fifteen thousand in making Liberty troop ships. German submarines hovered near the mouth of the Savannah River, while yet more venerable downtown homes were partitioned to make room for the rural labor arriving to grab at an unheard-of fifty dollars a week. Absentee landlords made a fortune.

As in past generations, Savannah's women helped entertain thousands of out-of-town soldiers at the U.S.O. headquarters in the old Savannah Volunteer Guard Armory on Bull Street. Grease-stained overalls and welding goggles were badges of honor to local *Rosy the Riveters* working tirelessly in the shipyards. With an independent spirit going back at least as far as Caty Greene, Savannah's ladies had begun taking on overdue social causes at the turn of the century. In 1920 the feisty League of Women Voters was organized. By then women were flaunting their personal preferences: shorter skirts, *form-fitting bathing suits*, and—horror of horrors—an interest in jazz and the new outrageously sexy dances like the Charleston and the Black Bottom. In this pantheon, one woman named Daisy is a story of triumph in itself.

Juliette Gordon Low
A Child Called Daisy

Savannah, home of traditional "Southern ladies," was ironically the birthplace of a woman who would become a prototype of modern feminists. She became a maverick in an era when few women ventured from the role of wife and mother. As she wrote from boarding school: *Mama, I can't keep all the rules, I'm too much like you. . . . I'll keep clear of big scrapes but little ones I can't avoid.* She would travel to remote areas of the globe and mingle with some of the most influential people of her day. In the end she overcame personal misfortunes to make a worldwide contribution to society.

Appropriately born on Halloween in 1860, Juliette Gordon Low's prosperous parents were Eleanor Kinzie Gordon, known as Nellie, and William W. Gordon, II. As a child, "Daisy," as Juliette was called, was considered neither intelligent nor a great beauty; her mother described her *as ugly as ten bears*. She would prove both judgments wrong. Her mother wrote in later life: *It makes me laugh now when I recall the estimate of her which was so completely reversed when she grew up and turned out to be such a genius.* Contrary to all expectations, Daisy would propel Savannah's name to prominence in the next century.

Perhaps Daisy's ageless capacity for fearless originality should not have been surprising. Her Chicago-born mother was well known for

Daisy Gordon is seated at right center amid her gala 1886 wedding party, with her English husband, William Low, standing behind her, all in the unchanged garden of the present National Girl Scout Center on Bull Street. (Courtesy of the Juliette Gordon Low Girl Scout National Center.)

her own wit and spirited escapades. Daisy was only four when she remarked to Union General O. O. Howard on the loss of his arm: *Well, I shouldn't wonder if my papa did it. He has shot lots of Yankees.* General William Tecumseh Sherman would roar with delight over his smallest unreconstructed rebel. Her friends always expected the unexpected from Daisy—her pet name in the family was "Crazy." Her brother Arthur wrote: *Given a certain set of circumstances, people will usually act in a certain way. Daisy's response was often that of a weird dream.* She marched through life to her own drum, obviously reveling in her eccentric reputation.

Despite the early deprivations of the Civil War period, Daisy was raised with rare advantages by her wealthy parents. Schooled in the North, she traveled throughout the United States and Europe, living life to the hilt with influential relatives and family friends. But she was not immune to tragedy. Daisy became almost totally deaf. At the age of twenty-five an earache, improperly treated at her insistence, resulted in partial deafness. Later, at her own wedding, a grain of rice lodged in her good ear, virtually destroying her hearing. It never deterred her, although this ironic misfortune might have served as an omen for her marriage.

In 1866 the Savannah belle married William Low—"Billow" as she called him—the only son of a wealthy British cotton factor, Andrew Low, who had married a Georgian. Juliette and Billow moved into the family home on Lafayette Square. Soon, however, they were spending most of their time in England.

Although their happiness was short lived, Daisy relished the life of the British aristocracy, making many upper-crust friends. Once asked by her niece how she became known as a social wit and mistress of repartee, Daisy replied: *I got tired of straining to hear conversations that weren't particularly interesting anyway. I decided it was simpler to take things into my own hands.*

Dividing her time between Savannah, England, and Scotland, Daisy enjoyed a life of relaxed affluence. Never content to idle, she explored many pursuits, once even carving a wooden mantlepiece for her English home, Wellsbourne House. She also took a class in blacksmithing, forging a set of gates, now in the garden of the Juliette Gordon Low Birthplace. The gates are not the work of an amateur, but of a talented artisan. Daisy also became an avid traveler, never deterred by discomfort or primitive conditions. But such long absences did not make Billow's heart grow fonder.

In 1901 her marriage exploded when the husband she adored deserted her for another woman, leaving Juliette devastated. Legal battles raged as she sought either reconciliation or financial support from her estranged husband. Yet throughout her trials she retained her irrepressible sense of humor. Ill herself, she nonetheless tried to mitigate her parents' anger at William, writing: *You had better be careful, Mama, how you pray for Willy's death. It looks as though God has gotten your orders twisted, and if you keep on, you may end by bringing about mine!* By 1904 Daisy reluctantly agreed to a divorce, but her husband died before the matter could be settled—leaving most of their estate to his mistress. Several trying years passed before Daisy was finally able to obtain a settlement under English law.

Feeling a failure and ravaged by the long legal disputes, Daisy spent the next several years flitting about the world. She became

Juliette Gordon Low, pinning the Golden Eaglet on a distinguished Girl Scout seven years after she founded the organization in 1912. (Courtesy of the Juliette Gordon Low Girl Scout National Center.)

depressed, writing: *I am just an idle woman of the world, with no real work or duties.*

That, however, was to change. The tragic collapse of her marriage with its depressing aftermath was the turning point of her life. Searching for some *worthwhile work* at the age of fifty-one, in 1911 she found it when she met the Englishman General Robert Baden-Powell.

Of her many lifelong acquaintances, it was Baden-Powell, founder of the Boy Scouts, who would have the most lasting influence on her life. They had much in common; he, too, was an individual with unorthodox ideas. Daisy became engrossed in Baden-Powell's Boy Scouts—soon progressing to an interest in the Girl Guides, the Boy Scouts feminine counterparts, begun by Baden-Powell's sister, Agnes. Daisy began organizing troops of Girl Guides in England and Scotland. Always a tomboy, she had fun working with girls in her new commitment.

Eventually Daisy decided to introduce Girl Guides to the United States. Arriving in Savannah, Daisy phoned a friend: *Come right over. I've got something for the girls of Savannah and all America and all the world and we're going to start it tonight!* The first Girl Guide troop, called a patrol, was founded in Savannah on March 12, 1912. Her niece, Daisy Gordon Lawrence, was the first member.

Daisy would spend the rest of her life establishing the Girl Scouts in America. After her resignation as president in 1920, she devoted her time to the international aspects of the movement. She was tireless, once crossing the Atlantic seven times in eleven months. Her sister Alice wrote: *I think Daisy's never seeing difficulties, and being absolutely uninfluenced by arguments, were an advantage to her, as it worked out.*

For Daisy, however, the work became her life and her fun. During the early recruitment days, her mother complained: *Daisy has the back drawing-room full of little girls, and is making Morrison [a servant] serve them a fussier tea than I would prepare for the President!*

She corralled her many influential friends to help her and used her deafness to ignore protests—*I knew you would be glad to help!* She supported the movement with her own money (overcoming an inborn frugality) as its momentum grew. By the time of her death in 1927, Girl Scouts in America had grown to 167,925 members.

What makes Juliette Gordon Low so special is that she was a woman with more human frailties and misfortunes than most, who persevered to make a difference. Daisy was not a saint, being often rash, at times parsimonious, frequently naive and foolhardy. She never could spell well, and her math was atrocious. But all was forgiven because Daisy Low could laugh at herself. She often told stories to her own disadvantage, learning from her mistakes and setbacks. One of her favorite poems she found carved over a fireplace in England:

> *Life is mostly froth and bubbles,*
> *Two things stand like stone.*
> *Kindness in another's troubles,*
> *Courage in your own.*

And she never ceased to enjoy life. As an old lady—ill, in pain, but hiding her suffering from her family and friends—the whimsical Crazy-Daisy did not hesitate to stand on her head at a national Girl Scout board meeting to better display the new sensible uniform shoes she wanted everyone to wear. Her family also reports that she unfailingly stood on her head each birthday to show the children how *young* she was.

In 1927 Juliette Gordon Low died of cancer at the age of sixty-seven, but her legacy lives on—today there are over three million American Girl Scouts. The organization has helped shape the characters of over fifty million members since it began in 1912, making it the largest girl-fostering group in the world. Her girlhood home, the Juliette Gordon Low Birthplace, at the corner of Bull and Oglethorpe streets, is now owned by the Girl Scouts of the U.S.A. Each year fifteen thousand Girl Scouts attend educational programs there, and another fifty thousand visitors from around the world tour the home.

Other Savannahians would also go forth to add prominence to their birthplace. Conrad Aiken, born in Savannah in 1889, became a Pulitzer Prize–winning author and returned sixty years later to live next door to his childhood home on Oglethorpe Avenue. As a child there, he was awakened one night by violent words and two gunshots. In his thinly disguised autobiographical masterpiece, *Ushant*, he described a boy entering his parents' bedroom who, *finding them dead, found himself possessed of them forever.* An intimate of T. S. Eliot and Sigmund Freud, he wrote four prize-winning novels and numerous short stories and poems, often expressed in universal and primordial image: *In a way I never stopped writing about Savannah.*

Flannery O'Connor, well-known southern author of startling imagination, was born in Savannah, although she spent her life after childhood in Milledgeville. Growing up on Lafayette Square during the Depression, she attended the nearby Catholic schools. As another Savannah writer, Chan Sieg, observed: "The dark sensitivities that characterize her mature work were nurtured in the shadow of the Catholic cathedral." Once irked at being categorized as a *Southern* writer, she retorted: *I have found that anything that comes*

Songwriter Johnny Mercer, back home in Savannah in front of the Alida Harper Fowlkes home on Orleans Square. (Courtesy of the Savannah History Museum.)

Charles Coburn with Marilyn Monroe and Jane Russell in *Gentlemen Prefer Blondes*, 1953. (Courtesy of the Savannah History Museum.)

out of the South is going to be called grotesque by the Northern reader, unless it is grotesque, in which case it is going to be called realistic.

Johnny Mercer, one of the most popular lyricists in the twentieth century, grew up in Savannah, his family name deeply imbedded since well before the Civil War. A winner of four Grammy popular song awards and also of an Oscar, the very names of his songs denote a nostalgic southerner who never lost his local *Geechee* accent. After he asked delighted listeners to *Pardon My Southern Accent,* he beguiled them *In the Cool Cool Cool of the Evening* in a slow region where many *La-zzz-y Bones* reside. He came back home to live on his beloved *Moon River.* His melancholy *Days of Wine and Roses* springs from the fiber of anyone with an ounce of southern blood. But friends and family in his later years most recall his greatest creation—spaghetti sauce that he lovingly labored over for hours.

Charles Coburn, the character actor familiar for corpulent upper-crust roles, called Savannah home. He learned his craft in the last years of William Jay's old theater on Chippewa Square. And the list of the prominent goes on, including "Captain Outrageous," Ted Turner, swashbuckling sailor who successfully defended the America's Cup by maneuvers honed in his boyhood on local inland waterways. Now he is merely content with ruling the world from Atlanta by his cable satellite television, with the reticent name of TNT, and with being the proud owner of the Atlanta Braves baseball team.

In 1991 the appointment of Savannahian Clarence Thomas to the U.S. Supreme Court was confirmed, making him America's second black Supreme Court justice, and the second justice from Savannah since the appointment of James M. Wayne over a century before. Brought up locally in the back-of-the-bus days in tiny Pinpoint near Savannah, his mother picked crabs while her studious son attended the rigorous Catholic school system. *Anytime you wanted to find him, you would have to go to the library,* recalled his mother. During his television appearance with President Bush, he movingly thanked his family and *the nuns, all of whom were adamant that I grow up and make something of myself.* Considering the threshold he now stands before, his recollections are ironic indeed: *My most vivid childhood memory of the Supreme Court was the "Impeach Earl Warren" signs which lined Highway 17 near Savannah. I didn't quite understand who this Earl Warren fellow was, but I knew he was in some kind of trouble.*

Savannah's personality was also formed by colorful and dynamic ethnic groups, which shaped her character with genes of their own.

In 1991 Clarence Thomas became the second Savannahian appointed to the United States Supreme Court. (Courtesy of the Savannah News Press.)

ERIN GO BRAGH—HERE COME THE IRISH!
"AN IRISHMAN ON THE 17TH OF MARCH—
AN AMERICAN ON THE 4TH OF JULY—BEAT THEM WHO CAN"

Every year on March 17—St. Patrick's Day!—one would assume that all of Savannah was Irish since 1733. In 1991 the estimate of out-of-towners attending St. Patrick's Day festivities was three hundred thousand, twice the in-town population. Two of those visitors from Dublin (Ireland, not Georgia) recently put things in perspective: *We've learned that Savannah has the second largest parade in the whole world, and New York the second best.*

What tradition! As any proud Irishman will tell you—as his grandfather told him—the St. Patrick's Day parade started in 1856. But would you believe 1824? Thanks to the fine research of William L. Fogarty in his book, *The Days We've Celebrated,* the earliest date may be 1818. The local *Gazette* of that year cryptically recorded on March 17—*Parade today, 9 o'clock.*

How can this be? Where did all those Irish come from, traditionally Roman Catholic since St. Patrick went to Ireland in A D 432? *Papists* were banned in writing in Georgia's 1733 charter—the gaggle of Counter-Reformation Protestants in the colony struggled for decades against the threat of the Spanish and French Catholics. Even by the new laws of 1776, only white male Protestants could vote. In Ireland it would not be until 1829 that a Catholic could own property or be elected to a seat in the British Parliament.

Actually this latter state in Ireland was a reason in itself; the more oppression at home, the more who leave home for elsewhere. Unlike China or France, settlement by strangers is the American

John J. Kelly, the fifth president of the Hibernian Society in 1856, was the first Catholic elected by the forty-four-year-old group. (Courtesy of William Fogarty.)

story, no better epitomized than in Savannah, and no more so than by the Irish experience.

Unlike the English, Jews, Salzburgers, and Scots, however, there is no neat *Mayflower* first boat of Irish that arrived on some early precise date. The closest nonequivalent was in 1734, when forty starving Irish convicts were tossed by storm into Savannah. Oglethorpe bought them at £5 a head and put them to work on communal farms as indentured servants. A year later they led a revolt, which was quickly put down. In 1756, four hundred Catholic Acadians from Nova Scotia took winter refuge in Savannah, but left because of the still prevalent antipapist mood. As individuals, the Irish came in lowly circumstances in those first decades, but not more numerous as servants than poor Scots, Germans, Dutch, or English. And there were exceptions to the trend. Henry Ellis, the cultured royal governor from 1757 to 1760, was Irish. By tradition a Catholic, Peter Tondee was the magnet of the Liberty Boys of '76; but Ellis was not Catholic, nor Tondee Irish.

Generally speaking, Irish-born predominance in Savannah before the 1840's was Protestant—more likely Presbyterian than Catholic—emigrants from the *Ulster plantation*. This was the same gene-pool as their inland Scotch-Irish "Cracker" kin, proliferating in Georgia since the 1770's. In 1812 the Irish formed the Hibernian Society in Savannah, the first forty-four members and four presidents of which were all non-Catholic, including a member of the Jewish Minis family. The group was usually composed of prosperous professionals. Typical would be member Michael Dillon. In 1818, at the age of twenty-six, he came from Ireland to Savannah. He opened a dry goods store and by 1821 bought the first of his thirty-seven slaves. In 1829 he joined the Hibernian Society. By the time he died in 1846, he had been on the city council seven times and left his family considerable property.

Despite the steady influx of Irish over the years, in 1843 a Catholic priest estimated *the Catholic population in the city hardly reached one thousand.* If less dominant than their Protestant kinsmen, they could at least look back on their own Catholic church site since 1791. In that year the Savannah city council granted a lot on Montgomery Street for a Roman Catholic church. This was the first locale of what would become St. John the Baptist, the congregation's present majestic cathedral on Abercorn Street, dedicated in 1876.

By that year Savannah was full of the Irish, now predominantly Catholic. This had been the trend for more than a quarter century, beginning in the 1840's. Even earlier, small clusters of destitute Irish sought refuge, as noted by Dr. William R. Waring's horrific report on the 1820 yellow fever epidemic: *In the summer of 1819,*

Grand Marshall E. C. Gleason leads the 1911 St. Patrick's parade on horseback. (Courtesy of Katherine Strickle and William Fogarty.)

fifty Irish immigrants arrived on the same ship, not one of whom survived til the frost. Around 1847 the great potato famines began in Ireland, driving millions of Irish to the United States, especially to major ports like New York, Boston, and Philadelphia. Those who reached Savannah would have been welcomed by veterans of the Mexican War, members of the Irish Jasper Greens. Dominated by working-class Irish Catholics, the company was formed in 1842, marching in continuous succession into the latest St. Patrick's Day parade.

Many others besides Irish-Americans might recognize their own tender family roots in an 1821 Savannah ad:

TO IRISH EMIGRANTS

Such persons in this country wishing to have any of their friends brought out from Ireland, may have a passage secured for them from a port in the north of Ireland to this place, by a first rate vessel to arrive here after the first of November next. Terms made known on application (if by letter, post paid) to the subscriber.

James Magee

Savannah, March 7, 1821

This steady recruitment resulted in nearly one of five Savannah citizens being Irish born by 1850. In the census ten years later the Irish population had doubled. By the exquisite analysis of Edward M. Shoemaker in his master's thesis, *Strangers and Citizens—The Irish,* over eighty percent of Irish immigrants in that decade came from Catholic counties in Ireland. Most Irish immigrants desperately needed a helping hand from both their kinsmen and the established mother church, if the Spellmans are a typical example. John and Elizabeth Spellman came to Savannah in 1850, both nearly fifty-years of age, with three children. Neither had an occupation. By the 1860 census, John had become a drayman and claimed $200 in personal property. They had no real property and lived on the seamy west side of town. But before that year they had—somehow—taken in a relative, Irish-born Catherine Spellman, with her two children. Even beginning in 1812, a minor class distinction, based on poverty, was implied by the charter of the Hibernian Society. The members were charged *to reach out the hand of friendship, to tender the aid of a delicate charity.*

Any Irishman today might recognize the still-legendary tug to the home sod by various toasts at the St. Patrick's banquet in 1829, the same year of the Catholic emancipation in their mother country. *Catholic Emancipation and Religious Freedom: Let every man freely choose his way, His Maker to Adore. . . . The Patriots of Ireland: May they never cease to exert themselves until they have wrestled from the Tyrant Monster, the liberties of which that country has been deprived.*

Mr. M. Hopkins then followed with a toast to put the proud Irish twinkle in every American's eye: *An Irishman on the 17th of March— an American on the 4th of July—beat them who can.*

A popular community leader after this time was the Reverend Jeremiah F. O'Neal. The forty-year-old priest came to Savannah in 1832 to help rebuild the crumbling Catholic structure, by then located on Drayton Street. Called "Old Hickory" by his parishioners because of his resemblance to Andrew Jackson, Father O'Neal happily provided community leadership by his wit, convictions, and deft political touch in the Protestant community. As the South moved toward secession over the following years, he was one of the movement's most visible leaders. His flock needed little nudging, the Irish in Savannah being among the most staunch secessionists. They had never opposed slavery. Those, like Michael Dillon, who could afford slaves, bought them. Those, like John Spellman, were too poor and powerless to oppose the trend; he and his class lived in the same part of town with the free blacks, competing for the same jobs. Both groups found heavy employment on the new Central of Georgia railroad, finished in 1847.

But "Old Hickory" O'Neal had little success in one crusade—that of the short-lived Catholic Temperance Association. By his eloquence and clout he actually had 403 members *sign the pledge* against ruinous drink by 1841. He was mirroring the same temporary movement in Ireland, also with his usual keen eye to improve the Irish image in Savannah. The group even marched as a unit in that year's parade. It was the society's only one, as it disappeared from existence, along with a parallel Protestant temperance group.

By 1850 the Catholic diocese was in Savannah. Father Peter Whelan, one of the first to serve there, is still remembered by the city. Irish born around fifty years before, he declined an offer to head the diocese, preferring to serve the downtrodden. By 1864 he was serving the thousands of Union prisoners at Andersonville, Georgia, where around fourteen thousand died under hellish conditions. Father Whelan was the only minister to live on site and actually enter the stockade. The short form of the Catholic last rites, Extreme Unction, was a too-common final duty for all untendered denominations. He was described as *a very old man, aging a year each day he served in Andersonville.* A Union prisoner from Illinois remembered him as *unwearied in his attention to the sick, and the whole day could be seen moving around through the prison, attending to those who needed spiritual consolation. He was evidently of such stuff as Christian heroes have been made.* When Confederate veteran Charles H. Olmstead and a group of his Fort Pulaski veterans followed Father Whelan's funeral procession in 1871, Olmstead remembered it *with a sense of exultation as I thought of the welcome that awaited him.*

Catholic clergy and proud Irish eyes watch a St. Patrick's Day parade in front of 1876 Cathedral of St. John the Baptist on Abercorn Street.

Another who gave his life for others was Bishop Francis X. Gartland. He died of yellow fever while helping to care for the hundreds lost in Savannah's 1854 epidemic.

But amid this bumpy—generally sad—long story, few good Presbyterians or Anglicans would have enough poetry in their veins or Celtic lilt in their soul to approach this 1840 St. Patrick's toast to Ireland's new shelter, Savannah: *Like a beautiful maiden too bashful to reveal her charms, she has hither to hidden them from our view, but now that we have unveiled them, they fascinate us even to idolatry.*

THE GREEKS

The Greeks had also arrived, but the gifts they bore for Savannah would pose no threat. Their thrifty natures and dedicated work ethics contributed considerably to Savannah's populace. Although there is evidence of individual Greeks as early as 1880, the great wave of Greek immigration to Savannah began around 1903. The first Greek Orthodox church was organized around 1900, later established in the old St. Paul's Episcopal Church on the corner of Barnard and Duffy streets.

Ties with the motherland were not broken during the early years, and never have been completely. Many families in Savannah conscientiously sent money back to their relatives in Greece. During the

Balkan War of 1912, the Volunteer Militia Greek Friendly Society, organized in 1910, departed for Greece to serve in the Greek army. These soldiers returned to Savannah at the end of the war, followed by another wave of Greek immigrants.

In 1918 a Greek school was started in order to familiarize Greek youth with the customs and language of the old country. Many citizens are still fluent in their native language—such as the five-term mayor, John P. Rousakis. But by the 1930's Savannah's Greeks were Greek-Americans. Beginning to consider themselves Americans, rather than displaced Greeks, many had joined the United States Army in World War I and earned their citizenship. The Greeks were becoming assimilated into the community, including local politics.

The present Greek Orthodox church, located on the corner of Bull and Henry streets, was founded in 1941. A Hellenic Center soon followed in 1951, to help maintain an understanding of Greek culture. Their annual fall festival is eagerly anticipated each year. The Greek food, music, and dance bring out the Zorba the Greek—even in the Crackers.

There is a local saying: *In Atlanta when you are introduced, they ask you what your business is; in Macon they ask you your religion; in Augusta they ask who were your ancestors; but in Savannah, they ask, "What would you like to drink?"* And so Savannah continues her Trustees' tradition of hospitality, warmly welcoming both the oppressed and the famous, the clan and the individual. And each year thousands of visitors fall in love with the city Conrad Aiken called *that most magical of cities . . . that earthly paradise.* But perhaps as Savannahian Arthur Gordon once said, *Savannah is not a city, it's a state of mind.*

THE PAST, THE PRESENT, THE FUTURE

HISTORIC PRESERVATION
SAVANNAH MID-CENTURY

Having generally failed to anticipate the demise of the cotton era, Savannah lethargically had pursued the diversification of its economy. By the 1920's, King Cotton was not only dead, but buried. The port was less active; Savannah turned in on herself. Then came World War II and the growth that fast-forwarded Savannah into the twentieth century. With the war's end, however, growth again came to an abrupt halt.

Although Broughton Street was still the shopping area, and although the business center remained downtown, the historic resi-

A 1925 drawing of the Savannah skyline by Christopher Murphy, one of Savannah's finest artists. (Courtesy of V. and J. Duncan Antique Maps and Prints, Savannah.)

dential district hibernated. *Out with the old—in with the new* was America's postwar motto; few cities looked more ripe for a facelift than moldy, ancient Savannah.

Luckily there was never a unified renewal plan to raze the old district, but decay and vandalism relentlessly took their toll. No one knew, or cared, how long before the proponents of progress would unite to put the corpse out of its misery, razing the historic buildings and replacing them with skyscrapers.

Property values in the area plummeted; even the stately homes around the squares degraded into slums—worth more dead than alive—their beautiful bricks of value to suburban builders.

Other detractions diminished the lure of the downtown district. Raw sewage polluted the Savannah harbor; and the stench—joined by sulfurous belches from the local paper company—permeated the city. Natives downplayed their *Savannah perfume* with a shrug and a smile: *Don't worry. It's just the smell of money.* Ship captains joked that they anchored in port to poison off their barnacles.

In 1946, a month before the International Monetary Conference held at the nearby Oglethorpe Hotel, visitor Lady Astor leveled her famous backhanded compliment: *Savannah is a beautiful lady with a dirty face.* The now infamous line shamed Savannah. A month later Lady Astor struck again: *Even if the International Monetary Conference has not put Savannah on the map, at least I have.*

Always an insular city, Savannah could no longer ignore her shabbiness. The city needed to do something, but she had no plan, no idea where to turn. By the mid-1950's Lady Astor might have described that face as ravaged by smallpox.

The Savannah Downtown National Historic Landmark District—affectionately called NOGS for *North of Gaston Street*—is the largest urban historic district in the nation. It consists of approximately 2.2 square miles, developed between 1733 and 1856 on land owned by the Trustees. Despite the decay, General Oglethorpe's venerated city plan never lost its splendor. As preservationist Audrey Rhangos explained: *We were more or less frozen in time for awhile. When things started happening in Atlanta in the '20's, they didn't happen here. And it gave us time to re-evaluate.* Since, in the words of a city planner, *Savannah was too poor to destroy herself,* her colonial layout was preserved almost intact from 1733—the most carefully conceived scheme for urban settlement this country has ever seen. The squares governed urban expansion without allowing formless sprawl; the transition from narrow streets to open squares provided *a wonderful sense of space in solidly built townscape,* according to the jargon of a national authority. Another expert from New York put it more bluntly: *The Squares—the Jewels of Savannah—guard them well.*

Savannah was a pedestrian's delight, but there were fewer and fewer to enjoy it. The residential centers of the city had moved south and east. Between 1900 and 1955 the wealth of magnificent architecture in the historic district was generally ignored. Demolition joined decay in taking its toll. The priceless buildings represented a succession of architectural styles: Federal, English Regency, Classical Revival, Italian Villa, Gothic Revival, Romantic Revival, Second Empire—Savannah had supported them all. Classic buildings by William Jay, John Norris, Charles B. Cluskey, William Gibbons Preston, and A. E. Eichberg were being lost.

As early as 1872, streetcar tracks had been laid through certain squares, and in 1912 only legal action prevented Lincoln Street from being routed through the vaults of the founding fathers in Colonial Park Cemetery. William Jay's architectural jewel, the Archibald Bulloch home on Orleans Square, was leveled in 1916 for a stolid municipal auditorium. Jay's Greek Revival U.S. Bank followed four years later. In 1921, because more streetcar tracks threatened the squares on Abercorn and Barnard streets, citizens formed the Society for Preservation of Parks in order to prevent further attempts at desecration. Only public opinion averted another plan to obliterate the squares with a broad avenue.

The fighting continued for years. In 1935 a proposed federal highway down Montgomery Street—never completed—demolished three squares. Franklin Square, directly in front of the First African Baptist Church, was eventually reestablished in 1983. More squares were threatened, and Jay's elegant Savannah theater burned in

The 1849 Andrew Low House, restored in 1928 by The Colonial Dames of America in the State of Georgia as their headquarters. Robert E. Lee sought a decent night's sleep there in 1870.

1948 (although this was no great loss by this time, due to insensitive revisions).

The destruction of the historic district arose from lack of understanding of the heritage involved. Prominent businessmen who cared nothing for *old* architecture assumed there was little to save. It would take the common citizen with deep emotional roots in Savannah to turn the tide. It was a close call.

Today proud Savannahians tend to look back on the 1950's as the decade that *saved* Savannah, but that is an oversimplification. Although the Historic Savannah Foundation, the city's contemporary flagship, was not organized until then, there were heroic contributions by individuals decades before.

During the waning years of the nineteenth century, one active Savannah philanthropist was Mary Telfair. Together with her sister, Margaret Telfair Hodgson, she donated money to build Hodgson Hall, home of the Georgia Historical Society. On her death she also bequeathed them her home on St. James Square. Today the Telfair Academy of Arts and Sciences is housed in the fine William Jay mansion built by her father.

During the 1890's many American heritage societies sprang up from patriotic roots. The most active were, and remain, the Daughters of the American Revolution (D.A.R.), the Colonial Dames, the Sons of the Revolution, and the Society of Colonial Wars. Beginning in 1898, these groups, in association with various city agencies, rescued Colonial Park Cemetery, marked Tomochichi's grave and the site of Oglethorpe's landing, and helped erect an imposing statue of Savannah's founder in Chippewa Square. In 1928 The National Society of

Today Trustees' Garden remains a vibrant area, the first proof that historic preservation could be economically profitable, as Mrs. Hansell Hillyer showed by this project in 1945.

The Colonial Dames in the State of Georgia purchased and restored the Andrew Low House on Lafayette Square as their headquarters.

Private preservation and restoration continued in a piecemeal fashion. In 1942 St. John's Episcopal Church acquired Sherman's old headquarters, the Green-Meldrim House, and had it magnificently restored as their parish house. James Habersham's Pink House on Reynolds Square was rescued by Alida Harper Fowlkes and converted to a charming tearoom, where Mrs. Fowlkes and her friends served as waitresses. The Pirates' House and adjacent ancient Herb House were likewise restored by Mrs. Marmaduke Floyd. The surrounding northeast section of the city drew the restoration attention of Stella Henderson. In 1951 Margaret G. Thomas bequeathed William Jay's 1819 Richardson-Owens-Thomas House to the Telfair Academy, and in 1953 the Wayne-Gordon Home on Bull Street was bought by the Girl Scouts.

These efforts would not be enough. Of the fifty priceless Savannah buildings recorded in the federal government's Historic American Buildings Survey in 1934, fourteen would be demolished later. But the seeds had been planted and would blossom into a consolidated program of preservation.

TRUSTEES' GARDEN

One major preservation project does predate the creation of the Historic Savannah Foundation. In 1945 the first real attempt at area restoration took place when the wife of Savannah Gas Company's chief executive resolved to renovate ten acres of dilapidated buildings near the gas works. Most Savannahians thought Mrs. Hansell

The demolition of the City Market in the 1950's would unite Savannah in the crusade for historic preservation. A particularly sterile parking garage now sits there like a thumb in the city's eye. (Courtesy of the Georgia Historical Society.)

Hillyer's scheme to renovate old clapboard cabins into modern rental units was a very foolish venture. As any astute business mind knew, new construction was much cheaper than restoration.

To the astonishment of Savannah, her strategy worked. A fashionable neighborhood was soon established on the original site of the Trustees' Garden. Best known now as the location of the Pirates' House Restaurant, Trustees' Garden was the beacon for others. It was a project that proved that preservation could be both aesthetic and economically profitable.

The Shot Heard 'Round Savannah

In 1951 a bill was submitted to the Georgia General Assembly, once again requesting permission to cut through the Habersham Street squares and make the street a boulevard. While preservationists concentrated on defeating this, another bill slipped past. It granted the city authority to raze the old City Market. The incident would ignite Savannah.

As a mark of farewell to an old friend, a gala costume ball was held in October 1953. Nostalgia was fused with anger. Savannahian Emory Jarrott recalled the general sentiment years later: *We fought a good fight and lost. There was nothing left to do but give the old market the kind of sendoff it deserved. . . . It was really ironic in a way. There was a feeling of resignation, but at the same time there was this determination that had started to grow, as if losing the market were the last straw. It was a disaster, but from the disaster grew Historic Savannah.*

At last Savannahians were shocked into concerted action. A group of old and new city leaders joined to combat further desecration of

Anna Hunter, the prime wit in founding the Historic Savannah Foundation in the 1950's. (Courtesy of Emory Jarrott.)

their heritage, but they were too late to save the market. It was demolished in 1954—for a parking garage, a remarkably hideous one to boot.

HISTORIC SAVANNAH FOUNDATION

As a direct result of the demise of City Market, the Historic Savannah Foundation was founded in 1955. Led by Mrs. Anna C. Hunter, a nucleus of seven women chartered the group, hoping to develop a long-range plan for saving the historic district before it was lost piecemeal. As Mrs. Hunter recalled: *We were off in a cloud of dust . . . I might say gunpowder.*

The group first met June 28, 1955. Jane Adair Wright, Elinor Grunsfeld Adler, Katherine Judkins Clark, Lucy Barrow McIntire, Dorothy Ripley Roebling, and Nola Roos joined Anna Hunter in her determination to save the historic district. The imminent demolition of the Isaiah Davenport House—the most outstanding example of Georgian architecture in the city—galvanized the group. The house, by then divided into tenement apartments, was to be razed to make way for yet another parking lot. Later, preservationist Audrey Rhangos reflected: *We needed one crisis, one central issue that would focus attention on the downtown area. This happened to be it.*

Others soon joined the group, including Walter C. Hartridge as an important advisor. Anna Hunter later joked: *To this day I can see Walter Hartridge ducking around corners or taking his phone off the hook to elude the pursuers.* Jack Rauers, the foundation's first president, along with Railford Wood, Hansell Hillyer, Alexander Lawrence, Reuben Clark, Freeman Jelks, and Lee Adler, were other early contributors— as were the Junior League and the *Savannah News/Press.*

Twenty-two thousand dollars was needed to purchase the house; the group raised it *(chicken feed today,* as Mrs. Hunter remarked a dozen years later). At the first general membership meeting in November 1955, a startling seven hundred members stepped forward. Mrs. Hunter observed: *Like a comic opera . . . lawyers protested in basso solos, the ladies raising treble obligatos (also raising funds) and the party of the second part remained incommunicado.*

The foundation raised the funds only hours before the wrecking ball would have swung. Local lore reports that when the wrecker, accustomed to razing historic buildings for their bricks, asked Lee Adler, *Where do you want your bricks put?* he replied: *Just leave them where they are for now.* Restored by the fledgling Historic Savannah Foundation, the house became the symbol of Savannah's rebirth and eventually also the group's headquarters.

The foundation determined to reawaken interest in Savannah's heritage, to convince the public of the economic benefits of restora-

Before being restored, the 1815 Davenport House had become a tenement, destined for demolition in 1955. (Courtesy of the Georgia Historical Society.)

Today the Davenport House is a tourist attraction, an excellent example of restoration to former Georgian splendor. (Courtesy of Hank Ramsey, Savannah.)

A 1968 photograph of Fort Jackson before restoration. Today it is a popular center for community affairs, such as the Scottish games and oyster roasts. (Courtesy of the Ships of the Sea Museum.)

tion, and to promote tourism. The sleepy Chamber of Commerce was closed on weekends, and there was no visitors' bureau.

During the next decade the foundation would deluge the city with a massive public relations campaign, arrange for a professional inventory of historic buildings, establish a revolving fund, and help establish a tourist and convention bureau within the Chamber of Commerce. Local banker Reuben Clark proclaimed: *We can have a $60 million tourist industry right now . . . all we have to do is develop it!* In their spare time the foundation members worked to improve the lighting and surfacing of River Street, and to persuade the Savannah Electric and Power Company to keep their corporate offices downtown.

Buildings in danger of leveling were saved. The Lachlan McIntosh House, the Francis Stone House, Mary Marshall Row, the Oliver Sturgis House, the Cluskey Buildings, and the Turner House—all were rescued. The foundation joined the effort to save Fort Jackson from demolition. When Emmett Park on Bay Street was scheduled to become *another* parking facility, the foundation, with the help of the Trustees' Garden Club, averted the situation.

Private rescues also continued. In 1961 the Hampton-Lillibridge House was saved by Jim Williams, among many he would eventually restore. The Mongin House on Warren Square was also privately restored by Mr. and Mrs. John Carswell. And in 1961 the Mills B. Lane family joined the restoration movement. Their invaluable commitment continues to this day. The most delightful legacy of Mr. Lane's boyish enthusiasm is the Ships of the Sea Museum on River Street.

Historic Savannah managed to halt Armstrong College's plans to expand in 1962. Located on Gaston Street in the old Armstrong mansion, the college proposed to tear down important buildings in the area. The foundation's purchase of six buildings from the college and the gracious donation of land by banker Mills B. Lane persuaded the college to move to the southside. One only need glance at the present United Way Building on Monterey Square, constructed by the college before relocation, to exalt in one of the foundation's greatest accomplishments. In a combination of both residential and business adaptation, all buildings in and around the old Armstrong complex have now been beautifully restored.

Yet there was still no systematic strategy involved; all of these buildings were saved at the eleventh hour. The foundation was heroically responding to threats, not anticipating them.

In order to change its crisis-oriented character, the Historic Savannah Foundation adopted a new real estate strategy of covenants to leverage the foundation's slim financing. The group vigorously promoted restoration by others, buying vulnerable buildings for resale to individuals for private renovation, thus transferring control of precious old buildings from those not interested in saving them to those who were. As preservationist Lee Adler observed: *In doing their own restorations, these people have become creatively involved in the life of the city.*

Soon, covenants were fine-tuned to require that the purchaser not change the exterior of the building, begin restoration within six months, and have it completed within eighteen months—plus give the foundation first right of refusal on any resale. This discouraged opportunistic speculation buying, with no serious intent toward restoration. And, by encouraging property to be restored as active structures with people living in them—not static museums—a vibrant, living community was created, adding to, not subtracting from, the city tax rolls. Oglethorpe and the Trustees would have beamed at its utilitarian simplicity, a reflection of many of their "outmoded" ideas.

The major breakthrough came in 1964 with the establishment of a revolving fund. Two hundred thousand dollars, which could scarcely buy or save a single restored house today, would revolutionize the foundation. Kept fluid through short-term commitment, recirculation of the limited supply of money guarantees the available funds for the purchase of endangered buildings.

The completed professional inventory of Savannah's 2,500 buildings in the historic district showed that more than forty percent had architectural or historic significance. Recognizing the need for aesthetic control of new construction, the foundation's *Preservation Plan for Savannah* established design guidelines to ensure that new construction was historically compatible with surrounding architecture. The plan recommended building heights, scale and proportion, landscaping design, even architectural details. The plan soon became a vital model for national preservation groups. Using it as a guide, and after years of wrangling, the city passed a Historic Zoning Ordinance in 1973.

Gradually, Historic Savannah moved into larger ventures. In 1963 the Troup Ward Urban Renewal project was initiated, taking advantage of federal housing funds for the first time. The foundation purchased eight area buildings for a mere $27,500. Promoting HUD 312 mortgage loans at an amazing three percent for thirty years, this fourteen-acre tract was restored as one of the first urban rehabilitation projects in the nation. At last, federal housing policies had stopped emphasizing new construction and provided homeowners

The first project to take advantage of federal housing funds, today Troup Square is surrounded by beautifully restored homes, and is one of the most popular areas in residential Savannah.

with an incentive to *restore*. A mere $4.5 million of low-interest HUD loans ultimately lured more than $40 million of private renovations into the historic district.

Commercial restoration was launched with the West Congress Street Revitalization project. In the Pulaski Square–West Jones Street Project, a thirteen-acre dilapidated area was returned to residential use with $38,000 from the revolving fund, which attracted over $1 million from private investors.

The most ambitious project that Historic Savannah has done to date was restoring the Scarbrough House. It had been vacant since the 1960's, when the first black Savannah public school closed its doors. Deteriorating rapidly, William Jay's tarnished jewel was in danger of demolition. Through the generous contribution of Mrs. Craig Barrow and $45,000 of foundation money, the house was purchased. Although sold, the house was reacquired by Historic Savannah in 1972, when the buyer could not afford to restore it. Renovating the house as a bicentennial project, Historic Savannah adopted the building as its headquarters. This was the foundation's first anchor in reclamation of the city's northwest quadrant. The foundation spent over $1 million on the rejuvenation of the Scarbrough House. By 1976 the house was opened to the public and designated a National Landmark.

Beginning to feel a sense of control over the problems of the downtown historic area, the Historic Savannah Foundation turned its attention to Savannah's Victorian District. Historic Savannah joined Savannah Landmark, along with the city's Community Development Program, to pioneer subsidy rental housing. Again, the combination of such diverse resources worked toward the same vibrant concept—average people in rejuvenated neighborhoods, both adding life to each other.

In 1974 the Victorian District was placed on the National Register, and in 1982 the boundaries were extended to include the 1870 city limits. Over 1,500 buildings of architectural importance are now in the expanded *historic downtown*.

By 1970 Historic Savannah Foundation had saved over 150 structures, resold to individuals who have in turn invested over $12 million. Although over seventy percent of the 1,100 important buildings in the original historic district had been stabilized, demolition continued to threaten the remainder, in spite of the Historic Landmark designation.

The Goose That Laid the Golden Egg

A dozen years after Historic Savannah Foundation's birth, Mrs. Hunter exclaimed: *I feel like the goose that laid the golden egg . . . and don't think we were not called geese.* She continued: *These nights I lie relaxed, smirking in my pillow, realizing the program is in good hands. "Historical" is now a prestige word—no longer called hysterical.* And well might she be proud. From 1955 to 1968 Historic Savannah Foundation was a voice of authority, heeded by city government and the business community. Although occasionally called Mrs. Hunter's *Hysterical Savannah* by foundation detractors, one male preservationist countered at the time: *They aren't twittering old ladies in tennis shoes. They use their brains, they work and they've got clout.*

With its innovative techniques, the foundation grew to be one of the most admired restoration groups in the nation. Historic Savannah popped up all over national magazines as a shining example to the rest of the United States. Tourists worldwide began taking note of all the lavish full-color publicity. Tax assessments in the city doubled or tripled as citizens invested millions in the historic area. Tourism, of little consequence three decades ago, added over $546 million to the local economy in 1990, spent by countless tourists.

With over two thousand members, the foundation continues to encourage individual restoration, provide consulting services, and to work with the city's Historic Review Board. A Tour of Homes and many other educational and cultural events are sponsored by the foundation annually. But the Georgia Week Celebration, inaugurated in 1965, remains one of Historic Savannah's most important functions. Before the whole extravaganza ends with a parade of school children in colonial garb, a week of school visitations reminds the youth of the diversity of their heritage. Doctors, lawyers, merchants— even one Indian chief—dress up as Oglethorpe, Tomochichi, Mary

There are still many beautiful homes awaiting loving restoration, as these before and after examples on Barnard Street attest.

Musgrove, Andrew Bryan, Paul Amatis, and ad lib *surprise* guests to help teach young school children how things *were*. Such efforts are not nostalgic play only, but fulfill the tenet long taught to the children by Sarah Parsons of the school system: *Savannah is like a mixed salad, all thrown together, but with each ingredient maintaining its own distinct, wonderful flavor*.

A new era has begun. In early 1991 the Scarbrough House was secured by the Telfair Academy of Arts and Sciences, placing all of the Jay buildings under the administration of the Telfair. Historic Savannah Foundation has moved its headquarters to Broughton Street in an heroic effort to encourage reclamation of that vital but moribund area. Other current priorities focus on reclamation of East Jones Street and fighting the Liberty Street Highway.

Preservation's Failures

Unfortunately preservationists have not always been victorious. One conspicuous defeat was losing architectural control of the new federal complex. The government *promised* that the Telfair Square buildings would be compatible with the surrounding historic structures, commensurate with guidelines spelled out in the *Preservation Plan for Savannah*.

A prestigious architectural competition was held to select the design choice—the first for a new federal building in the nation. Savannah preservationists trustingly let down their guard. What happened! A visitor only has to wince at the massive complex to realize that Savannahians' faith was anchored on shifting sands. Deep in the federal labyrinth, faceless gnomes came out at night to slyly modify the winning plans from that exalted competition. Designs were changed; proposed materials were mutated. Cunningly the resultant scale and mass were kept correct, but Savannahians were not deceived. The exterior's mismatched glossy tiles—apparently chosen by the mistress decorator of an I.R.S. accountant—evoked both tears and laughter from Savannahians. But it was no joke.

Many, including the mayor, howled that the ghastly complex looked like a massive bathroom. One architect is said to have quipped: *You shouldn't make a judgment until the shower curtains are hung*.

An earlier battle was also lost, which, rightly or wrongly, seriously hurt the Historic Savannah Foundation, ultimately pitting *pure* preservationists against the very *progress* they sought. As the story goes, in 1969 Historic Savannah actively solicited development of a hotel on River Street, convinced it would revitalize the area. A gentleman's agreement was reached with local developers that the new hotel would replace only the mass torn down—so important to maintaining compatibility with the surrounding historic buildings. When the developers returned with plans for a towering fifteen-story structure, friction erupted, splitting the executive committee.

The dissenters found a National Trust consultant to recommend against a high rise in the historic district; but the foundation approved the new plans, as did the Chamber of Commerce. It was again Savannah brother against brother in an awkward civil war.

Accusations of conflict of interest flew. Opposing board members resigned. The protesters united with others in the community to fight the construction; a *Save the Bay* group sprang up, followed by a lawsuit.

What is today the Hyatt Regency Hotel is the compromise. Local opinions vary as to whether a reasonable compromise was reached. Instead of being outrageously tall, the building ended up remarkably fat, its modern glassy midriff lurching out over antique River Street, dwarfing everything in sight—even the magically stupendous ships who now cower past. Albert Scardino, the notably outspoken Pulitzer Prize–winning editor of the defunct *Georgia Gazette*, called the building *the Death Star* that crashed on the nineteenth-century river area—straight out of the film *Star Wars*. He added: *The tragedy of Savannah's Hyatt is that it need not have been so rude, so insulting, so brutal.* But the hotel has been wildly successful with tourists, and immediately, local "Old Boy" functions rushed there as if nothing had happened.

The eventual developer replied to complaints: *I've spent millions of dollars in development and done things right. I don't think tourists are coming to see old houses.*

And the problems continue. The supervision of a historic area is an ongoing task, and careful surveillance must be maintained. Aesthetic control can slip so easily in the obviously human struggle to balance needed progress with Savannah's priceless heritage.

Crime (a major concern in the area), stagnant property values, and the loss of low-interest HUD loans have put a damper on individuals' incentives to restore. Broughton Street, once the heart of the city's shopping district, is filled with vacant, deteriorating buildings. Like most main streets in the country, it has relinquished its once precious role to suburban shopping malls. Many plans have been proposed—a new one is now under discussion—but the problem remains and the answer is not yet clear. Perhaps Historic Savannah Foundation's move of its headquarters to Broughton Street will be an incentive for others.

Individuals from nonhistoric areas often have no empathy with the heartache involved in maintaining the character of a historic district, demolished decades ago in their own steel and glass cities. The state

The Savannah College of Art and Design

Sidewalk Art Festival for the Savannah College of Art and Design. Many languishing old buildings—such as the old armory on Madison Square—have been superbly restored by the college.

Department of Transportation (DOT) still threatens Savannah with a parkway straight down tree-lined Liberty Street. The state clearly has difficulty recognizing that a major highway through a historic area is an aesthetic disaster, one that threatens to poison the golden goose that delivers nearly half a billion dollars in tourist income each year.

All is not complacent within the preservation community itself either. Splinter groups have developed. Discontented with Historic Savannah, new organizations have evolved with their own priorities and ideas for solving the problems they perceive. Sadly, one cohesive organization is generally more effective than several working independently, but so far on major threats—like the Liberty Street freeway—the groups have managed to man the same barricade.

The establishment of the Savannah College of Art and Design (SCAD) has been the latest and biggest boost to the historic district. This school has befriended numerous derelict white elephants, restoring the buildings in vibrant, tasteful style. Of course, this being Savannah, there are dissenting opinions. More sedate residents resent the lively students. Downtown parking, always a problem, has been a major issue with the influx. But there has been god-sent restoration, and the city bustles with new vitality.

The struggle never ends. Yet, like ardent preservationists, there are others who conscientiously stand guard over Savannah's historic buildings. As in any old city, Savannah has her tales.

On February 12, 1917, William Washington Gordon, II, was seen by his daughter-in-law leaving his dying wife's bedroom. *With an expression of grave gladness,* he was dressed in his familiar gray suit. Back in the bedroom his children attended his wife, Nellie, whose dying expression *took on the radiance of a bride, going to meet her bridegroom.*

As he did daily, Gordon descended the classic spiral stairs of their home on Bull and Oglethorpe, then exited the front door. Left in his wake downstairs was an old black butler, moved to tears of shock and joy. And small wonder—William Washington Gordon had been buried five years before in Laurel Grove Cemetery.

Few of the dozens of *beings* in Savannah who still go bump in the night have such specific identity. Only a minority are regularly *seen,* such as by staff members at the Gordon home even decades later. Now a national Girl Scout museum, it was there that one guide recounted to Margaret DeBolt, author of *Savannah Spectres,* how she saw Nellie Gordon on a late Sunday afternoon: *Well, suddenly I heard a kind of rustle, and a figure was there above me, in the center hall. I recognized Mrs. Gordon from the picture in the library. I don't know who was the most startled. She drew back as though to say, "Oh, I thought you'd all gone!!"* When the maintenance man comes in early in the morning, he claims to often glimpse an elderly woman at the dinner table *wearing a long blue robe, with flowers all over it.* He believes the whole family *continues life as usual when we all go home.* Visiting Girl Scouts periodically see an old woman of different dress in the gift shop—usually invisible to adults.

William Washington Gordon, II, and his wife, Nellie, in front of their carriage on Oglethorpe Avenue at the turn of the century. Perhaps you are looking at one or more ghosts. Even the carriage is still alive, activated for special occasions. (Courtesy of the Juliette Gordon Low Girl Scout National Center.)

Not only does Mrs. DeBolt relate dozens of such spooky stories—and quaint legends—but she visited many of the haunted sites with a young student of the paranormal. *Strong vibrations* were the result, mingled with the sincerity of average people who *had* witnessed unearthly things. Consider the account of two young antique dealers, visiting a friend for a drink in his apartment above the Richardson-Owens-Thomas House museum. Around twilight one Sunday, the two guests both saw a fourth man—in his mid-thirties, around 175 pounds, and with black hair—join them. As one described: *I had a feeling he was a guest in the home and had just come in from outside, maybe from riding. . . . He was dressed in the style of about 1830, wearing a cutaway tail coat, black or dark blue, light tight pants, and a white ruffled shirt. . . . My partner and I looked at each other and nodded, to be sure we were both really seeing him.* The host noticed nothing as the apparition eased around the room for ten minutes before exiting by a guest-room door.

Certainly the most researched specters in town reside on East St. Julian Street, in the Hampton-Lillibridge House. Built in 1796, it was moved from another site on Bryan Street. From the beginning workmen were spooked by sounds and mounting, bizarre, little things. While the owner, Jim Williams, was away, neighbors heard a woman clearly singing. The parents of a judge watched a dance on the top floor for several hours. Again—nobody was home. When the spirits became menacing, the house was formally exorcised in 1963 by an Episcopal bishop, the Right Reverend Albert Rhett Stuart. Despite the ritual, strange noises and occasional apparitions persisted. Two families of physicians have lived there since Williams, neither noting the high drama of his tenure. In the 1980's, however, one new owner's wife was alone in the house. *I heard the music others had talked about. . . . It started very softly, from somewhere above me, getting louder. I didn't wait to hear more; I was out of the house!* Several psychics have visited to report their sense of a feminine presence there. Dr. William G. Roll, of the American Physical Research Foundation, spent four nights in the house, interviewing three dozen people who had observed bizarre things there. His conclusions ruled out any explainable physical phenomenon.

One may also contemplate ghostly legends while enjoying a meal in the historic surroundings of the Pirates' House and 17Hundred90 restaurants. In the former there is a long history of strange noises and lights on the top floor. Employees are too spooked to go up there alone. A psychic named Lorraine Warren visited in the 1980's and while standing near the cellar stairway, sensed *the smell of old blood, the feeling that something evil happened to some young men.* There are rumors that an underground passage was present there, by loose tradition the last exit long ago of young men being shang-haied to sea. Other more whimsical traditions relate to the haunting wails of pirates, such a Jean Laffite and Captain Flint.

In the 17Hundred90 Restaurant is a more palpable unseen presence attributed to "Anna," who is said to have committed suicide when her lover left for the sea. Occasionally, on lonely Sunday afternoons, footsteps are heard on the stairs, toilets flush, and the phone rings with no one on the other end. When the young psychic in Margaret DeBolt's book visited, he strongly sensed two disturbed spirits, neither of them "Anna": *One is a young girl, very unhappy, from about the 1820's . . . not a presence that would harm anyone. . . . The second presence is a black cook, a big aggressive woman, from about the 1850's who wears several bracelets and does not want another woman in her kitchen. . . . I would also say she was quite involved with voodoo.* A former owner, who does not believe in ghosts, was working alone in the kitchen on a Sunday afternoon. Hearing the jangle of a woman's bracelets behind her, she next received a hard push, as though to get her out of the way.

There have been several isolated sightings of gray ghosts attributed to Confederate soldiers in houses on Drayton, Abercorn, Harris, and Gordon streets. As told to a friend, one appeared to an employee of an insurance company on Drayton Street at 7:30 in the morning. *The scariest thing about the man was his eyes . . . in worse shape than the rest of his face. They had worms and things in them. . . . And yet . . . the main emotion was not fear, but sympathy.* Charles C. Jones, Jr., a Savannah mayor during the Civil War, recorded in great detail his encounter with a female ghost in a house on State Street in 1857. She was *emaciated in figure . . . attired in a loose morning gown of grave color . . . her hair, lifeless and sandy in its hue, was parted in the middle . . . her countenance denoted more than sorrow. There was . . . an absence of life and hope and love pitiable in the extreme.* After she disappeared before his incredulous eyes, his burning cigar and the wet ink on his legal papers verified that he was not dreaming. Later a woman in the neighborhood affirmed that it was "Miss Jane," of identical melancholy description, who moved *specter-like about her house, taking note of little.* In Jones's lifetime and since, "Miss Jane" was never reported again.

In Savannah many other incidents are attributed to disturbed spirits, such as the *presence* on West Perry Street who is drawn to electric calculators. According to the apartment occupant, *I would leave it turned off . . . when I went to sleep, and awake to find it on, and numbers on it.* Another one downtown—among other things—makes periodic phone calls to help out the owner. A presence called *the Judge* cohabits with a family on Victory Drive, riding the elevator up

Meta Thomas, repressing a smirk as she poses in period family clothes. Perhaps the ghost at the Richardson-Owens-Thomas House is a similar joke; perhaps not. (Courtesy of the Georgia Historical Society.)

and down at all hours—until politely, on sleepy request, now confines its joy rides to the daytime.

Another legend relates to Miss Margaret Thomas, last owner of the Richardson-Owens-Thomas House. Dressed in an old long gown and shawl corresponding to her portrait, she is supposed to appear regularly in her garden waiting for a carriage. Or it may not be her; a specter of similar appearance quit hanging around doing the same thing sometime in the 1950's.

Miss Thomas, however, did enjoy dressing up in period clothes when holding old-fashioned birthday parties with her friends. In 1951, the year after she died, a staff photographer from the *Savannah Morning News* showed up at her former home for a human interest story. Her old friends had decided to carry on Miss Margaret's birthday custom. Entering the old parlor lit only by flickering birthday candles, he found the tradition-clad elderly ladies mysteriously seated around a small table. Expecting to see an apparition, the young man whispered, *Where's Miss Thomas? She's dead, poor dear,* came the surprised response.

We have had cursory conversations with half a dozen people in attempting to verify some of the ghost stories romantically recycled about Savannah. In most cases the incidents are contradictory or exaggerated. Others cannot be so easily dismissed. We often noticed a reluctance to be candid. It was not the hesitation of appearing a fool, but more a quiet empathy and respect for the melancholy spirit itself—a private, personal matter. But lack of candor is not the same as lack of truth. In a few conversations we have no doubt that perfectly sane people believe themselves to be repeatedly in the presence of what—in this world—only fits the description of a ghost.

Perhaps Hamlet's advice to Horatio after seeing the ghost of his father bears remembering: *There are more things in heaven and earth, Horatio, / Than are dreamt of in your philosophy.*

THE FUTURE

Savannah has often been a city too complacent with what she had. Some residents, frustrated and angered by this smug self-satisfaction, have turned their backs on Savannah and walked away. One to do so was Dr. John M. Harney, editor of the *Savannah Georgian* in 1818. His parting shot was:

> *May all your free citizens, wealthy or poor*
> *Be bribed for their votes, as they have heretofore!*
> *May every quack Doctor be patronized still,*
> *And his talents be judged by the length of his bill;*
>
> *May all your quack Lawyers find themes for their tongues*
> *And their brains get the applause that is due to their lungs;*
> *May your miserly merchants still cheat for their pence,*
> *And, with scarce any brains show a good deal of cents!*
> *Now, to finish my curses upon your ill city,*
> *And, express in few words all the sum of my ditty,*
> *I leave you, Savannah—a curse that is far*
> *The worst of all curses—to remain as you are!*

There also, however, has been another spirit alive in Savannah— the spirit embodied by the Trustees' charter, by George Whitefield's Bethesda, by Dr. Waring's selfless dedication to yellow fever victims, by the seven women who united to start Historic Savannah. And it is this spirit that has saved the city's soul. Whether future generations will know or—worse—*care* about her priceless heritage is a painfully open question. However, James Oglethorpe, Tomochichi, Andrew Bryan, and Anna Hunter would relate to the words of another with a Savannah connection, Khalil Gibran, in this portion from his best-loved work, *The Prophet*. Published in 1923, his original drawings from the book reside in the Telfair Academy of Arts and Sciences.

You have been told also that life is darkness, and in your weariness you echo what was said by the weary.

And I say that life is indeed darkness save when there is urge,
And all urge is blind save when there is knowledge,
And all knowledge is vain save when there is work,
And all work is empty save when there is love;
And when you work with love you bind yourself to yourself, and to one another, and to God.
And what is it to work with love?

. . . .

It is to charge all things you fashion with a breath of your own spirit,
And to know that all the blessed dead are standing about you and watching.

FURTHER READING

Many fine books are available on Georgia's COLONIAL PERIOD, but they vary in approach and scope of information. Our favorite overview is Webb Garrison, *Oglethorpe's Folly: The Birth of Georgia* (Lakemont, Ga., 1982), which is both readable and loaded with documented information not usually found in other general books, such as Clifford Sheats Capps and Eugenia Burney, *Colonial Georgia* (Nashville, 1972). The Beehive Press has taken the straight-up approach with two superb, thick volumes of colonial letters: Mills B. Lane, ed., *General Oglethorpe's Georgia* (Savannah, 1975), in which the colonists speak for themselves, if often in lengthy mundane minutiae. Phinizy Spalding, *Oglethorpe in America* (Chicago, 1977), is short but reflective in its examination of the Trustees' actions in those fragile first years. The delightful details concerning the Creek Indians' visit to England came from Helen Todd, *Tomochichi, Indian Friend of the Georgia Colony* (Atlanta, 1977).

Other works on the colonial period include Rodney M. Baine, "Philip Thicknesse's Reminiscences of Early Georgia," in the *Georgia Historical Quarterly*, 74 (1990), 672–698; Elfrida De Renne Barrow and Laura Palmer Bell, *Anchored Yesterdays: The Log Book of Savannah's Voyage Across a Georgia Century in Ten Watches* (Printed by the Ashantilly Press of Darien, Georgia, for the Little House, Savannah, Georgia, 1956); Ira L. Brown, *The Georgia Colony* (New York, 1970); Kenneth Coleman, ed., *A History of Georgia* (Athens, Ga., 1977); E. Merton Coulter, ed., "A List of the First Shipload of Georgia Settlers," in the *Georgia Historical Quarterly*, 31 (1947), 282–288; Mills B. Lane, *Savannah Revisited: A Pictorial History* (Savannah, 1969); Peter Marshall and David Manuel, *The Light and the Glory* (Tappan, N.J., 1977); Royce C. McCrary, Jr., *History of the St. Andrew's Society, Savannah, Ga.* (Savannah, 1972); Rabbi

Saul Jacob Rubin, *Third to None: The Saga of Savannah Jewry, 1733–1983* (Savannah, 1983); and Thomas L. Stokes, *The Savannah* (Athens, Ga., 1979).

A delightful and complete work about the ROYAL CROWN CITY is W. W. Abbot, *The Royal Governors of Georgia, 1754–1775* (Chapel Hill, N.C., 1959). The prerevolutionary tensions are well covered in Ronald G. Killion and Charles T. Waller, *Georgia and the Revolution* (Atlanta, 1975), filled with telling letters and documents that convey those windy times. See also Capps and Burney; and Zell Miller, *Great Georgians* (Franklin Springs, Ga., 1983).

On the REVOLUTIONARY PERIOD, see Alexander A. Lawrence, *Storm Over Savannah* (Athens, Ga., 1951), which is the definitive source on the 1779 siege of Savannah. Other works include Robert S. Davis, Jr., "The British Invasion of Georgia in 1778," in the *Atlanta Historical Journal*, **24**, no. 4 (1980), 5–25; Franklin B. Hough, comp., *The Siege of Savannah* (Spartanburg, S.C., 1975); Charles C. Jones, Jr., ed., *The Siege of Savannah by the Fleet of Count D'Estaing in 1779* (New York, 1968); Benjamin Kennedy, ed., *Muskets, Cannon Balls and Bombs: Nine Narratives of the Siege of Savannah in 1779* (Savannah, 1974); Killion and Waller; and *The Remains of Major-General Nathanael Greene* (Providence, R.I., 1903), a report of the Joint Special Committee of the General Assembly of Rhode Island.

Works dealing with the POST-REVOLUTION period include Malcolm Bell, Jr., *Savannah, Ahoy!* (Savannah, 1959); E. Merton Coulter, "The Great Savannah Fire of 1820," in the *Georgia Historical Quarterly*, **23** (1939), 1–27; Thomas Gamble, comp., *A History of the Municipal Government of Savannah, 1790–1901* (1901); Thomas Gamble, *Savannah Duels and Duellists, 1733–1877* (Spartanburg, S.C., 1974); William Harden, *A History of Savannah and South Georgia* (Chicago–New York, 1913); Archibald Henderson, *Washington's Southern Tour, 1791* (Boston–New York, 1923); John F. Stegeman and Janet A. Stegeman, *Caty: A Biography of Catherine Littlefield Greene* (Providence, R.I., 1977); Robert L. Usinger, "Yellow Fever From the Viewpoint of Savannah," in the *Georgia Historical Quarterly*, **28** (1944), 143–156; William R. Waring, *Report to the City Council of Savannah on the Epidemic Disease of 1820* (Savannah, 1821); and W. T. Williams, *Reception of General Lafayette in Savannah, March 19, 1825* (Savannah, 1883).

On the issue of slavery, see Malcolm Bell, Jr., *Major Butler's Legacy: Five Generations of a Slaveholding Family* (Athens, Ga., 1987); Sidney Kaplan, *The Black Presence in the Era of the American Revolution* (Washington, D.C., 1973); Mills B. Lane, *Savannah Revisited*; and Thomas L. Stokes, *The Savannah*.

On Savannah during the CIVIL WAR, Alexander A. Lawrence, *A Pre-*

sent for Mr. Lincoln: The Story of Savannah from Secession to Sherman (Macon, Ga., 1961), is indispensable. As is his custom, Lawrence emphasizes quotations from major and mundane characters, lending a you-are-there feeling. Richard Wheeler, *Sherman's March* (New York, 1978), is a collection of first-hand impressions of the crushing of Georgia from the Union point of view. Robert E. Lee's 1870 visit to Savannah comes mainly from Charles Bracelen Flood, *Lee: The Last Years* (Boston 1981), a superb and moving book.

Two books provided a comprehensive overview of RECONSTRUCTION: William B. Hesseltine and David L. Smiley, *The South in American History* (Englewood Cliffs, N.J., 1936), an outstanding, brief account of the period; and C. Mildred Thompson, *Reconstruction in Georgia: Economic, Social, Political, 1865–1872* (Savannah, 1972), a detailed overview. Alan Conway, *The Reconstruction of Georgia* (Minneapolis, 1966), and Edward Chan Sieg, *Eden on the Marsh: An Illustrated History of Savannah* (Northridge, Calif., 1985), are also good general sources.

For an excellent, definitive view of Savannah's black community at the time, see Robert E. Perdue, *The Negro in Savannah, 1865–1900* (Jericho, N.Y., 1973). Frances Butler Leigh, *Ten Years on a Georgia Plantation Since the War* (London, 1883), and Robert Manson Myers, *Children of Pride: A True Story of Georgia and the Civil War* (New Haven–London, 1972), are wonderful personal reminiscences. Other details may be gleaned from Sidney Andrews, *South Since the War* (Boston, 1868); William Starr Basinger, "Personal Reminiscences of William Starr Basinger, 1827–1910," a manuscript in the archives of the University of Georgia Library, Athens; Charles Carleton Coffin, "Four Years of Fighting" (Boston, 1899), in Richard Wheeler, *Sherman's March*, p. 149; E. Franklin Frazier, *Black Bourgeoisie* (New York, 1957); George Spencer Greer's letter to his wife from the flagship *Philadelphia*, Charleston Harbor, June 9, 1865 (courtesy of Carl Espy); and William Harden, *A History of Savannah and South Georgia*. For extensive material on the life of Robert E. Lee, see Charles Bracelen Flood; and Ralston B. Lattimore, ed., *Lee* (Philadelphia, 1964).

POST-RECONSTRUCTION and the TWENTIETH CENTURY cover a wide period of Savannah's history. The following works are recommended for further study: Thomas Gamble, *History of the Municipal Government of Savannah, 1790–1901* (Savannah, 1901); Mills B. Lane, ed., *Savannah Revisited*; and Edward Chan Sieg—all of which are good overall views of the time. Juliette Gordon Low is well covered in Gladys Denny Shultz and Daisy Gordon Lawrence, *Lady From Savannah* (New York, 1958–1988). On the Irish, see William L. Fogarty, *The Days We've Celebrated: St. Patrick's Day in Savannah* (Savannah, 1980); and, for additional details, Edward M. Shoemaker, "Strangers and Citizens—The Irish" (master's thesis), a copy of which is in the Savannah Public Library. Savannah Jewish history is well covered in Rabbi Saul Jacob Rubin, *Third to None*; and on Greek history, see *St. Paul's Greek Orthodox Church Anniversary Brochure* (Savannah, 1982).

Information on various individuals came from Robert Coles, *Flannery O'Connor's South* (Baton Rouge, La., 1980); Betsy Fancher, *Savannah: A Renaissance of the Heart* (Garden City, N.Y., 1976); Flannery O'Connor, *The Habit of Being* (New York, 1979), ed. by Sally Fitzgerald; and *The Third Annual Report of the President of the Savannah and Tybee Railroad Co.* (Savannah, 1889).

On some Savannah organizations, see Malcolm Bell, Jr., *The Oglethorpe Club* (Savannah, 1970); Preston Russell, *The History of the Georgia Society of Colonial Wars* (Savannah, 1988); and the *Savannah Yacht Club Directory* (Savannah, 1988).

Additional information on auto racing in Savannah can be found in Julian K. Quattlebaum, *The Great Savannah Races* (Athens, Ga., 1957).

The Historic Savannah Foundation is an especially helpful source for information on the development of preservation in Savannah. See especially Beth Lattimore Reiter's excellent articles: "The Savannah National Historic District" and "Preservation in Savannah Prior to 1955." Also excellent are Audrey Dunn Rhangos, "Historic Savannah Foundation," in the *Georgia Historical Quarterly*, **63**, (1979), 173–179; and Anthony Wolff, "The Heart of Savannah," in the *American Heritage*, **22**, no. 1 (1970), 54, which provides an outsider's view.

Margaret Wayt DeBolt, *Savannah Spectres and Other Strange Tales* (Norfolk, Va., 1984), contributed most of the information used in the ghost stories segment.

INDEX

Page numbers in italics indicate illustrations.

Peter Beney

A native Tennessean, PRESTON RUSSELL is a graduate of Tulane University and Vanderbilt Medical School. The chairman of Savannah's 250th anniversary celebrations in 1983, Dr. Russell maintains his interest in American history by creating historical miniatures and painting. BARBARA HINES is a native Savannahian whose family roots go back to colonial Georgia. She received her bachelor of arts in history from Agnes Scott College. When not involved in her business of resource management, she is an avid world traveler and writer. Both authors delight in Savannah's diverse and vibrant heritage.